ANIMAL T
AND T
GEMSTONE KINGDOM

"*Animal Totems and the Gemstone Kingdom* has already earned a space on my shelf of favorite books. I've long believed in the power of animal totems, but only Margaret's compendium links an animal with its unique gemstone, relaying the messages conveyed by both. Magic and meaning come together in this one-of-a kind resource, which I'll be using daily. This book is irreplaceable."
—**Cyndi Dale**, author of *Energetic Boundaries*

"Margaret Ann Lembo brings the animal and gemstone kingdoms together in an inspiring and enlightening way in this must-read reference book. With divine messages from animals, gemstones, and the angelic realm, including affirmations and questions and answers to contemplate and guide you, Lembo has created a spectacular guide you will turn to time and time again. Written in Lembo's engaging style, you'll easily discover deep and long-lasting connections to the animals and their associated gemstones. *Animal Totems and the Gemstone Kingdom* should be in everyone's personal library."
—**Melissa Alvarez**, author of *Animal Frequency* and the *Animal Frequency® Oracle Cards*

"Margaret Ann Lembo shares a new connection between the animal and crystal/gemstone realms, further acknowledging their guidance for us. It is imperative that humankind listens to the nature realms of Mother Earth at this time, to ensure our reconnection and ascension into Unity Consciousness. The wisdom imparted in *Animal Totems and the Gemstone Kingdom* helps to remind us that there is so much support and re-empowerment available, if we can be open to receive it. With the heart-felt messages from the animals and their stones, each page offers us great opportunities for doing so!"
—**Madeleine Walker**, author of *The Whale Whisperer* and *Animal Whispers Empowerment Cards*

ANIMAL TOTEMS AND THE GEMSTONE KINGDOM

Spiritual Connections of Crystal Vibrations and Animal Medicine

Margaret Ann Lembo

FINDHORN PRESS

Findhorn Press
One Park Street
Rochester, Vermont 05767
findhornpress.com

Findhorn Press is a division of Inner Traditions International

A CIP record for this title is available from the Library of Congress
– ISBN 978-1-84409-742-5 (print)
– ISBN 978-1-84409-762-3 (ebook)

Text design and layout by Thierry Bogliolo
Cover design by Richard Crookes

10 9 8 7 6 5 4 3 2 1

Printed and bound in China by Reliance Printing Co., Ltd.
This book was typeset in Trajan Pro and Bernhard Modern Standard

To send correspondence to the author of this book, mail a first-class letter
to the author c/o Inner Traditions • Bear & Company, One Park Street,
Rochester, VT 05767, and we will forward the communication.

CONTENTS

To Vincent Velardez, my husband. All creatures love him.
His loving, caring way is a blessing for every animal that crosses his path.

ACKNOWLEDGMENTS

There are many people to thank and acknowledge. As the saying goes, "It takes a village," and I am blessed with an amazing network of support in my life. To complete a book like this, many days and nights are spent in seclusion to research, contemplate, and listen to the guidance. I am very grateful to so many, starting with the teachers and authors I've learned from over the years.

My first introduction to the power of animal medicine came from the book and card deck *Medicine Cards: The Discovery of Power Through the Ways of Animals* by Jamie Sams and David Carson. My understanding of the interconnectedness of all life was further deepened by Jamie Sams's book, *The Thirteen Original Clan Mothers*. My gratitude goes to these two inspirational authors and practitioners.

My knowledge continued to grow as I studied the work of Ted Andrews, an important mentor to me as an author. I had the honor and privilege to host him as a speaker at my conscious-living bookstore, The Crystal Garden, and interact with him on several occasions. Through his firsthand storytelling, as well as from my favorite books, *Animal-Speak* and *Animal-Wise*, my connection with animals as allies on my spiritual journey advanced. Though Ted crossed over in 2009, I remember him fondly and cherish his lessons.

As I wrote this book, I found myself calling on my good friend and fellow author Joan Ranquet, to get her take on the characteristics of certain animals. Joan is an animal communicator and the author of several books on animal communication. She also teaches communication with all life. I am grateful for Joan's input based on her personal experiences communicating and interacting with members of the animal kingdom and more.

It is a wonderful gift to be a Findhorn Press author and to carry Findhorn's imprint on this book, along with some of my other books, decks of cards, and CDs. In 1975, I read *The Magic of Findhorn* by Paul Hawken. I had just moved to South Florida with my parents, and I clearly remember reading this book while sitting in a doctor's office waiting room with my mom. I looked up and said, "Mom, the people in this story garden like you do and talk to the plants—and listen—just like you taught me." From that day on, I became enthralled with the Findhorn Community and often included the teachings of Findhorn in the many workshops I've taught.

Findhorn is a community that had humble beginnings. In the early 1960s, Eileen Caddy, Peter Caddy, and Dorothy Maclean moved into a caravan community (trailer park) in Moray, Scotland, on the eastern shore of Findhorn Bay. Eileen Caddy, a spiritual teacher, received guidance that was instrumental in the founding of this intentional community.

The evolution of the community stems from their organic gardening practice to supplement their food supply. By listening and following guidance, they grew their food and their spiritual community. After fifty-five years, it is a thriving ecovillage and educational center.

Fast forward to 2011. My first book, *Chakra Awakening: Transform Your Reality Using Crystals, Color, Aromatherapy and the Power of Positive Thought*, had just launched, and I knew I wanted to publish a young reader's title with the same type of information found in my book. When I answered the phone at The Crystal Garden one day and a US sales rep for Findhorn Press was on the other end wanting to tell me about Findhorn's new releases, I asked him if he knew of any publishers who might be willing to publish a young reader's title on crystals, colors, and chakras. During our conversation, I learned about the people who would later become my colleagues and publisher. (I love synchronicity and the circles of life as we walk the wheel of life!)

I am grateful for publisher Thierry Bogliolo, and for Carol Shaw, who has supported my journey with Findhorn in many ways. I appreciate Carol's kindness and social media support. I am grateful for Gail Torr, publicist in Los Angeles, for so many great placements for me as an author, as well as for the work I published with Findhorn Press and their imprint, Earthdancer Books. I am grateful for Sabine Weeke, who has procured foreign rights for the young reader's title *Color Your Life with Crystals* and a number of oracle decks. Thank you to Elaine Harrison for radio spots and article placement in the UK.

Words cannot express (though they should) my gratitude for my personal editor, Carol Rosenberg. She is a treasure as a wordsmith. I am so grateful that she fixes and polishes my work, yet keeps my voice in all the publications I produce. Thank you, Carol!

There are many magazine editors who publish my columns, for which I am grateful. Thank you to Cynde Myer of *Spirit Seeker* magazine in Missouri, who offered me my first regular column. Thank you to Andrea de Michaelis of *Horizons Magazine*, Sherry Henderson of *Oracle 20-20* in the South, Mary Arsenault of *Wisdom Magazine* in the Northeast, Yolanda Pulakis at *Awareness Magazine*, and all the staff at *Sedona Journal of Emergence*.

Thank you to everyone on the team at The Crystal Garden. Their good work, reliability, and dedication make it possible for me to work from my home office while writing my books and creating affirmation decks and audio products. I can rest easy, knowing that all is well. Special thanks to Caitlin Ten Eyck, Pam Moore, Angelina Kessler, Katrina Duff, Phyllis Lamattina, and Vincent Velardez.

AUTHOR'S NOTE

My interest in the teachings of nature, plants, and animals started in the garden with my mother. Thanks to the time spent talking to and listening to the plants and flowers, the turning of my attention toward a spiritually rich life also grew in the garden. As I child, I felt as if I could hear what dogs were thinking as well as feel the presence of angels at all times. My ability to "see" angels was experienced as an inner vision. As time went on, I realized that when I quiet my mind, clear my emotions, and eliminate preconceived notions, my perception filter allows for more vivid visions and messages.

Thus, I learned that it's easier to link with all life telepathically. Angels, archangels, and masters are always divinely influencing us, and we are always receiving messages from all of nature for our contemplation. The seen and unseen are real worlds, and these beings and energies help guide and light our path.

As a young girl, I watched all the popular Saturday morning cartoons—from Bugs Bunny and Daffy Duck to Woody the Woodpecker and Heckle and Jeckle, and many more. I realized then that although these animated and anthropomorphized animals had been created in someone's mind and appeared as entertaining images on a screen, the inspiration for them came from the animals themselves. Animals do communicate with each other as well as with humans. With Mickey Mouse and the rest of the Disney animals and plants, Walt Disney opened a pathway in our consciousness to the possibility of interspecies communication and messages beyond the norm. Shows like Captain Kangaroo heralded a new type of children's TV in the mid-1950s, featuring human-animal communication with Mr. Moose, Bunny Rabbit, and Dancing Bear. It's been a long time since I watched Saturday morning cartoons, but today's modern kids probably can't fathom a world in which animals don't talk.

With these few examples, it's not far-fetched to believe that we can work with animals on an energetic level through symbolism and intuition. It's also not far-fetched to believe that animals communicate with us.

After many years of personal experience with rocks, crystals, and gemstones, I began writing books on colors, crystals, and the power of positive thought. The more I wrote about gemstones as a matching vibration for positive thoughts, angels, archangels, and the like, the more I realized that there are matching gemstones for the various animals and their position in the wheel of life.

I was drawn to the lessons found in the cycles of life early on my spiritual journey, which led me to the wheel of life, which created a bridge between animals and their connection with cycles of life through the seasons. The wheel of life drew me toward the teachings of the ancient ways in Italy, Peru, and North America. Many realizations have come to me from spending time observing the wheel of life, so I incorporated those realizations into this book, as well as into all of my teachings.

It's my intention to continue to open up our consciousness so that we can all grasp the interrelatedness of all life on planet earth. Like the butterfly, it takes just a little "flutter of my wings" to make big results. Within these pages, you will have the chance to read, contemplate, observe, and understand yourself and your life a little better, as I have done as I wrote this book.

INTRODUCTION

The connectedness of everything on our planet—from rocks and crystals to plants and animals—is the foundation of this book. As the title suggests, *Animal Totems and the Gemstone Kingdom* links messages and lessons from the animal kingdom to the vast, supportive energetic world of crystals and gemstones.

The characteristics of animals—from birds and insects to mammals, fish, and reptiles—relate to our human walk on this planet, providing us with lessons and helping us mindfully focus our intentions for our life experiences. Animal medicine offers us a powerful signpost for self-knowledge and clarity on life's challenges. When a creature from nature appears to you repetitively or in some out-of-the-ordinary way, it is time to pay attention and find the message that nature is bringing you. This requires mindfulness and contemplation. Read the messages within these pages and take time to think about what these characteristics symbolize for you.

Remember, everything is energy, and all energy has a vibration. Plants and animals hold an energetic vibration. Rocks and crystals hold an energetic vibration. Colors hold an energetic vibration. Energetic vibrations reveal themselves to us as symbols and signs, offering us clues to light our path. Being aware of these signs and symbols is important for gaining the insight we are looking for to keep us on our desired course in life. Maintaining mindfulness is the key to self-actualization, which allows us to create our vision. Actualization is simply the action that makes something real in our lives. Mindfulness is our living experience, clearly realizing and being conscious of our thoughts and feelings in the present moment.

Crystals, minerals, and stones hold the history of the earth and all that this planet has to offer you to evolve your soul and spirit in this incarnation. The color, formation, and manner in which the stone grows offer a teaching to know yourself and your life purpose. It takes time and inner reflection to understand the messages and clues found throughout the gemstone kingdom.

Matching the teachings of gemstones with the teachings of animals provides you with an even deeper understanding and a life filled with "aha" moments. The spiritual fulfillment you seek is available to you in so many ways, and this path of working with gemstones and animal medicine is just one of many.

Understanding symbolism and the messages around you—*and* within you—at any given moment helps you to be consciously present and to know yourself better. This book is written with the intention of helping you to be consciously present, so that you can create the change or transformation you want in your life, understand a situation or interaction better, or gain more insight into your relationship with another, or with yourself.

With regard to the animal totem's complementary crystals and gemstones, these were each handpicked based on the color, chakra association, and the oracular message of the gemstone. When discussing how a crystal supports you, it is meant in a metaphysical way.

How to Use This Book

Use this book as a tool for self-observation, self-discovery, and as a path toward self-realization, self-empowerment, and personal growth. *Animal Totems and the Gemstone Kingdom* does the following:

- Provides the meanings of animals showing up in your life in various ways.
- Offers an understanding of crystals and gemstones to help you maintain focus on your intention for self-actualization.
- Introduces you to angels, archangels, and master guides to provide guidance and spiritual understanding.
- Opens your awareness to the cycles of life and the constant spiral upward for higher understanding through animal messages within the wheel of life.
- Provides affirmative thinking to assist in achieving your goals and aspirations.
- Brings a message from the animal and the gemstone for deeper self-understanding.

There is so much to learn from observing the characteristics and qualities of all beings—especially the animals here on Planet Earth. Through observation, you can derive symbolic meanings and teachings as they apply to you personally. As you observe certain animals showing up repetitively, let yourself take the time to discover what that animal might be teaching you. Each and every one of us is gifted with signs and symbols placed in our path. When you pay attention to the signs, you have an opportunity to develop your spiritual nature, which is unique to you and you alone.

You can read this book straight through, or you can read the introductory material and then use the entries like a directory. Refer to the appendices to find the associations for each animal.

Each entry, appearing in alphabetical order by the animal totem, contains the following:

Characteristics and Symbolic Meanings of the Animal:

This part starts out with a series of questions for your consideration. Take a moment to decipher if these questions resonate with you at this time. The qualities and characteristics of the animal are symbolically related to aspects of your life for reflection to garner a deeper understanding of yourself.

Animal's Vibrational Matching Gemstone:

The complementary gemstone is an ally to further support your ability to maintain focus on your intention for self-actualization.

Divine Influence:

Introduces you to the angels, archangels, and master guides available to support you here on earth and to provide guidance and spiritual understanding.

Animal's Location on the Wheel of Life

Based on the teachings of the seasons and moon positions, the wheel of life entry gets you thinking about the times of year and seasons of life. As it opens your awareness to the cycles of life, you can spiral upward for higher understanding through the animal's position on the wheel.

Contemplate This

Think about what this animal represents for you. Contemplation is the key to help you dig deeper for a more profound understanding of the teaching it brings at any given moment in your life.

Message from the Animal

Provides a direct message for application in your daily life in a practical way and for deeper self-understanding.

Animal's Affirmation

Provides affirmative statements to assist in achieving your goals and aspirations.

Message from the Gemstone

Provides a direct message for use in your daily life. Incorporate the gemstone in your jewelry choices or in the stones you keep nearby to support you.

Additional Gemstones for the Animal

There are many gemstones that support varying aspects of the message offered from the animal. The gemstones listed in this entry can enhance your awakening experience.

Here's an example of how you might use this book: On a given day, you see and/or hear a woodpecker in your backyard. Later, you notice a woodpecker on a TV program or in a meme on social media. Maybe you also see one in a movie or on a billboard. Perhaps a vehicle passes you on the road with Woody Woodpecker plastered on the side. When you pay attention to "sightings" like these, you can pick up this book to find out what Woodpecker might be trying to tell you. Read the entry, contemplate the animal's teaching, use the affirmations, connect with the vibrational matching gemstone, request the angels' assistance, and then consider taking action.

Here is another example: If there is something you want to create or strengthen in your life, you can choose to call upon a certain animal and go straight to that entry. For instance, if you are developing the heartfelt energy to be in a monogamous relationship, you can call on Penguin or Flamingo. If you are working on being more sociable, perhaps Wolf or Monkey can guide you. And if you are taking a big leap forward and wish to transform yourself, Frog or Butterfly may be a good ally for you.

In each case, use the matching stones to focus on your intentions to create and maintain positive change in your life. The stones are intended to help you maintain mindfulness in your connection with the animal ally and its message. When working with gemstones, create a matching intention and focus on the positive aspects of the intention. Pair the gemstone with an affirmation to amplify that intention. If you're interested in knowing more about the crystals and gemstones, you can read about them in my book *The Essential Guide to Crystals, Minerals and Stones*.

How to Find Your Totem Animal

Every animal has gifts, talents, and qualities. The qualities are the animal's "medicine," to assist in healing, growing, and learning on many levels. Once you meet with, connect with, or know your animal totem, you have the opportunity to draw upon the gifts that animal brings and use it in your everyday life. After all, that is the purpose of finding your power animal—to use their medicine in your everyday life. (By the way, the terms *power animal*, *spirit animal*, and *animal totem* can be used interchangeably.)

You may ask, "How do I know which animal is my totem?" I recommend you start by noticing your affinity for certain animals in your life. Second, take note if a particular animal consistently shows up in your life for a period of time. Third, your power animal will show up in your dreams, on shamanic journeys, and during meditations. For example, I realized that Owl is one of my main totem animals because Owl continuously showed up in my life. They were in trees where I lived (in the city), and I could hear them. Little owls sat on the railing outside my condominium door when I came home late at night. Owls appeared in my dreams. Owl appeared on my left shoulder during shamanic journey experiences. Eventually, I recognized that when Owl appears in my life, I need to pay attention to that which is hidden or not obvious. Now, I imagine Owl on my shoulder for every shamanic journey I experience.

Similarly, Spider made itself known to me. Unfortunately, I first recognized Spider showing up because I was bitten by Spider at almost every Sacred Circle Gathering—a medicine wheel event—that I facilitated for over a decade. After that, Spider would show up in more amicable ways. Most of the time, Spider is quite large and obvious when it has a message for me. When Spider appears in my life, I receive the message as a signal that I need to write, write, and write some more.

* * *

As you embark upon the journey presented in this book and in your life, keep this in mind: Nature nurtures us; we are nature. As we step out of our narrow perspective and into the world of observing all life, from a passing dog to a ladybug on a leaf, there are many teachings to help awaken and energize spiritual fulfillment. So many people are seeking their purpose. The age-old questions "Why am I here?" and "What is my life purpose?" continue to arise. Self-observation is key.

Messages from Animals Totems
and
Their Vibrational
Matching Gemstones

1. Ant and Red Calcite

Are you methodical and organized? Have you relaxed into the flow of working well with others to accomplish tasks as a team? Do you do what you say you will do? Ant totem is an ally that will help you work with others in a harmonious and organized manner. Ants are industrious and responsible. They get the job done and have a clear focus on their goal and responsibilities. Ant helps you keep up with your responsibilities with focus.

Ant is a social creature. They live in colonies and depend on each other and protect each other. Ants have great strength and follow through on their tasks. When a trail of ants comes into your life, reflect on your part in your social structure. Look at your responsibilities and how you fulfill your role. Call on Ant when you need strength that you perceive to be bigger than you can fathom. Ant is also a reminder to find the sweetness in life. Ants are constantly sniffing out food and sugary treats. Use this characteristic to encourage resourcefulness in find the joy in life.

Ant medicine plays a part in stories found in texts about Spider Woman, a deity in the Navajo religion and Hopi cosmological teachings. Spider Woman is considered the creator of humans and a great benefactor. There is an old Hopi story about the people who had many differences and had forgotten their connection with the creator. They had lost their conscience to act with integrity. Those who remembered how to walk in balance on the earth and harmoniously with each other were guided to an opening in the earth: an ant mound. They were invited to live with the ants while the creator cleansed the world with fire. The ants were gracious hosts and had storerooms of food. However, it took a while for the world to cool, so when the food stores started to become depleted, the ants just kept feeding their guests and tightening their belts. And that's why, it is said, that ants have tiny waists! During their stay, the people learned from the ants how to be a good and generous neighbor to houseguests. This particular story offers many morals, especially the value of listening to guidance and staying aligned with spiritual teachings.

Ant's Vibrational Matching Gemstone: Red Calcite

Red calcite holds the energy of staying organized and getting things done in an intelligent, sequential manner. Red calcite is the perfect stone to use when an activity requires physical endurance. On a spiritual level, red calcite amplifies the understanding of the teachings of Native American spirituality, the way of the Good Red Road (walking the road of balance). Its energy lends itself to a stronger connection with Mother Earth and earth-centered spirituality. It is a tool for grounding and focus in medicine wheel ceremonies, sacred circles, and altars related to Native American ceremonies. Use it to help you to tap into higher forces for the good of the community.

Divine Influence

Call on Archangel Ariel to help strengthen your personal endurance when you are faced with challenges and the Angel of Divine Remembrance to help you remember to walk on this planet with respect for all life.

Ant's Location on the Wheel of Life

Ant is located on the eastern portion of the northeast quadrant, where wisdom, clarity, and experience bring understanding of the interconnectedness of all life.

Contemplate This

Are you paying attention to the details and staying organized? Do you have to complete a project and need a team to make it happen? Are you patient with yourself and others? Ant medicine signals that it's time to get organized and maintain focus to achieve a project or goal. Remember to ask for help, delegate, and work together with others. The old African saying "It takes a village to raise a child" applies to you now.

Message from Ant

Take notice of your ability to work harmoniously with others. Be sure you are prepared for the future and have supplies in store for unexpected storms or delays in obtaining food. Cultivate ways to be welcoming and gracious with guests in your home, as well as with those who come into your business.

Ant Affirmation

I stay focused on the task at hand. I am an intelligent being with the ability to focus on complex tasks. It is easy for me to complete all that I need to do. I am patient with myself and those around me. It's easy for me to ask for help when I need it. I am blessed to be part of a community.

Message from Red Calcite

Perhaps you need a burst of energy and enthusiasm and a bit of motivation to get things done. It's time to get things moving. Use your creative energy to manifest your heart's desire. Take the time to connect with Mother Earth. Perform a simple ceremony stating your intention, and watch how you move forward to complete your goals.

Additional Vibrational Matching Gemstones for Ant

Azurite, charoite, clear quartz laser wand, dumortierite, fluorite, magnetite octahedron, sapphire, trilobite, yellow jasper, and zebra jasper.

2. ANTELOPE AND RUBY

Are you quicker to understand what's going on than other people are? Or do you feel like everyone else gets what's happening and you keep missing the point and the opportunities? Are you trying to get motivated to act? Are you mindful of taking more than you need for daily survival needs?

Antelope totem is an ally that will help you improve the quickness of your mind. The energy of Antelope is beneficial when you are shoring up and supporting your crown chakra on all levels—mentally, physically, spiritually, and emotionally. On a mental level, learn to adapt to the changing landscape of your life and understanding. On a physical level, support your brain with the right nutrition and right use of food and supplies. On a spiritual level, take the time for contemplation, meditation, and prayer. On an emotional level, embrace your feelings and integrate any emotions that need extra attention.

Antelope is also known as pronghorn and belongs to the same family as gazelles—the Bovidae family. An antelope's horns (which both the male *and* female have) remain with them for life, which is usually eight to ten years in the wild. Their top speed is 43 miles per hour! If Antelope leaps into your life, acclimate to your conditions and rapidly move forward. Take time to reflect on the lessons you've learned—both intellectual knowledge as well as the understanding of life. Antelope signals that it may be beneficial to think about where you want to be eight to ten years in the future. Observe the messages, for they lead you to a better understanding of your life purpose.

Antelope's Vibrational Matching Gemstone: Ruby

Ruby aligns you with higher consciousness. It helps you be aware of the spiritual and mystical experience of the unity of the universe. Ruby is the stone to use when you need extra energy around your ability to adapt and take action quickly. Just like the energy of Antelope, look to this gemstone to amplify your inner core strength. Keep a ruby on hand with the intention to strengthen your clarity and decisiveness. Ruby helps you do what needs to be done for any given situation. The red vibration of this gem enhances your vim and vigor, increasing your stamina and endurance.

Divine Influence

Call on Archangel Ariel to help you increase your vitality, Archangel Camael to help you to move forward with great force, and Archangel Uriel for wisdom and to enhance your ability to make decisions.

Antelope's Location on the Wheel of Life

Antelope is located at the northern portion of the northwest quadrant, where wisdom is integrated.

Contemplate This

Have you been trying to understand why things are the way they are? Do you wish you could be quicker to grasp scenarios in your life and around you? Are you paying attention so that you only gather what you can use to avoid waste? Recognize that every day you have the opportunity to realign yourself with the highest good. Think about what activities improve your courage to take action swiftly. Create new pathways for thinking by training your mind to look at things in new ways. Observe the benefits gained through meditation.

Message from Antelope

Take action, and do it now! Be alert. Pay attention. Swiftness and immediate response are important. Engage in activities that strengthen your courage to take action swiftly. Improve your mental abilities through mind exercises and meditation. Maintain focus, and persevere. It is time to establish guidelines for honoring all life by avoiding situations that waste time and resources. Do things that amplify good health and vitality.

Antelope Affirmation

Vital life force flows vibrantly through me. I am strong and healthy. I am adaptable and take immediate action. I am an intelligent being with the ability to focus on complex tasks. I am blessed to have a deep understanding of the truth. I am grateful for mental clarity.

Message from Ruby

It is time to take steps to improve your endurance and overall ability to think through complex problems promptly. Know that you are an intelligent being and that you can accomplish whatever you put your mind to. Engage in illuminating activities, such as meditation, contemplation, and inner reflection. Strive to better comprehend the nature of reality.

Additional Vibrational Matching Gemstones for Antelope

Fluorite, Mookaite jasper, red calcite, red jasper, red tiger's eye, sapphire, sunstone, tiger iron, golden topaz, and vanadinite.

3. ARMADILLO AND AMBER

Are you trying to maintain a sense of safety? Have you been attempting to set boundaries? Do you feel honored by others? Do you feel like you are being taken advantage of or taken for granted?

Armadillo totem is an ally that enhances your ability to stand up for yourself and set proper boundaries. Just as Armadillo digs and lives in burrows below ground, you can use that same vibration to go beneath the surface of what is apparent to have a deeper understanding of yourself and your interactions with others. With Armadillo as an ally, you are shielded from negativity as you look closely below the surface to know the truth. Skills of discernment are important. Use this shield only when necessary.

Whenever you want to avoid people in certain places or types of situations, call on the energy of Armadillo to support you. Make it your intention to establish a clear, energetic vibration that keeps others from invading your energy with hurtful words or bad intentions. While Armadillo has a tendency to roll up and hide, be mindful that your armor is to be used only when absolutely necessary. The best of everything is always available to you, so avoid missing out on experiences and fine-tune your ability to discern and feel out situations and people.

Armadillo's Vibrational Matching Gemstone: Amber

Amber helps you transform negative thoughts or beliefs. It clears your mind of incessant chatter and is a grounding force for you on your spiritual path. Amber filters out other people's energy. As you raise your vibration, you may find you are more sensitive to the thoughts and feelings of others. Amber is a cleansing stone that comes from the resin of a tree—most often a pine tree. Both pine and amber have a protective energy that creates a filter for, and a barrier from, negative psychic energy and unwanted influences. As you gain understanding on your part in your relationships with others, Armadillo and amber help you clear out unwanted energy from energy-sucking acquaintances, friends, colleagues, and family members.

Divine Influence

Call on Archangels Jophiel and Seraphiel to help you understand and break unwanted repetitive patterns.

Armadillo's Location on the Wheel of Life

Armadillo is located at the western portion of the southwest quadrant, where inner reflection and the healing of relationships and patterns occur.

Contemplate This

Are you hiding behind an emotional wall to avoid getting hurt again? Have you opened up to release patterns of the past? Armadillo signals that it's time to go beneath the surface of your consciousness to discover the energetic vibration attracting people and situations to you that don't honor and respect you. Remember, it is up to you to recognize your magnificence first and then others will naturally recognize it in you, too!

Message from Armadillo

It is time to find your confidence and courage. How comfortable are you with saying no? You have the personal power you need to establish boundaries, so use that power. Remember to be discerning, and you will be protected. Discernment is your best tool to feel safe and sound. Maintain empathy for others, but remember that you must take care of yourself first. With life experience, you will know when to protect yourself and when to let your defenses down.

Armadillo Affirmation

I have the courage to set boundaries with love and grace. I am protected. Experiences from the past empower me. I am discerning about the people I allow into my circle. I am mindful of being in peaceful places to support my loving vibration. It is safe to be powerful in loving ways. I find strength through vulnerability. It is safe for me to be seen and acknowledged.

Message from Amber

Establish clear boundaries by surrounding yourself with a protective shield to deflect any negative energy that comes your way. Decide what is acceptable in your space and in your life, and open yourself to receive all that is acceptable. The level of clarity you bring to deciding what is okay will help filter out what is unwelcome. Ancient wisdom resides within you, and when you subconsciously tap into it, it can keep you protected and transform your life.

Additional Vibrational Matching Gemstones for Armadillo

Ametrine, black tourmaline, charoite, desert rose, golden calcite, danburite, hematite, orange calcite, pyrite, and yellow jasper.

4. BADGER AND AMETRINE

Are you being assertive or aggressive? Are you comfortable standing up for yourself? Can you balance and temper the manner in which you defend your sacred space?

Badger totem is an ally that brings strength while at the same time encouraging aggressive behavior. People with Badger medicine tend to be both assertive and aggressive. They have the confidence, strength, and courage to stand up for themselves and what they want. They have the oomph and motivation to reach a goal with follow-up and determination. If you realize that Badger is a strong part of your personality, take the time to observe yourself, and temper aggression so that it is more gentle assertion. Be mindful, so you don't rip others to shreds!

Badger is known as the "keeper of the medicine roots." If Badger appears in your life, find the resources necessary to heal the situation from the source or origin point that needs healing. Inner reflection is necessary to achieve this goal.

Badgers are diggers. They dig and dig. This is the primary action of their daily life. It is through digging that they find their food underground. Look to Badger as an ally to help you find the source of personal satisfaction deep within yourself. Feed your mental, emotional, and spiritual bodies by looking deep within for sustenance. Through the inner search, you will find your truth and stand strong in the world with courage. The words or biting comments of others won't find a way into your consciousness and affect you. Like Badger's loose outer skin, biting energy from others can't injure you.

Badger's Vibrational Matching Gemstone: Ametrine

Ametrine is a powerful spiritual tool, containing the power of amethyst to transform and transmute negativity and the power of citrine to boost self-confidence to achieve your heart's desires. The purple vibration helps transform and transmute negative emotions and releases the hooks that others have in your emotional body. The yellow encourages the ability to discern the right people, places, and situations that you allow into your life. With ametrine in hand, use the complementary colors—purple and yellow—to promote balance by connecting the crown chakra and the solar plexus chakra. Focus on Divine will, not the small lower ego will, to manifest in your life. Amethyst and citrine facilitate high connections with Ascended Masters and spiritual teachers.

Divine Influence

Call on Archangel Haniel to help you align with Divine communication, balanced determination, and your soul's purpose.

Badger's Location on the Wheel of Life

Badger is located in the southern portion of the southwest quadrant, where transformation and personal growth take place.

Contemplate This

Do you fight for what you believe in? Are you aware of how your energy affects others? Do people let you know that you hurt their feelings? Take notice of how you are coming across and soften your energy. Loving-kindness comes through when you make it your intention to be assertive instead of aggressive. You can transform and transmute any challenging situation. Draw on your confidence, and shine your light. It is safe for you to powerfully assert yourself!

Message from Badger

Take the time to observe yourself and determine if you are being assertive or aggressive. Prepare yourself to get through challenging situations by using a variety of healing modalities, including essential oils, herbs, and active venting. Find creative ways to release pent-up feelings. Drumming and even primal screaming can be profoundly healing, or simply give yourself permission to have a good cry.

Badger Affirmation

It is safe for me to be powerful. I am deter-mined and see projects through to fruition. I am determined to achieve my goals and dreams. I move forward with focus and deter-mination. Confidence and courage are mine. I have a deep understanding of myself and the circles of life around me. I communicate softly regardless of what I need to express.

Message from Ametrine

This is the time to release a bad habit, addiction, or a relationship that is no longer for your highest good. To make changes in your life, don't let your inner critic tell you that you can't do it. Start healing by looking within, and reflect on the source of the challenge. It's time to take action and be determined and confident enough to make the necessary changes to transform your life!

Additional Vibrational Matching Gemstones for Badger

Amazonite, black obsidian arrowhead, charoite, chrysocolla, dogtooth calcite, emerald, rhodochrosite, and selenite rose.

5. BAT AND GALENA

How well do you observe your surroundings? Do know what situational awareness is and how to use it in your life? Do you listen well and hear how people respond to you?

Bats navigate not by vision but by echolocation, which is also known as biosonar. It is a navigation system in which bats send out high-frequency sound and listen for the "echo" that bounces off nearby objects. When Bat shows up in your life, pay attention to what others are saying about you in response to your words, actions, or feelings. Notice how your words and communications reflect back to you. Bouncing ideas off others can be beneficial at this time.

Dusk is the time that bats typically leave their roost to hunt for food: insects. They are our environment's natural pest control and reduce the need for pesticides in the area they live in. Sunset may be the time to feed your soul and decrease the need for non-natural substances to relieve stress.

Bats are pollinators and drop seeds that take root. If you have Bat medicine, take action at dusk on any projects you want to come to fruition. Also spend some time in a garden, or do some gardening. Nature is nurturing—the vibration of being among plants and flowers feeds deeper parts of your soul.

One interesting tidbit is that the fruit bat became the logo for Bacardi rum when Doña Amalia noticed a colony of fruit bats living in the eaves of the distillery. According to Cuban and Catalan folklore, Bat represents good fortune, and because of this association, it also represents persistence and determination. With Bat in your life, have faith that success is on the horizon.

Bat's Vibrational Matching Gemstone: Galena

On a vibrational level, galena's reflective qualities align you with the openness to receive feedback from others. Use galena when you want to hear information or messages that may be a bit more obscure. While it is a mineral that aids you in seeing the silver lining, it also helps you refine and gain clarity. Galena is a grounding stone, so it helps you to be realistic when you want to emphasize the brighter side of a situation. Galena amplifies your ability to channel or increase your intuitive abilities. Use it when you delve into any of the intuitive arts. Because of its conductive qualities, this stone sharpens your ability to "tune into the right channel."

Divine Influence

Call on Archangel Gabriel to help you hear and listen to the obvious and less obvious communication.

Bat's Location on the Wheel of Life

Bat is located on the west path, where connection is made with the mystery, the nocturnal patterns in nature, and the voice within.

Contemplate This

Do you listen to your inner voice? Are you aware that you have an internal guidance system? Listen to that still, small voice within to find the answers you seek. Take notice of the signs and symbols around you, and contemplate their meaning. Through the integration of all the guideposts on your path, you have the power to find your way to feed your soul and fulfill your life purpose.

Message from Bat

Observe and listen. Cultivate projects you've started. Tend to projects requiring attention, just as you tend to a garden, so that they can come to full bloom. Bat is associated with clairaudience, the ability to hear messages from within. Encourage the flow of inspiration through you, enabling you to embrace change and the possibilities for your future. Listen to the feedback from others for guidance and direction, and contemplate their input. Make your own decision on how to move forward with determination.

Bat Affirmation

I'm grounded, focused, and tuned in to the Universe. I listen and really hear what others are saying. I pay attention to all that is around me and use the information as clues to make my life easier. My creative projects bring me prosperity and abundance. Guidance from my higher self lights my path. I trust my intuition and my internal guidance system. I take time for inner reflections.

Message from Galena

Get focused and look for the silver lining. Worries about finances do not have to plague you. The time has come for you to share your message, based on what you really want. Channel all your energy with strong intention, and watch your prosperity roll in! Take notice of what is reflected back to you or what energy is returned to you based on what you sent out.

Additional Vibrational Matching Gemstones for Bat

Azurite-malachite, blue lace agate, blue calcite, clear quartz singing crystal, celestite, and Picasso stone.

6. BEAR AND MAGNETITE OCTAHEDRON

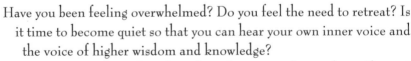

Have you been feeling overwhelmed? Do you feel the need to retreat? Is it time to become quiet so that you can hear your own inner voice and the voice of higher wisdom and knowledge?

Bear totem teaches the value of going within and just "being." Bear teaches us the power of awakening the consciousness below the surface of our awareness in order to know the truth. The still, small voice within is available to everyone. With a little effort, turn off all outside distractions, and find your way into a place of non-doing and just being. Bear teaches that retreat, or doing nothing, is sometimes more powerful than taking action. The symbolic energy of Bear and the cave signal a time for inner reflection. Just as a bear uses its energy stores during the long winter for nourishment, you can use your inner wisdom stored in your consciousness to guide you.

Bears can hear beyond the frequency of humans. Bear medicine is a reminder to be quiet enough to hear, as it is within the silence that you find answers. Bear experiences life through scent because its olfactory abilities are extremely sensitive, one hundred times greater than a human's sense of smell. Pay attention to your sense of smell, both on a physical level as well as on a level beyond the physical. Clairolfaction is the ability to intuitively pick up a smell that doesn't physically exist as a scent particle. Observing the scent of a place or space is beneficial as it brings you feelings of well-being and safety, leading to relaxation. However, if the aroma is offensive, you should be on guard.

Bear's Vibrational Matching Gemstone: Magnetite

Magnetite puts a spotlight on the spiritual component of taking the time to release incessant chatter in your mind. It is through the release of the chatter that there is the opportunity to awaken your consciousness through self-awareness. In the "no mind" and "no thought" consciousness, the structure of magnetite octahedron aligns you with the vibrational energies of bringing Heaven to Earth. It is a reminder of "as above, so below," and to ultimately create your reality from the inner cave of your consciousness. The energy of magnetite helps you attract what you need, although it is likely already within you. Bear and this mineral both teach that you should draw out what you don't need—filter and discern.

Divine Influence

Call on the Angel of Inner Reflection to help you look within your own consciousness and know the truth.

Bear's Location on the Wheel of Life

Bear is located on the northwest quadrant, where inner reflection is enhanced.

Contemplate This

Are you feeling mentally, physically, or spiritually depleted? Do you need to recapture your essence down to the very cells of your being? Pay attention to the signs and symptoms of overwork, lack of nutrition or rest, and reenergize yourself. There is great value in going within to refuel and sort out your thoughts. Establish the space to rest, regenerate, and rejuvenate. Go into your cave, rest, then emerge renewed.

Message from Bear

Slow down. Go within. Stop doing; just be. Quiet time is necessary. It is time to be reclusive and quiet. Experience contemplative thought. Find your balance by avoiding the company of others. Be aware enough to know when it is time step out of the inner world and give birth to ideas and projects that were realized during the solitude.

Bear Affirmation

I take time for inner reflection. Contemplative thought help me to reveal and process thoughts and feelings. I awaken my awareness through quiet time and meditation. I am a clear channel, and my filters allow me great mental clarity. My observations strengthen my spiritual nature and improve my inner foundations for knowledge and wisdom.

Message from Magnetite

Take time for inner reflection and self-observation to expand your spiritual foundation. Be a magnet for all the good things in life. Balance your life with times of inner work and then take action on all the realizations and "aha" moments received during that time. Establish safe surroundings, and magnetize financial success and good relationships. Stay grounded and focused.

Additional Vibrational Matching Gemstones for Bear

Azurite, brown agate geode, brown jasper, honey calcite, lodestone, moonstone, muscovite, golden sheen obsidian, rainbow obsidian, and sodalite.

7. BEAVER AND EPIDOTE

Is your focus on your home and family? Are you ready to start your own family and build the life of your dreams? Are you looking for your life partner?

Beaver totem is an ally that offers added energy toward manifesting your life partner, dream home, and family. Beaver is also an ally to help you formulate good plans for retirement and the golden years. Beavers are one of the largest rodents, growing up to 4 feet long and weighing 60 pounds. They live in the water and take special care in building their home. They mate for life and will find another partner if their mate passes away. Beaver brings to your life the energy of home, hearth, and lifetime companionship. Beaver is a perfect totem when you are building or renovating a home.

Call on Beaver medicine to help you get moving and make your dream come true. Because beavers live in the water, they also encourage you to deal with emotions. Use your intention, and ask to receive clarity and understanding regarding your emotions and what might be preventing you from manifesting what you truly desire. Visualization and imagination are what create your life. What will you imagine?

Beaver's Vibrational Matching Gemstone: Epidote

The gemstone epidote increases your mental capacity to integrate the true meaning of love and abundance into your understanding of the world. With this stone in hand, think from your heart and the truth will be yours. Use this heartfelt truth to make your decisions. Epidote aligns you with parallel realities in which you already know how to love freely. This stone awakens the realization that there is plenty of love to go around. It is a good stone to improve relationships in which jealousy tends to be an issue. Like the energy of Beaver, epidote reminds you that there is plenty of everything to go around, including good health, sufficient income, and unconditional love. You just need to be industrious and take action. You'll find that you have an abundance left over to share with others.

Divine Influence

Call on Archangel Raphael to help you heal your emotions.

Beaver's Location on the Wheel of Life

Beaver is located in the southern portion of the southwestern quadrant, where healing on all levels, including emotions, occurs.

Contemplate This

Are you taking action to bring your dreams to reality? Have you created the home and/or life of your dreams? Do you know how to build your life as you want it to be? Take action, and envision your future by tapping into the part of you that knows how to create reality. Recognize that there is plenty of everything to go around to construct your reality, so your basic needs are met, with plenty to share.

Message from Beaver

Focus on home and family. If you want a family, have faith that you are worthy of enjoying a love-filled home with children. If you are getting closer to retirement, determine the type of living arrangements that will make you feel safe and happy. To achieve this goal, take action to deal with emotions that must be healed or balanced. Find the home you want to live in, and live in it. Don't wait. Remember, thoughts and actions create beneficial results. Imagine yourself with a perfect mate who enjoys building a life together. Recognize the people and situations in your life that are already in place that make you feel at home, safe, and secure.

Beaver Affirmation

My thoughts and actions create favorable results. I am the builder of my life through my dreams and imagination. I enjoy the fruits of my labor through good work and an open heart. I relish helping others, and I am happy to do good deeds. I am grateful to spend time with friends, family, and my loved one. I have fun!

Message from Epidote

You are ready to take action to achieve your dreams and desires. Believe that you can overcome the challenges. It's time to move beyond the pains of your past and build the joys of your future. Breathe deeply, and take action to move forward with ease and grace to create your reality.

Additional Vibrational Matching Gemstones for Beaver

Agate, amber, carnelian, fluorite, honey calcite, petrified wood, orange calcite, pyrite, rose quartz, pyrite, and sardonyx.

8. Bee and Honey Calcite

Are you involved in a creative project or thinking about starting one? Do you have some great ideas? Are you taking action on those ideas? When was the last time you stopped to embrace all that nature offers, or at least stopped to smell the flowers? Bee totem is an ally for gardeners and farmers. Bees are essential for life on this planet; all plant life relies on bees for pollination, which is necessary for the fertilization of plants and reproduction. When Bee shows up in your life, it is time to cultivate concepts or projects through action. Do what needs to be done, and make things happen. It's time to be productive!

Call on the energy of Bee if you are trying to get pregnant or come up with a new idea. Align with the energy of Bee when you are working toward reproducing or producing a fruitful outcome. Bee is especially helpful when you need to put energy into making sure that everyone is responsibly doing his/her part in a larger project. Bee totem will help you work with others with a clearly defined understanding of your part in the community. Bee is a good ally when you want to be very organized, have clearly defined roles, and dedicated workers who are interested in the greater whole. Community is a keyword for Bee totem because of bee's ability to work with others to produce a sweet outcome.

Bee's Vibrational Matching Gemstone: Honey Calcite

Honey calcite reminds you of your emotional connection to all that is. With this stone in hand, go to a natural environment such as a desert, stream, mountain, ocean, or lake to calm your emotions, regain your composure, and find your inner peace. The brown energy of honey calcite helps you realize your spiritual connection with Mother Earth. Use this stone to connect with nature spirits. If the energy of Bee has you working overtime, relax with this gemstone to restore balance and remember to enjoy the sweetness of life. Honey calcite is a good stone to use to embrace the power of gardening as emotional therapy. This stone provides a sense of safety and security.

Divine Influence

Call on Archangel Uriel to help you focus on guiding humanity toward stewardship of Mother Earth and keeping our bee population healthy and active.

Bee's Location on the Wheel of Life

Bee is located in the western portion of the northern quadrant, where the harvest is converted into wisdom.

Contemplate This

Are you ready to be all that you can be? Do you recognize and embrace the sweetness of life? Do you work well with others for the good of all concerned? It's time to get organized and be productive. It is always a fertile time for you to manifest and create. Enjoy this fertile energy, and share it with others. Be open to working with others to accomplish what needs to be done in the community. Build your life and your community with joyful, sweet experiences.

Message from Bee

Using up all your time being busy and working too much compromises your ability to relax, and relaxing too much compromises your ability to be productive. Find the balance between relaxation and productivity. Take time to smell the sweetness of life around you. Remember that your life's activities are more productive and enjoyable when you take time to appreciate them.

Bee Affirmation

I am fertile with great ideas. I am focused and creative. It is easy for me to be creative and bring a project to fruition. Building and creating are joyful experiences for me. I take the time to enjoy the sweetness of life. It's very enjoyable for me to work in harmony with others.

Message from Honey Calcite

Do you need to increase your ability to get things accomplished with joy? Do you need some self-motivation to accomplish your list of things to do? Be creative to get things moving in the right direction, and use your energy to manifest your heart's desire. Align with Mother Earth in a ceremonial way, and stay focused on your intention. Enjoy the harmony of joyfully working with others in order to complete goals.

Additional Vibrational Matching Gemstones for Bee

Amethyst, blue calcite, citrine, golden calcite, golden topaz, magenta-dyed agate, malachite, and red calcite.

9. BEETLE AND CHAROITE

Are you ready to experience a metamorphosis? Is there a part of your life that needs to be transformed? How is your behavior and energy affecting the people around you? Are you letting the energy of what others are throwing out affect you too much?

Beetle totem is an ally to help you work through challenging situations by maintaining a strong outer protection while still being flexible. Beetles are members of a group of over 400,000 insects with a hard exoskeleton, providing them with flexible "armor." When Beetle shows up in your life, be open to changes or suggestions being offered but continue to maintain your own sense of self.

As with many insects, beetles communicate using pheromones. Pheromones are used to locate a mate as well as to signal the location of a source of food to other beetles. The presence of Beetle alerts you that there are messages and signals being sent to you by your friends, family, coworkers, and colleagues that affect you vibrationally. Even though it is silent, be aware that these vibes you are picking up on are real.

Found widely in ancient Egyptian hieroglyphs, Beetles are a symbol of the sun. Many stories relate that because dung beetles roll their eggs in dung to protect them, Beetle's message is one of how new life emerges following burial in a dark and safe space. In some interpretations, it means we might need to roll around in "mud" to transform challenging situations! While there is value in experiencing the darkness that often accompanies transformation, be sure to look for the lesson and move forward to the other side of the experience.

Beetle's Vibrational Matching Gemstone: Charoite

Charoite assists when you are in the process of spiritual transformation. Beetles go through a complete metamorphosis, a keyword for the gemstone charoite. Turn to this gemstone when your own body structure is changing. Call on this energy to align with the strength needed to move forward with transforming your body. A mineral for sorting out the details, charoite untangles chaotic thoughts and sheds light on confusing circumstances and complex situations. Initially, the intensity of the chaos expands in order to draw attention to the key elements that require attention. The transformational properties of charoite expand your ability to set boundaries and amplify your personal power, just like Beetle with its strong armor.

Divine Influence

Call on Archangel Zadkiel to help transform and transmute challenging situations.

Beetle's Location on the Wheel of Life

Beetle is located on the south path, where the path of transformation is illuminated.

Contemplate This

Are you finding that life feels out of control? Do you need to sort out exactly what's going on to get to the reason for the chaos? Do you feel like you need an outer shell of protection during this cycle of your life? Take the time to go within, and call on the angels and the Divine to light your path. Ask for the help you need from trustworthy friends and colleagues. Allow your "village" to provide you with the inspiration and guidance you need to transform your life.

Message from Beetle

Take notice of the energies you are picking up from others. Believe yourself when you are receiving feelings, and try not to discount your hunches. Ask for the support you need. Remember to remain flexible, even though you may need a strong shield around you right now. Have faith, and trust that the experience will help you evolve.

Beetle Affirmation

I trust my internal guidance system. I am deeply intuitive and take action based on my intuition. I comprehend the details of everything set before me. I am enveloped in a protective shield. As change takes place, I am transformed. The good is revealed in challenging situations.

Message from Charoite

Contemplate all the energy that is being sent your way in words, thoughts, and emotions. Develop a deep understanding of yourself and the circles of life around you. Take the time you need to quiet your mind and sort through the chatter and feelings to determine which are yours and which are coming from others. Define and clarify the direction of your life to help you stay aligned with the Divine and on target with your purpose. Trust your intuition.

Additional Vibrational Matching Gemstones for Beetle

Amber, amethyst, black onyx, black tourmaline, girasol quartz, galena, hematite, magenta-dyed agate, and red tiger's eye.

10. BLUEBIRD AND PERIDOT

Are you happy when you wake up? Do you find gratitude with the new day dawning? Will you let yourself be happy? Has the blue-bird of happiness flown into your life?

Bluebird totem is an ally that helps you find happiness. Bluebirds have been symbols of happiness for thousands of years; they are found in many cultures, from pre-modern China through today. Plays, movies, and songs epitomize blue-birds as the harbinger of happiness. Navajo culture recognizes the mountain bluebird as a totem associated with the rising sun. Call on Bluebird to enliven that part of you that is joyful and happy. Let this bird be a reminder that you have the spiritual fortitude and self-confidence to ex-plore new pathways for delight and pleasure. When Bluebird shows up in your life, it may be an omen to protect and defend your home and hearth. Bluebirds compete for nesting locations and are quite territorial. Find your courage, and stand up for yourself and your space. Be like Bluebird and know that it is acceptable for you to be territorial when others are trying to take away the peace and harmony of your home. Spruce up your home and make your nest more comfortable and colorful to nurture and elicit feelings of well-being. Helpful to gardeners, bluebirds are insatiable consumers of insects, so they are good at get-ting rid of pests. If you need to rid your life of annoying people or other nuisances, call on Bluebird to help remove the energy that is not for the highest good.

Bluebird's Vibrational Matching Gemstone: Peridot

Peridot helps you transform jealousy into love and happiness. With peridot and Bluebird as your allies, you will easily focus on love, compassion, acceptance, and gratitude. Observe the past, and use memories to support you as you move forward in life with confidence. It is time to forgive and forget past injustices. Forgive, repent, have gratitude, and focus on the vibration of love that is inherent in all life. Peridot helps you maintain your world as it is and then transform anything that is not for your highest good with clear intention to create the reality you wish to have.

Divine Influence

Call on Archangel Sabrael to help deflect feelings of jealousy, negativity, and posses-siveness of others and of yourself.

Bluebird's Location on the Wheel of Life

Bluebird is located on the east path, where clarity abounds.

Contemplate This

Have you been upset about how life is changing? Are you experiencing a struggle over your space or territory? Are you open to being happy the majority of the time? Right now, where you are, happiness is available to you. Find the source of your unhappiness. Take a look around on a level that is beyond the physical to perceive if there are energy and vibrations with your ability to be happy. Great happiness is available to you as you release worn-out life situations and perspectives.

Message from Bluebird

This is a time of great happiness. With a greater understanding of yourself and further inner exploration of your finer qualities, self-confidence increases and general happiness ensues. Embrace this gift to live a charmed and enlightened life as well as to help others attain freedom from suffering and to find happiness and peace themselves.

Bluebird Affirmation

Great happiness is normal in my life. I am authentically happy for the good fortune of others. My friends, family, and colleagues are happy for my success. I know that my accomplishments are the result of good thoughts and energy. I send out positive vibes and look forward to meeting up with them in the future.

Message from Peridot

You may be in the process of healing after a period of struggle. Perhaps you are feeling jealous of someone's good fortune or you perceive that others are jealous of you. Stay focused on the goodness in your life. Remove your attention from other people's success and accomplishments, and focus on your blessings. Uncover what you can do for yourself to increase your happiness.

Additional Vibrational Matching Gemstones for Bluebird

Apophyllite, clear quartz, citrine, gold tiger's eye, golden calcite, kyanite, peacock copper, rhodonite, rose quartz, and selenite.

11. Blue Jay and Angelite

Are you aggressive? Are you being bullied by someone? Do you speak up for yourself and establish clear boundaries? Is someone invading your space?

Blue Jay totem is an ally that will help you find your voice and your courage when you need to protect your space, family, business, or emotional field. Blue jays are aggressive and territorial. Call on the energy of Blue Jay when you need to speak up for yourself and establish a clear picture of acceptable and unacceptable behaviors from others regarding your personal space. When Blue Jay shows up in your life, it signals a time when it is important that you find your voice. It is time to express what needs to be said for the highest good of all concerned.

Blue Jays are seed spreaders. They enjoy acorns of the great oak tree and are sometimes responsible for new oak trees finding a place to take root. In fact, blue jays are said to have been responsible for reseeding the oaks after the last glacial period. Therefore, Blue Jay carries a message of encouragement from the oak tree to stand tall to overcome all odds— even if you are in a situation where you are being verbally disrespected. There is another message that carries the energy of both the oak and Blue Jay: Be adaptable and flexible when outside influences are affecting your personal space. Be courageous and bold.

Blue Jays are known for storing their food for later. This characteristic makes Blue Jay an ally to remind you to always have food in your cupboards. Being prepared and having a plan in place for the future is a key lesson.

Blue Jay's Vibrational Matching Gemstone: Angelite

Angelite helps restore balance. This stone helps you formulate your plan on how and when you will express yourself. As a throat chakra stone, it aids in aligning with Divine timing so that the time and place of the communication is ideal. Heavenly blue angelite is a good stone for attracting Divine intervention through communication with the angels. With angelite on hand, call on the angels to help you with your emotional upsets. If you feel the need to cry or if you are experiencing internal emotional angst, touch this stone and gaze at the calming blue color while you form the thought or prayers asking your angels to help you.

Divine Influence

Call on your Guardian Angel to help you recognize that you are protected and the Angel of Communication to help you find the courage to speak up and set boundaries.

Blue Jay's Location on the Wheel of Life

Blue Jay is located on the southern quadrant, where transformation of emotional challenges and self-empowerment are experienced.

Contemplate This

Is there a bully in your life? Are the words and actions of a coworker, friend, spouse, or family member intimidating you? Is it time to look at yourself to observe if you, in fact, are the bully? Allow yourself to be calmed by the vibration of the color blue. Be mindful of how you let others talk to you—and how you talk to them.

Message from Blue Jay

This is a time when you need take a look at how you interact with others. Observe if you are imposing your energy on others. Have your words been less than loving? On the other hand, perhaps you need to defend yourself. Have the courage to speak up. Look at how you use your power over others and how others use their power over you.

Blue Jay Affirmation

I communicate with ease and grace. I attract people who are kind and respectful in the manner in which they interact with me. It is safe for me to set boundaries in loving ways. I deserve to be respected. I am prepared in every way. I tap into the courage and strength that resides deep within me.

Message from Angelite

Quiet your mind, and give yourself permission to communicate with the angels and other spirit guides. Remember, true communication includes listening as well as speaking. Get clear on how far you'll allow someone to push you before you speak up for yourself. Contemplate how you may be bullying someone else. Invite the angels to gently orchestrate your interactions with others.

Additional Vibrational Matching Gemstones for the Blue Jay

Amazonite, aquamarine, blue calcite, blue lace agate, celestite, citrine, indicolite, lapis lazuli, and sodalite.

12. Buffalo and Sardonyx

Are you using your resources fully and completely? Do you let food or other things go to waste? Do you honor your food and the sources that brought your meal to your table?

Buffalo totem is an ally that helps you maintain your connection with the spiritual source of your life. The American buffalo, which is known as bison, is a massive animal that once freely roamed the prairies. Buffalo medicine holds the energy of prayer and gratitude. One of the teachings of White Buffalo Calf Woman, who brought the pipe to the people, was to help people remember God–Creator–Great Spirit and pray. White Buffalo portends a time of peace in your life. In general, Buffalo signals a time to be extra mindful in food preparation and ingestion.

Buffalo gave his whole body to the Great Plains Indians, and they respected Buffalo by only taking what they needed and finding a way to use every part of the buffalo. You, too, can establish a practice in which you place leftover parts of your food into a compost bin and leave the non-compostable food for the wild animals so that nothing goes to waste.

A beautiful lesson from this vibration of non-waste is to focus on gratitude for the food you have from its earliest inception. While preparing the food, focus on the process of how it grew and everyone who was involved throughout the process of getting that food to your counter for preparation. Keep your awareness on gratitude for the many people who were involved, from planting to harvesting and from packaging to delivery. When you do this, your food will be much richer and blessed as you ingest it. This is Buffalo's teaching. Open up to receive and begin saying your prayers of gratitude before the fruits of your labor are manifested.

Buffalo's Vibrational Matching Gemstone: Red and Black Sardonyx

Red and black sardonyx provide stabilization and the strength required for the endurance, energy, and fortitude to create prosperity and good fortune. After all, Buffalo signals a time of prosperity and abundance. With sardonyx in hand, you can begin transforming your energies into tangible results. Prosperity and abundance are the result of actions you've taken to bring in income. Sardonyx's rich, bold colors are a grounding force; this combination helps you maintain a strong foundation and provides you a firm springboard for tangible results.

Divine Influence

Call on the Angel of Gratitude to help you maintain focus on the blessings in your life.

Buffalo's Location on the Wheel of Life

Buffalo is located on the northeast quadrant, where wisdom and gratitude for life's experiences are practiced.

Contemplate This

Are you increasing the flow of financial resources into your life? Have you stopped for a moment of gratitude today? When was the last time you prayed? Clear your mind, and establish a focused intention regarding abundance and prosperity. Setting an intention provides a strong foundation for prayer and visualization. Count your blessings, from the mundane to the extraordinary.

Message from Buffalo

Take time to stop and be grateful for every little thing. Experience the magical manifestation of extraordinary wealth and abundance on all levels. Use everything, and waste nothing. Reuse, reduce, and recycle. Buffalo have been near extinction in the past, reminding you to take and use only what you need. Have gratitude for all that you are and for your unlimited potential. Waste nothing, and enjoy every morsel life has to offer.

Buffalo Affirmation

All that I need is available to me. I am truly blessed. Prayer is a powerful resource for me. In my mind are loving thoughts for everything that helps me live a happy life, including people I don't know. I am grateful for all the gifts that come into my life. I have extraordinarily good fortune in all aspects of my life.

Message from Sardonyx

A clear mind and focused intention provide a strong foundation for accomplishments. Recognize all your accomplishments. Practice gratitude for all the blessings in your life. Have gratitude for all that you are and for your unlimited potential. Enjoy every morsel life has to offer, and waste nothing. With this stone in hand, amplify your loving prayers and focused intentions to contribute to world peace.

Additional Vibrational Matching Gemstones for Buffalo

Amethyst druzy, angelite, celestite, copper, jade, howlite, rose quartz, ruby in zoisite, seraphinite, and serpentine.

13. BUTTERFLY AND PHANTOM QUARTZ

Have you been thinking about making a few small changes in your life? Are you willing to experience a fairly big result or series of outcomes that change the course of your life? Have you noticed that something feels different? Is your direction changing?

Butterfly totem is an ally for when you are about to make a significant change in your life. The butterfly effect is a theory that the slightest change can have very big effects somewhere else. With this in mind, even the smallest of changes in your perception or the way you think can change your life significantly. Your choices in this moment through realizations and the way you look at things make up your life experiences. Just as a butterfly begins as an egg and goes through many stages to reach the point of metamorphosis, you, too, have the opportunity to create your reality in stages with every thought, word, feeling, and action.

When Butterfly appears in your life, take the time to observe your situation and become aware of imminent changes. You may be on the precipice of a new chapter of your life or a new way of looking at life. Participate in the changes instead of letting the changes happen to you. Be the change, and alter the trajectory of your path. The gentle energy of Butterfly is a perfect reminder that you have the courage you need in the face of changes and challenges. Metamorphosis is the keyword for Butterfly because of the profound levels of transformation in the cycles of its life.

Butterfly's Vibrational Matching Gemstone: Phantom Quartz Crystal

The phantom quartz crystal contains ghost-like images of crystal faces caused by a pause during the growth of the crystal. The pause at each cycle of growth—the egg, caterpillar (larva), chrysalis (pupa), and adult butterfly—is symbolic of the pause that creates these ghost-like images in the crystal. This energy helps you gain clarity on repetitive emotional patterns throughout the various stages of your life. It is helpful for uncovering the cyclical nature of how you engage in relationships so that you can break recurring themes and move forward in a healthy way. Phantom quartz is a stone of transformation and change. It helps release the ego's attachment to behaviors and situations.

Divine Influence

Call on Archangel Zadkiel to help you process your spiritual transformation and cultivate the freedom to be all you can be.

Butterfly's Location on the Wheel of Life

Butterfly is located on the north path, where an evolutionary cycle of the wheel is completed.

Contemplate This

Do you go with the flow? Is change imminent? Are you able to accept a new life or a new way of being? The winds of change are blowing into your life. Make a choice to be the objective observer. In that decision, realize that your filters and the manner in which you were socialized deter your ability to be the objective observer. Go beyond the norm and use self-observation as a tool to make small changes in your life.

Message from Butterfly

You are blessed with autonomy. Recognize and integrate that you are free from external control or influences. This independence opens a new chapter with unlimited potential. This transformation will give you the freedom you have been seeking. Transform and transmute the old, and allow yourself to open to a new start. Express joy and happiness as you spread your wings.

Butterfly Affirmation

I embrace the hard-earned lessons of the past to catapult me into a bright and positive future. I easily adapt to my changing environment. Change is good. I recognize that all changes bring better life situations. Opportunities constantly present themselves to me. I recognize opportunities and take immediate action. I allow myself to spiral upward to higher awareness.

Message from Phantom Quartz

Observe what needs to be cleared away and renewed in your life. Look at where you've been, and realize there is so much more you can do, learn, and grow. Release patterns of your past and heal the issues once and for all. Emerge from your chrysalis and be free. Know that you are evolving and improving yourself on all levels.

Additional Vibrational Matching Gemstones for Butterfly

Amethyst, ametrine, charoite, green aventurine, green calcite, orange calcite, pietersite, pink calcite, purple-dyed agate, and tiger's eye.

14. CAMEL AND AZURITE-MALACHITE

Are you adaptable? Do you easily align and realign with life's current situation? Have you felt like you are subjected to whatever blows into your life, unable to adjust to the situation? Are you prepared? Do you have all your basic survival needs in place?

Camel totem as an ally helps you establish a mutually beneficial relationship with people, your surroundings, and any life situations that arise. Camel is adaptive. Its feet are designed to not sink when walking on sand. The broad base of Camel's feet teaches the importance of establishing a good foundation. When Camel shows up in your life, it's time to look at core issues that may need to be dealt with so that you have a sturdy foundation for your life's work. It's time to balance and align your health, your vital energy, and your ability to have plenty of money to pay for your core needs of food, shelter, and water. Camel also signals a time to heal relationships with others and find the right balance of adjusting to how other people are without losing yourself in the process. Like Camel's feet, avoid sinking into the "sand" of relationships.

Camel signals a time to save money and resources for the future. The humps on the camel's back are filled with fat, not water, so they have a reserve if they can't find food. Preparedness and basic survival are two key teachings from Camel. Camel teaches you to have your core basic needs met to navigate this life with ease.

Camel's Vibrational Matching Gemstone: Azurite-Malachite

Azurite-malachite represents the physical blending of two copper-carbonate minerals, which is symbolic of a symbiotic relationship. This copper-based stone, a mineral associated with prosperity and abundance, reminds you of living physical association. It helps you recognize that having plenty for yourself and plenty to share deepens your relationship with financial success. Use this stone as a conduit to maintain a grounded connection with the physical world. Azurite-malachite is a combination stone that helps all your body's systems to work together. Azurite promotes mental clarity and the proper flow of knowledge, which provides the information so you can make clear connections to recognize what is necessary to do to adapt and be prepared.

Divine Influence

Call on the Angel of Adaptability and the Angel of Abundance to help you be prepared in any life situation.

Camel's Location on the Wheel of Life

Camel is located on the southwest quadrant, where change and learning life lessons take place.

Contemplate This

Have you been taking good care of your health? Do you put money away into a savings account or have investments for the future? Are you ready with extra food in your pantry or freezer in case of an emergency? Take a good inventory of your relationships, your health, your financial situation, and your food stores. Put habits into place that cultivate healthy relationships, a healthy lifestyle, and a healthy bank account.

Message from Camel

Take an inventory of the food in your home, and determine if you have enough if there is a situation where you can't get to the store or if some other situation arises and the stores are closed. Survey your bank accounts and other stashes of money. Create a backup plan, and make sure everything is in place. You will feel more secure and safe in your daily life knowing that you've done what is necessary to take good care of yourself.

Camel Affirmation

My body is healthy. The cells in my body naturally regenerate and rejuvenate. I treasure the lessons I learn through being in relationships with others. I am prepared! I have plenty of everything I need and plenty to share. I am flexible and adaptable. I objectively observe circumstances and seize new opportunities as situations naturally shift and change in my life.

Message from Azurite-Malachite

It may be time to be more flexible. Observe yourself mentally, physically, spiritually, and emotionally to determine if you need to be more easy-going. Notice if those around you are in flow with your predominant intention. Trust your intuitive senses to know and act on gut feelings and insights. Look at patterns that no longer serve you, and replace them with new patterns of abundance, adaptability, and preparedness.

Additional Vibrational Matching Gemstones for Camel

Emerald, green aventurine, green tourmaline, Isis clear quartz point, jade, leopardskin jasper, Mookaite jasper, tree agate, pyrite, rutilated quartz, and tourmalinated quartz.

15. CARDINAL AND RED GOLDSTONE

Do you find that you often have to set boundaries to protect your personal space? Have you tried to communicate in a creative and melodic way? Do you like to sing? Are you interested in theology?

Cardinal totem is an ally for personal power and inner strength. Align with Cardinal's energy when you need to speak up for yourself and communicate with confidence and courage. Cardinals are songbirds and establish their territory with their song. They communicate with their life mate and other birds with their chirps and varying patterns of sounds. Let Cardinal help you when you need to find your voice to say what you need to say. Use different tones and ways of expressing yourself. For example, if you normally have a booming voice, try using a softer tone, or if your voice is normally high pitched, consciously lower your pitch.

The male's red coloring is distinctively brighter than the female cardinal, which is typically duller, depending upon the region. Cardinals received their name from early settlers because their red crest reminded them of the red biretta worn by Catholic cardinals. When Cardinal flies into your life, it signals a time to delve into higher spiritual teachings and academia.

Cardinals mate for life. Cardinal is a good ally to help you attract or maintain a lifelong partner and a stable household. While cardinals will not use the same nest again once their offspring have left, they tend to remain nearby.

Cardinal's Vibrational Matching Gemstone: Red Goldstone

Red goldstone is a man-made glass containing crystallized copper. Legend says that the original formula for this glass was gifted to monks near Murano, Italy. This little gem amplifies your brilliance. The vivid sparkles within help remind you of your magnificence and encourage you to shine your light brightly with confidence. This confidence can be called on when you need to assert yourself and courageously establish boundaries. Red goldstone aligns you with higher consciousness. It helps you become aware of the spiritual and mystical experience of the unity of the universe.

Divine Influence

Call on the Angel of Relationships, the Angel of a Happy Home, and Archangel Chamuel to help you manifest and maintain healthy relationships and home-life experiences.

Cardinal's Location on the Wheel of Life

Cardinal is located on the northwest quadrant, where the peace of home and hearth resides.

Contemplate This

Do you need more courage to set boundaries? Improve your ability to notice when people are true to their word, or not. Focus your attention on improving your knowledge base. Stay focused and concentrate, so that you can align with the higher knowledge that is accessible to all. It is beneficial for you to integrate complex scholarly subjects of higher education. Furthering your education will improve your confidence. As you strengthen your courage, you will have the guts to stand up for yourself and be empowered.

Message from Cardinal

Establish more effective ways to communicate. Find the courage to express and demonstrate your love to your partner through healthy communication. Spend time at home together, and enjoy your stable environment. Shift the tone of your voice to garner a better or different response. Listen to each other, and develop a stronger spiritual connection with each other.

Cardinal Affirmation

I am grateful for my stable home environment. I am blessed to live with the love of my life. It is easy for me to voice my feelings and intentions. I enjoy learning new things. I am smart enough to realize that I can always discover new information. I create the perfect space to learn.

Message from Red Goldstone

Increase your ability to be successful in all endeavors, including financial success, fertility, creativity, family blessings, happy home, healthy body, and much more. Make a decision to magnetically attract the perfect life partner or cultivate your existing relationship. Nurture and nourish the relationship you have with your significant other as it develops and evolves over the years. Seek to educate yourself in areas where you feel your knowledge may be lacking.

Additional Vibrational Matching Gemstones for Cardinal

Andulasite, blue calcite, clear quartz, fluorite, garnet, green tourmaline, lapis lazuli, red jasper, Mookaite jasper, pyrite, ruby, tabular quartz, and vanadinite.

16. Cat and Hiddenite

Are you independent, or are you dependent on others due to emotional attachments? Do you consider yourself to be flexible? Do you take the time to observe situations before taking action?

Cat totem is an ally for you when you need to be more flexible in various life situations and find balance between your dependent and independent behavior. For over 5,000 years, cats have been domesticated companions to humans in many civilizations. Cat is quite coordinated and has considerable elasticity. When Cat shows up in your life, you are being called to stop and observe yourself in order to determine how you can become more flexible.

Just as a cat stalks its prey, "stalk" your own emotions, actions, and reactions in order to uncover the source of repetitive patterns in your relationships, career, or any aspect of your life with gentleness and ease. The resulting realizations most often provide you with self-understanding and self-confidence. Cats are naturally intuitive. There are many people, including reputable researchers, who believe that cats have psychic abilities. Having Cat as a totem and a companion in life improves your intuition through resonance.

Cats can be nurturing and comforting as well as independent. Although they appear emotionally detached, they are loving companions. Cat's purr is a healing vibration. Most often, a cat's purr indicates contentment, although they may purr when they are nervous or sick. It has been said that when a cat purrs while on their human companion's lap, the sound and vibration contribute to the reduction in the time it takes to heal from broken bones, muscular challenges, and even infections.

Cat's Vibrational Matching Gemstone: Hiddenite

Hiddenite helps you improve intuitive insights. Keep it nearby when you delve into psychic development and training. Hiddenite can be used as a shield when you are feeling empathic. When you are feeling extremely sensitive, you can use hiddenite with the intention to be a buffer for the thoughts, feelings, and physical challenges of others. This stone is an excellent tool to relieve your mind of the incessant chatter in your everyday life, as well as when you meditate. Due to the lithium content within hiddenite, use this vibration to release mood swings and improve stable emotions. Use this stone to bring mental peace and serenity.

Divine Influence

Call on Archangel Camael to help you release out-of-balance emotions and the Angel of Flexibility to help you improve physical and mental balance.

Cat's Location on the Wheel of Life

Cat is located on the southwestern quadrant, where inner transformation and maturity is integrated.

Contemplate This

Do you need to be more flexible? When you observe yourself, do you perceive that you are mentally, physically, spiritually, and emotionally balanced? Look at each layer separately to understand how your thoughts affect you and others (mental). Check in with your physical structure to ascertain if your body is stiff or flexible (physical). Notice if you are a clear conduit of the Divine (spiritual). Take a moment to check in and feel your feelings. Notice your actions and reactions to others, on both the inner and outer space (emotional) levels. Observe yourself and those around you in order to be mindful of the predominant intention.

Message from Cat

Be alert, and observe your surroundings using all your senses. Take time to stretch and maintain your physical flexibility. Relax and curl up with your loved ones. Let yourself lie down and take a nap when you feel the need to rest. Use your voice to comfort yourself and others through song or humming. The sound and breath of your hum will slow your breathing and soothe you.

Cat Affirmation

It is easy for me to comfort myself and feel nurtured. I am calm. I am detached from drama. I am tranquil. My intuition is strong. It is easy for me to feel, sense, or know how others feel. I can tell the difference between my feelings and the feelings of others. I am flexible. I observe myself and all that is going on around me.

Message from Hiddenite

When you have a lot of worrisome thoughts and/or notice that you are extremely sensitive to the thoughts, feelings, emotions, and physical challenges of others, it's time to find mental peace and tranquility in your life. Spend time meditating to relieve your mind of the incessant chatter. Observe life in a detached manner, and focus on what is truly important.

Additional Vibrational Matching Gemstones for Cat

Amethyst druzy, azurite-malachite, labradorite, leopardskin jasper, lapis lazuli, lepidolite, moonstone, selenite, trilobite, and unakite.

17. Clam and Orthoceras Fossil

Are you shy and introverted? Are you filled with great ideas that you keep to yourself? Are you conscious of the underlying thoughts, feelings, and emotions that have made you who you are today?

Clam totem is an ally for you if you feel shy, reserved, or uncomfortable revealing your thoughts and feelings. There is a time for everything, which includes spending time in your inner world, although it is beneficial if these times occur occasionally rather than are the norm. Clams are ocean creatures that clean and filter water through their bivalve tissues. They constantly strain the water around them in search of food, which typically consists of bacteria or microscopic algae. Align with the energy of Clam and its beneficial filtration system to clean out what might be stopping you from emerging from your shell and being part of the vibrant experience of life.

Working with Clam medicine is great for sifting through emotions that feel like they are buried deep within the sands of your consciousness. On a symbolic level, Clam's filtration system represents emotions that are polluted with the remnants of the past. Use Clam medicine when you are in the process of releasing toxins in your physical body, as well as in your emotional body. Let that energy support you through your process.

Clam's Vibrational Matching Gemstone: Orthoceras

Orthoceras fossils help you get in touch with your subconscious and the deep inner feelings you have for yourself and others. Use orthoceras to fully comprehend the old adage "What goes around comes around" on an emotional level. Use it to stop the repetitive patterns in your life that cause you emotional distress. Orthoceras is beneficial for healing intestinal disturbances, for promoting proper absorption of nutrients, and for keeping the body hydrated. Use the vibrational couple of orthoceras and clam to aid in the proper integration and assimilation of information as well as nutrients. The ancient energy of orthoceras provides a deeper understanding of oneself through enhanced memory retrieval of previous incarnations. This fossil is ideal to use during regression therapy and later to capitalize on memories of past experiences and the lessons learned through them to awaken you to your life's purpose in this incarnation.

Divine Influence

Call on Archangel Haniel to help you align with your soul's purpose.

Clam's Location on the Wheel of Life

Clam is located on the northeast quadrant, where the understanding and wisdom that come from life experiences are recognized.

Contemplate This

Have you been feeling overwhelmed? Are you trying to sort through thoughts, feelings, and details to make sense of everything? Are you able to absorb and digest all that is happening, both physically and emotionally? Take the time to make lists and journal in order to sort through things. Drink water to filter impurities out of your physical body, and use meditation to clarify your mind. Let yourself open up in order to lighten up your life and cultivate good relationships.

Message from Clam

Pushing for new insights or understanding and trying to force information through your consciousness can be futile. Relax your body, mind, and spirit, and allow your subtle bodies to absorb what is truly important. Turn to water to help you cleanse and clear your body, mind, and emotions. Visit the ocean, a pool, or any nearby body of water.

Clam Affirmation

It is easy for me to take time for contemplative thought. I am observant of thoughts, words, feelings, and actions. The way to my future is clear and bright. My mind is free of unhelpful thoughts. My focused intent aligns me with my highest good. I easily move forward in life, using the lessons of my past as positive steppingstones to my future. My digestive system is healthy. I easily absorb and process all that goes on around me.

Message from Orthoceras

Cultivate the clarity you need to make important changes in your diet (including your mental diet!) to maintain healthy digestion. Put your awareness on the proper functioning of your gallbladder, liver, pancreas, spleen, and kidneys. Honor periods of growth in order to integrate the teachings of those past emotional lessons. Assimilate the various aspects of your life, your consciousness, and your emotions and then relax, knowing that the information will be retrievable when required for future use.

Additional Vibrational Matching Gemstones for Clam

Amber, ammonite, clear quartz, elestial quartz crystal, magnesite, petrified wood, smoky quartz, turquoise, and yellow jasper.

18. COYOTE AND MALACHITE

Are you conscious of the various intonations of your own voice as well as the voices of others? Do you pay attention to those cues? How well are you integrating the lessons from life experiences?

Coyote totem is an ally to help you navigate life's lessons. Coyote has been part of many stories, creation myths, and teachings passed down by indigenous cultures. The trickster (an anthropomorphized coyote) teaches lessons of self-observation. It is through recognition of your mistakes and the extraction of a lesson learned that you can integrate and, hopefully, find humor in the experience. Laughter is one of the keys to the transformation of a negative lesson into one where you can laugh at yourself. Through true integration and a lesson learned, knowledge and wisdom become a factor in the experience.

When Coyote steps into your life, pause and listen well. There is a lesson to be learned. Coyote is a very vocal animal, which makes Coyote an ally to storytellers, who teach morals and lessons through the narration of tales. Coyotes express themselves in a variety of ways: howls, yips, barking, whining, whimpering, and high-pitched sounds. Coyote medicine teaches you to enhance your communication style by using your voice with varying inflection, cadence, and other speaking patterns. Additionally, Coyote's vocal skills enhance your gift of clairaudience (the ability to hear messages from within) and telepathy (the ability to hear what is being projected through thoughts, feelings, and mental pictures).

Coyote's Vibrational Matching Gemstone: Malachite

Malachite helps you get to the heart of a matter. This stone reminds you that when patterns are repeated in relationships, there is a lesson to be learned. This stone helps you grow emotionally, as well as mentally and spiritually, as you recognize the emerging patterns. With the aid of Coyote medicine and malachite's bull's-eye effect, know your truth, speak your truth, and live your truth. Swirl into the center of your own consciousness to know when you need assistance, and use lessons from song lyrics, stories, movies, novels, articles, and tales from friends and relatives to help you through transitional periods of learning lessons.

With malachite in hand, examine the deeper recesses of your mind and life experiences. Follow the swirling patterns in order to symbolically encourage your mind to find answers, uncover truths within stories and lyrics, and deepen your life experience.

Divine Influence

Call on Archangel Raphael to help you heal and transform on all levels and guide you to another level of self-awareness.

Coyote's Location on the Wheel of Life

Coyote is located on the south path, where transformation, learning, and the integration of life lessons are made possible.

Contemplate This

Are you able to laugh at your mistakes? Do you take the time to learn from them? Have you felt like life is playing tricks on you? Observe yourself and the series of events that led up to perceived mistakes. Find the humor and levity in the situation. Allow the energy of the lesson to help you mature and grow. Transform and transmute stuck emotions through sound and song. Rewrite your story and achieve your full potential.

Message from Coyote

Your repetitive patterns in life are important to recognize so that you can prepare to emerge from the maze you've created. Walk the labyrinth, and find the higher spiritual purpose for all of your challenges and lessons. As you discover which patterns no longer serve you, remove them and replace them with new patterns. Look for the emerging patterns of joy, harmony, and inner peace. Embrace them, and continue forward in your evolutionary spiral upward.

Coyote Affirmation

I focus my attention on my behaviors and their results in order to learn from the past. I recognize repetitive patterns. I choose patterns of love, compassion, and kindness. Laughter and compassion for myself help heal emotional wounds. I am responsible. I stay with matters until they are settled, and I then understand them. I accept myself and have tolerance for my way of being as I learn and grow.

Message from Malachite

Perhaps you've been spiraling, round and round, trying to find the answers to improve a situation in your life. Meditate on remembering your sacred contract and life purpose. Change the mental composition of your thoughts. Break down old repetitive ways of thinking, and reconstitute them with a new storyline. Restructure thoughts, giving them new life with a positive twist.

Additional Vibrational Matching Gemstones for Coyote

Amazonite, ammonite, angelite, blue lace agate, chevron amethyst, Picasso stone, tabular quartz, turquoise, and vanadinite.

19. CRAB AND TRILOBITE

Do you see things from all perspectives? Can you find different approaches to life situations? What kind of signals are you sending out into the world?

Crab totem is an ally that aids you in finding your unique path and your ability to shift and change directions when necessary. Crabs are known for walking sideways and their ability to walk in any direction. This characteristic is a quality to remember when you are approaching something head on and it's just not working. Let Crab's energy remind you that different perspectives and approaches can be beneficial.

Crab has a hard outer shell, which is a symbol of protection of the emotional body. As an aquatic creature, Crab's medicine is associated with your inner feelings and emotions. Crab must soften its hard shell to molt; otherwise, the hard shell prevents it from growing. To grow, your hard outer shell must soften; true growth comes through vulnerability. The value of having the hard outer shell, for you and Crab, is to protect you from unwelcome predators. Symbolically, this shell can aid in having a strong sense of self and the ability to set boundaries.

When Crab sidles into your life, let yourself release crusty old energy and emotions so that you can evolve and allow for personal and spiritual development. Crab, as an ally, can assist you when you want to attract the perfect mate and the most authentic understanding friends. Once you have let go of the emotional walls, you are free to send out various types of signals through vibratory means, just as the crab does for its mating process. Signals include your appearance, your scent, and even the sounds you emit. Whether you are sending out mating signals or platonic vibes, Crab is a surprisingly good ally to have on your side.

Crab's Vibrational Matching Gemstone: Trilobite

Trilobite is a fossilized marine creature from more than 500 million years ago. This fossil can help you uncover crusty feelings and emotions that are affecting your decisions and actions. Use trilobite to release these unwanted memories. A trilobite fossil is a good tool to help you turn off your filter so that you aren't jaded by your personal experiences all the time. Trilobite helps you sort out your emotions so that you can be pure and unfettered by emotional baggage. At the same time, symbolically, the filtering system of trilobite keeps unwelcome energies from interfering with the process. Trilobite is a good fossil to work with in order to become highly sensitive while still being protected from others' energies.

Divine Influence

Call on the Angel of Balanced Emotions to help you have healthy relationships and a happy life.

Crab's Location on the Wheel of Life

Crab is located on the eastern portion of the southeast quadrant, where perspective is integrated and the emotional body is healed.

Contemplate This

Determine which feelings are yours and which feelings have been imposed upon you by society or other people. Write down your thoughts; journaling can help you sort out your feelings so that you can release any emotional walls you may have set up for protection. Gain perspective, and clear the pathways to self-awareness. Through emotional balance, you can find alternatives for enjoying your life. Balance your mind with your heart and emotions.

Message from Crab

You may be in need of protection. Being very sensitive to the feelings and emotions of others, you may need to spend time alone in order to feel balanced. You are a highly sensitive person and extremely intuitive. Use your intuition as a filtering system to keep unwelcome energies from interfering with your inner peace. It is important to recognize when it is safe to let those boundaries down in order to let others into your life.

Crab Affirmation

I easily accept the things that happen in life. I readily absorb life experiences. It's easy for me to filter out the unnecessary and retrieve good energy. I discern what's important. My emotions are balanced. My ability to see and know the truth is exceptional. My digestive system functions optimally. I gratefully receive guidance from my ancestors.

Message from Trilobite

Drink enough water, and take time to immerse yourself in healing waters, such as a bath or a refreshing pool. Water purifies your body and mind. Hydrate yourself inside and out in order to maintain fluidity at all levels of consciousness. Allow the natural flow to detoxify your body, mind, and emotions. Clarity provides you with a higher understanding and an avenue to deal with emotions in a balanced way.

Additional Vibrational Matching Gemstones for Crab

Aragonite, black tourmaline, Botswana agate, elestial quartz crystals, jasper, howlite, orange calcite, smoky quartz, and unakite.

20. CROCODILE AND ORANGE CALCITE

Do you have a tendency to conceal yourself and your motives from others? Do you need to keep your mouth shut about something? Are you patient? Are you resistant to change?

Crocodile totem is an ally to assist you when you want to keep your plans or projects a secret from others. Ambush is Crocodile's method of hunting, which requires the use of its extraordinary sense of smell and sight while mostly submerged and out of sight. Patience is a key trait of Crocodile, because it waits for its prey to come nearby and then makes a surprise attack. Crocodile medicine doesn't mean you need to attack, but rather, take mindful action at exactly the right moment. The teaching for you is that there are times when keen senses and waiting patiently out of view until just the right moment is more powerful than taking immediate action.

Crocodile supports you during times when you know you need to let go of the old way of doing things. On the other hand, if you've achieved a tried-and-true method of doing things that has worked for many years, then crocodile can be your ally as well. Crocodile has powerful jaws that bite down with incredible pressure, although, if Crocodile's mouth is being held shut, it cannot open its mouth. Crocodile teaches you when it's important to keep quiet and wait for the right time to speak.

Crocodile signals you to notice if you're holding on to something and won't let it go. Adaptability is one of this reptile's traits. Crocodile hasn't changed much since the age of dinosaurs; they have had to adapt to changing environments and behaviors for over 80 million years! Experience over the millennia has given Crocodile an evolutionary advantage, as they've learned to observe patterns and actions of their prey. Watch and wait.

Crocodile's Vibrational Matching Gemstone: Orange Calcite

Orange calcite helps you become conscious of repetitive patterns and clarify what shifts to make for your evolution. When you are in the process of changing your reality, it is beneficial to be the observer. This tool gives you the ability to see if you are stuck in a rut or limiting belief systems. Orange calcite helps you adapt to your changing environment, as you realize that change strengthens your soul's evolutionary journey. This stone is especially effective in working with the emotions that arise due to sudden changes. Use orange calcite to encourage patience and release impatience into realizations and understanding so that you can take action at exactly the right moment.

Divine Influence

Call on Archangel Gabriel to help you conceal your intentions while you patiently experience quiet introspection and Archangel Zadkiel to help you transform situations and adapt.

Crocodile's Location on the Wheel of Life

Located on the southwest quadrant, where transformation occurs and introspection garners realizations

Contemplate This

Are you good at seeing patterns of behavior in others? When Crocodile swims into your life, become the objective observer in order to assess situations and the best time to take action. With patience and keen observation, you can make decisions based on information, remarks, statements, and clear consideration. Opportunities abound. Do you feel like you keep missing promising opportunities? Have faith. Allow yourself to recognize this powerful force and believe that you are always in the right place at the right time with the right people.

Message from Crocodile

Be the objective observer. Notice the patterns and habits you have created in your life, and make the same observations of those close to you while withholding judgment. Release assumptions, and interpret situations based on facts. Use all your senses to determine when to reveal yourself and your intentions. Timing is important. Believe that Divine timing is at play in your life. Adapt and go with the flow of the evolutionary tides of your life.

Crocodile Affirmation

I am flexible and adaptable. I trust in the relaxed movement of the day. I objectively observe circumstances

and seize new opportunities as situations naturally shift and change in my life. There is no resistance, only willingness to go with the flow. I have Divine timing. I am always in the right place at the right time with the right people.

Message from Orange Calcite

When trying to gain some clarity in some part of your life, begin to notice the larger-than-life signs and messages all around you. Perhaps it's time to believe what you see or perceive. Honor your intuition and your ability to see the truth. Make a stronger connection with Mother Earth and ground yourself with earth-centered spirituality. Integrate the meanings of the messages from your surroundings to guide you on your path.

Additional Vibrational Matching Gemstones for Crocodile

Blue calcite, blue lace agate, Botswana agate, optical calcite, peridot, and turquoise.

21. Crow and Lodestone

Are you getting warning signals? Is someone trying to tell you something you aren't understanding or hearing? Are you being a good communicator with your loved ones and your community?

Crow totem is an ally that will help you when you acknowledge your intelligence and support you during times when you must solve problems. Crows are very good communicators, so call on Crow when you need to sharpen your communication skills. They caw loudly, which sometimes serves as a warning to their companions that a predator is near. A crow's call isn't always a warning, though. In some instances, they are being territorial or arguing over food.

Surround yourself with people who will watch your back and warn you of danger. Pay attention to the caw of your spirit guides and angels who send you messages through symbols all the time. Notice your surroundings, and remember that a warning isn't always a negative thing. An opportunity may be presenting itself. Crows have a special place in supporting you in life. They have mystery and magic woven into their history. When Crow flies into your life, look for sudden gifts, surprises, and messages.

Crows are social birds; a flock of crows is called a murder, and each flock has a distinct dialect. Cultivate good communication skills with your close-knit group so that you hear what is being communicated and you are being heard as well. Crows mate for life. Invite Crow to be your ally if you are looking for a lifelong partner. Crow contributes energy to your intention not only to have a mate for life but also to raise a family with your mate.

Crow's Vibrational Matching Gemstone: Lodestone

Lodestone is beneficial to keep nearby when you want to improve both spoken and telepathic communication. The energy of this stone helps you read between the lines in order to truly grasp what is being said or written. A stone of good luck, lodestone helps you focus your attention on creating a world filled with good fortune for yourself and your loved ones. Maintain a positive outlook using the energy of magnetism inherent within this stone. It is a magnet for all of the good things in life. Invite loyal and trustworthy people and situations into your life, with lodestone in hand. In fact, use the magnetic quality of lodestone to attract your lifelong partner or improve your existing relationship.

Divine Influence

Call on Archangels Gabriel and Haniel to help you hear and heed messages.

Crow's Location on the Wheel of Life

Crow is located on the southeast quadrant, where clarity increases and relationships heal.

Contemplate This

What are you drawing into your life? Are you getting alerts or warnings to pay attention? Do you trust your intelligence? You may be receiving prophetic or predictive indicators of things to come. There are many ways to hear and learn. Sometimes, you are the one who is warning others; sometimes, people or nature are sending you signals as a warning; and other times, you must pay attention because an opportunity may be in your path.

Message from Crow

Listen. There are messages all around. You are being alerted to pay attention. Spend time with your friends, and cultivate your connection with others. You will feel supported by being with your community, and your friends will know they can depend on you, too. If you've been considering entering into a relationship, whether it is a romantic relationship or a business relationship, first gain clarity regarding what you want in that relationship.

Crow Affirmation

Messages come to me in many ways. I am an objective observer. I am mindful. My intuition is getting stronger and comfortable. I pay attention to guidance from the Divine. I am a magnet for all the good things in life. I align with my spiritual strength. My consciousness is awake. I am aware. I allow love and a strong connection with my life partner.

Message from Lodestone

You are a magnet for all the good things in life. You likely enjoy scholarly activities or mind-bending projects. It is time to embrace concepts that may seem too challenging at first glance. You have a brilliant mind and good problem-solving capabilities. Are you a good listener? Are you heard and understood? Maintain a positive outlook, using the energy of magnetism inherent within the stone to alert you to what is around you.

Additional Vibrational Matching Gemstones for Crow

Black obsidian, black tourmaline blue lace agate, celestite, cathedral quartz, fluorite, magnetite octahedron, moldavite, scolecite, and selenite.

22. Deer and Rhodochrosite

Are you a bit shy about asserting your power? Do you find it uncomfortable to set boundaries? Do you know how to use your gentle yet powerful strength?

Deer totem is an ally that will help you connect with your sensitive nature, your strong intuition, and your gentleness. Deer is an animal of power. If you have Deer medicine, you can transform challenging situations through your self-confidence and firm yet gentle approach to life situations.

Doe, a female deer, enjoys the company of other does and their young. If you are a woman, this characteristic invites you to use Deer medicine to connect with circles of women for camaraderie and support. Regardless of your gender, Doe invites you to cultivate a group of supportive friends.

If Deer has bounded into your life, mindfulness is key. The ability to separate yourself from a potentially dangerous situation is crucial for your well-being and those around you. Deer are fast and agile. They quickly assess the situation and can be off and running, sometimes up to 35 miles per hour. This characteristic of Deer medicine can help you to evaluate your circumstances and quickly flee, if necessary.

Exercise and improve your physical strength in order to increase your core energy for those times when you want to speak up for yourself and the situation calls for it. There is a direct correlation between your physical strength and your self-esteem. It is one of the objectives in physical fitness and exercise programs to improve personal behavior and assertiveness training. Use Deer's energy as an ally for you when you want to be light on your feet on a physical level and quick to assess your setting on a mental and emotional level.

Deer's Vibrational Matching Gemstone: Rhodochrosite

Rhodochrosite emanates gentle vibes while at the same time amplifying your ability to set boundaries. This nurturing, heart-centered gemstone supports you in becoming comfortable with asserting your inner strength. It amplifies your intention to be powerful in loving ways. Use rhodochrosite to help you have the confidence and know-how to improve your health and physical strength. The loving vibration of this gem lends energy to improved mental and emotional well-being. Use rhodochrosite as an ally to rid yourself of subconscious fears in order to have the courage to assert yourself.

Divine Influence

Call on Archangel Auriel to help you focus on a strong physical body and overcome fears.

Deer's Location on the Wheel of Life

Deer is located on the east path, where illumination and clarity are offered.

Contemplate This

Situational awareness is always essential for your safety, but especially when Deer has come to your attention. It is important to have the courage and confidence to take action. Let experiences from the past empower you as you learn and grow. Make positive changes based on the situation at hand. If you need to, leap away from uncomfortable circumstances, if you are feeling uncomfortable based on your observations. Take time daily or multiple times a week to improve your physical strength and stamina.

Message from Deer

You are magnificent. Believe in your magnificence, and embrace your power. You are strong enough to set boundaries with others and lovingly assert yourself. Allow yourself to recognize this powerful force and believe that you have the right to stand up for yourself. Add swift movement to your exercise program, such as walking or running, to be sure to maintain a strong, agile body.

Deer Affirmation

Power and strength are mine. I have the courage to set boundaries with love and grace. I am protected. I adapt to new situations easily. It is safe to be powerful in loving ways. I express my power with loving-kindness. Love vibrates through the sounds I make. I exercise regularly, and I am physically fit.

Message from Rhodochrosite

You might be lacking confidence in your abilities. Be adaptable. It's time to take action. Gently assert yourself. Be determined and confident, and make the necessary changes to transform your life! Acknowledge your magnificence as well as your shortcomings, and focus on what you do well to increase your self-esteem. Trust that it is safe to be powerful.

Additional Vibrational Matching Gemstones for Deer

Amber, amethyst, ametrine, blue calcite, citrine, golden calcite, golden topaz, orange calcite, red goldstone, and sunstone.

23. DOG AND IOLITE

Are you craving companionship? Do you feel loved? Are you surrounded by loyal people who love and like you unconditionally?

Dog totem is an ally that helps you attract loyalty and unconditional love. Unconditional love includes acceptance, tolerance, compassion, and kindness toward all beings. Dogs love unconditionally and offer companionship. Dogs are humans' best friends. They are loyal, affectionate, and dedicated. Like their human companions, dogs just want to love and be loved. They want to please you.

Dog medicine brings you the vibration of compassion and understanding. Dogs bring comfort through hugs, cuddles, and their very presence. The magnitude of their joy and happiness when you arrive (sometimes even from another room) is beyond measure. Their reaction is priceless. When Dog comes into your life, observe your willingness to offer unconditional love and acceptance. Take note of your ability to be a loyal, compassionate, and kind friend. In many ways, dogs are altruistic. They have selfless concern for their human companions. Selflessness is a practice of concern for the welfare of others. Your canine companions often take actions for the benefit of others at their own expense. Call on the energy of Dog medicine to assist when you are pursuing altruistic pursuits.

Dog helps you align your relationships with comfort, love, and true companionship. Dog medicine relates not only to the faithfulness of the relationship you have with others but also (and especially) to the faithfulness of the relationship you have with yourself. Dog helps you attract loving, authentic, and supportive colleagues, family, and friends and helps you feel safe and protected.

Dog's Vibrational Matching Gemstone: Iolite

Iolite is a reminder to focus on being loyal to yourself and loving yourself unconditionally. Keep iolite with you when you want to attract a best friend or a circle of trustworthy companions. The blue color of iolite elicits true blue energy and is calming. When you feel peaceful, it helps you allow love, adoration, and companionship into your life, which like that of a dog is healing and nurturing. Iolite supports altruistic work that affects many people. It helps you give of yourself to benefit others. Iolites amplifies Dog medicine's vibe of dogged determination.

Divine Influence

Call on the Angel of Loyalty and the Angel of Unconditional Love to help you set an intention to attract thoughtful, loving friends who honor you on all levels.

Dog's Location on the Wheel of Life

Dog is located on the south path, where healing one's heart and relationships is made possible.

Contemplate This

Are you yearning for companionship? Would you like to attract loyal and supportive friends into your life? Do what it takes to make yourself happy. Devote time and energy to doing things that make you feel protected. Be your own best friend first, and gain clarity on what you are looking for in your friendships. You'll start to see an increase in loyal and caring friends in your life as soon as you decide that you are willing to accept their love in your life.

Message from Dog

Take a look deep into yourself to check in on your own level of fidelity and dependability. Is yours or someone else's loyalty in question? Are you building relationships with trustworthy and reliable people? You can benefit from a connection with an animal companion for overall well-being. Consciously decide to create happiness and harmony, and you will naturally attract unconditional love and good friends.

Dog Affirmation

I attract loyal people into my life. I cultivate and maintain meaningful relationships. I am loyal and faithful. I am blessed with great friends, companions, and colleagues. I am loving. It's easy for me to express my love. I willingly share my love and my life with others. I am filled with happiness and have an exuberance for life. My spiritual life is full. I love to share my blessings with others!

Message from Iolite

Dog medicine can attract relationships into your life that will provide loving companions or a mutually satisfying relationship. It is safe to allow others to do nice things for you and shower you with gifts. Permit blessings and love to pour into your open, receptive heart. It's time to receive with grace. Decide what types of people you want in your life, and know that you can attract them.

Additional Vibrational Matching Gemstones for Dog

Citrine, Dalmatian jasper, green aventurine, green tourmaline, emerald, jade, lapis lazuli, pink calcite, rose quartz, sapphire, and sardonyx.

24. DOLPHIN AND BRUCITE

Have you found that you feel much better after spending time at the shore? Are you a sociable person? A playful person? Do you enjoy being part of a group?

Dolphin totem is an ally that reminds you that play is a vital part of a happy life. If you think about it right now, when was the last time you played? Did you play with others? Play benefits your relationships, your mood, and is an effective way to cultivate joy. Dolphins are naturally playful mammals that live in pods of anywhere from two to 12 dolphins. The members of the pods develop strong bonds and assist one another as needed.

When Dolphin appears in your life, it signals a time to pay attention to communication from others as well as your ability to communicate effectively. Dolphins use a variety of sounds, such as clicks, whistles, moans, and squeaks, to express themselves. The clicks are part of echolocation, which allows them to perceive the distance of objects around them. These characteristics remind you that it's important to maintain situational awareness and be open to receiving information or communication beyond ordinary means. Telepathy is a form of communication available to you as a human that is beyond the ordinary. Trust those telepathic messages, and be the objective observer.

Notice whether you hold your breath when you are waiting for something less than pleasant to happen or breathe deeply and cultivate ways to flow with the experience. Change is always present. Every day and every moment are open to a new reality. It's up to you to create your reality.

Dolphin's Vibrational Matching Gemstone: Brucite

Brucite (especially the pastel-blue variety) is extraordinarily helpful for communicating with the spirits of the oceans, lakes, and rivers. Communing with nature enables you to realize the oneness of all life, thereby expanding your spiritual awareness. Brucite also expands your mental pathways so that you can more easily generate new ideas. It helps you venture outside your regular way of thinking and use your mind in different ways to achieve new results in your life. When it is especially necessary to remain hydrated, brucite is a good reminder to drink plenty of water. Use this stone to energetically enhance your body's ability to integrate oxygen into your cells.

Divine Influence

Call on Archangel Thuriel to help you effectively transmit your words, thoughts and feelings telepathically.

Dolphin's Location on the Wheel of Life

Dolphin is located on the northeast quadrant, where growth to the next level occurs and new cycles begin.

Contemplate This

Do you notice that you hear or know what people think, even if they don't say it out loud? Are you aware of the thoughts and feelings of animals and nature? Be aware of your breath's ability to align and balance you. It is time to accept that you are a naturally good communicator and embrace your ability to express yourself. Communing with nature enables you to realize the oneness of all life. Allow your connection with nature to expand your spiritual awareness.

Message from Dolphin

Take notice of how well you go with the ever-changing flow of life. Take a deep breath, and get in touch with your emotions. As a mammal of the water, Dolphin reminds you that it is beneficial to pay attention to your feelings, embrace them, and breathe through your feelings. Spend some time by the ocean, and connect with the healing energy of the salty seawater and its cleansing properties to support your health, physically and emotionally. Not near an ocean? Saltwater purifies body and mind. Get into a bathtub with some bath salts, or use a salt lamp to help realign you.

Dolphin Affirmation

I listen and really hear what others are saying. I understand what others are communicating, including what isn't spoken aloud. Peacefulness and playfulness are mine, now and always. Every breath I take increases my life force and vitality. I am in touch with my emotions. I breathe in life completely. It is easy for me to relax into the ebb and flow of life.

Message from Brucite

Go with the flow, and find a unique way to perceive your reality. It's a good idea to increase your intake of water or take a walk by a lake, ocean, or river. Connect with nature and flow with the current. Your ability to telepathically communicate (send and receive nonverbal messages) improves when you daily form the conscious intent to eloquently express what isn't said.

Additional Vibrational Matching Gemstones for Dolphin

Amazonite, angelite, apophyllite, blue lace agate, blue calcite, celestite, indicolite, kyanite, and larimar.

25. DOVE AND OPTICAL CALCITE

Do you find love and peace in all you do? Are you striving to make a deeper and higher connection with the Divine? Are you ready to make peace with someone in your life?

Dove totem is an ally that will help you remember the love that you are and the peace within yourself. Dove has been a symbol of life and peace for a long time. According to the biblical story of the Great Flood, when Noah released a dove from the ark to find land, the dove returned with an olive branch. During ancient Roman times, the olive branch was used as a plea for peace. The phrase "to extend the olive branch" is still used today to make a request for a peaceful interaction. Because Dove is closely associated with this symbol, this ally signals to you that it's time to make peace with someone or something that has upset you. Dove helps you instill and invoke general peace and spiritual enlightenment in your life, and heralds the opportunity to be a transformational person in the lives of those you touch.

Dove is also a symbol of the Holy Spirit. In historical artwork, the dove has been a Christian icon symbolizing the descent of the Holy Spirit over the heads of apostles or those being baptized. Dove's presence reminds you that you are a spiritual being having a human experience.

When Dove flies into your life, pay attention to how the sound of your voice may affect others. Observe yourself and notice if your voice is soothing and gentle or harsh and hard. Is your manner of speaking unfriendly or welcoming like Dove's coo? Dove teaches you to align your voice to a sweet low sound that still has the power of a stronger use of your voice.

Dove's Vibrational Matching Gemstone: Optical Calcite

Optical calcite amplifies your connection with the Divine. It complements Dove medicine, which awakens your spiritual body and connects you with your Divine spark within. With this calcite in hand, focus on the light within you. It helps you recognize that you have a spiritual body filled with light. Optical calcite, well known for its clarity, is a tool that helps develop your clairvoyance as well as the other five "clairs" (or extrasensory gifts). Optical calcite invites you to acknowledge and use your spiritual sight, hearing, and all your senses on a metaphysical level.

Divine Influence

Call on Archangel Gabriel to help align you with inspiration and Archangel Haniel to help open you up to Divine communication and align you with your soul's purpose.

Dove's Location on the Wheel of Life

Dove is located on the south path, where love is transformed and actualized.

Contemplate This

Do you nurture dreams of peace? Do you fill your heart with love and peace? It is time to invoke Dove as a messenger in order to allow the gentle, loving vibration of purity and peace to embrace you in your life. Let yourself feel supported, and ignite the light of hope in your heart. Open up, so that Divine inspiration can enlighten you and bring you clarity in your heart and your mind. Through personal revelations and aha experiences, you have the gift of a higher power enlightening your consciousness.

Message from Dove

Be a messenger of peace and love. Be the peaceful one who brings positive change into the lives of those with whom you interact through gentle guidance, storytelling, or inspired writing. Cultivate the timbre of your voice to sooth and comfort. Form the intention that love and kindness are emanating through your words and voice. Listen to inner guidance. Pay attention to the dreams and symbols that fly into your life to guide you on your path of peace and love.

Dove Affirmation

I speak with loving-kindness. I am liberated and confident. Love vibrates through the sounds that come through me. The tone of my voice is perceived as peaceful and calm. I easily and honestly communicate what is on my mind. I speak eloquently. I effortlessly align with inner peace. I allow love, calm, and tolerance to integrate with my consciousness.

Message from Optical Calcite

You may be trying to gain some clarity in some part of your life. Larger-than-life signs and messages are all around you. Believe what you see or perceive. Honor your intuition and your ability to see the truth. Find peace with the truth so that you can stay aligned with love. Align with peaceful energy in order to bring about enlightened activity, serenity, personal power, and transformation from anger.

Additional Vibrational Matching Gemstones for Dove

Amazonite, amethyst, blue calcite, celestite, clear quartz, danburite, Herkimer diamond, kunzite, rose quartz, scolecite, and selenite.

26. DRAGONFLY AND AMETHYST CATHEDRAL

Are you caught up in an illusion? Do you see life situations with clarity? Are you ready to move forward and take swift action in your life?

Dragonfly totem is an ally to help you see life with great clarity and take action. Dragonflies have extraordinary eyesight and quick, agile flight. The power of Dragonfly helps you sort reality from illusion. If you are caught up in illusion, Dragonfly's energy can assist you in seeing the situation clearly and help you take speedy appropriate action.

Dragonfly is symbolic of pure water. Water is symbolic of uncovering and understanding emotions and feelings. When Dragonfly appears in your life, it is time to awaken and recognize your emotions and feelings and then take rapid action to create the life you want. Ask yourself, "What do I want?" Define your desires and take action. It is your life. You create it with your thoughts, feelings, words, and actions. Dragonfly and its iridescent wings flutter into your life as an opportunity to separate illusions from the dream. To manifest anything, you must be able to envision your goal or intention in your mind's eye and take action to materialize it.

Call on Dragonfly's vibration in order to be awake in life. Regardless of the daily illusions you may hold dear, you have the power to transport yourself out of that perception and fly higher in order to see life from a greater perspective.

Dragonfly's Vibrational Matching Gemstone: Amethyst Cathedral

Amethyst cathedral transforms and transmutes what is holding you back from seeing a different reality. Release the stories blocking your happiness and fulfillment of your dreams. Amethyst cathedral helps you interpret the intuitive insights you receive to help you in your daily life. The combination of Dragonfly and the violet light of amethyst enhances your ability to transform challenges into positive and powerful experiences. Use amethyst to envision yourself in the life you want to create as if it already exists. Create the illusion of actualization and manifestation, and surround it with the violet light of amethyst. Envision the situation changing to what you do want, versus how it currently is.

Divine Influence

Call on Archangel Auriel to help you realign your awareness away from subconscious fears and Archangel Gabriel to help you interpret your dreams and enhance inner knowing.

Dragonfly's Location on the Wheel of Life

Dragonfly is located on the southwest quadrant, where dreams and transformation are manifested.

Contemplate This

Are there situations in your life where the truth needs to be revealed? Are you ready to break through the illusions that others have erected, or perhaps the illusions you've created? It's time for you to work through the emotions that create misconceptions, both for yourself and those that you create for others. Use your dreams as a tool to balance your emotions. It is easy for you to transform the challenges of your past in order to let your true nature shine through. Wake up from the illusion.

Message from Dragonfly

You have an opportunity to break down illusions, uncover the truth, and overcome fears created by the illusions in your mind. Spend time in or near water in order to tap into your emotions and feelings and gain a deeper understanding of yourself. Allow the translucent wings of Dragonfly to help you see and understand the dream. Do something about your life and what you want to create. There is no better time than the present moment!

Dragonfly Affirmation

I am ready to transform my life into one filled with truth and clarity. My emotions are balanced. It's easy for me to transform and transmute challenging situations. I pay attention to my dreams, interpret them, and take action based on my findings. My understanding of symbols helps increase my self-awareness.

Message from Amethyst Cathedral

Journey into the depths of your consciousness to visualize and imagine your life as you want it to be. Use the power of creative visualization to script out various ways to direct and unfold your future. Expand your mind to realize your potential and reveal your own truth. Set up your sleeping quarters for restful sleep and dream recall, and rest well. Use the sleep state to dream potential realities and cement the manifestation. Practice the reality in dreams, both awake and asleep.

Additional Vibrational Matching Gemstones for Dragonfly

Chevron amethyst, dioptase, Herkimer diamond, labradorite, opal, opalite, peacock copper, pietersite, rainbow moonstone, and window clear quartz.

27. Duck and Pink Calcite

How do you cope when your emotions are running high? Do you find comfort when you are in the water? Are you adaptable? Are you yearning to feel the comfort of a family unit?

Duck totem is an ally that you can call on when you want to feel emotional balance. Ducks are waterfowl with special plumage designed to provide temperature control and waterproofing. Like Duck, you can delve into your watery emotions without losing your ability to stay afloat and remain in balance as you feel your feelings.

Ducks are adaptable in their ability to feel at home in trees, on land, or in water. Their clawed, webbed feet make it possible for them to grip different types of surfaces. Whether they are on a slippery surface, swimming, diving, or perching on a tree branch, they can adapt with ease. Ducks remind you to feel secure in various situations while maintaining a sense of balance and ease. Use the energy of Duck medicine to help you adapt to situations that cause intense emotional reactions.

Mandarin ducks are the ultimate symbols of love and marriage in Southeast Asia. It is said that Mandarin ducks are faithful lifelong mates and good luck symbols for a happy marriage. Their image or statue is used in classical feng shui to energetically adjust the environment to improve love relationships. In some feng shui traditions, the placement of a statue or a picture of a pair of ducks is used to encourage the energy of a happy family. Duck medicine is helpful when you want to just relax into your feelings and emotions and enjoy being with your family.

Duck's Vibrational Matching Gemstone: Pink Calcite

Pink calcite is a stone of good relationships, happy marriage, overall happiness, and comfort. Pink calcite activates loving thoughts by transforming less-than-ideal musings into thoughts of self-love, thereby increasing your ability to love and receive love from others. Hold this stone when you are concentrating on thinking positive and uplifting thoughts about yourself and others. Pink calcite activates the opening of your heart chakra so that you can release feelings of hurt or fear. Feelings of anger and frustration can be assuaged by keeping this stone nearby. It is also a useful stone for meditation or contemplation when you are working through your emotions.

Divine Influence

Call on Archangels Auriel and Muriel to help you release subconscious fears and balance emotional reactions and feelings and Archangel Chamuel to help you attract good romantic and platonic relationships.

Duck's Location on the Wheel of Life

Duck is located on the south path, where relationships are transformed.

Contemplate This

Do you need more sweetness in your life? Are you gentle with yourself in your words and thoughts? Treat yourself with kindness. When you treat yourself well, you can cultivate loving relationships with family and friends, and create a family-friendly environment. Be your own best friend, and be the best friend you can be to others. Love and accept your emotional nature. Release any and all beliefs that are associated with the lack of feeling loved or being loving. Transform it with self-nurturing, kindness, and compassion.

Message from Duck

The love of your life may be waiting to meet you, or perhaps reigniting your soul-mate connection with your partner is the order of the day. Maybe you are ready to start a family. Cultivate and nurture the loving relationships that are presently in your life, and change your mindset to think as "we" rather than as "me" to attract or renew more love into your life. You have the ability balance your emotions and improve confidence within relationships. Remember that when there are no expectations or assumptions, there are no disappointments.

Duck Affirmation

I am blessed with nurturing vibrations wherever I go! I am gentle with myself. I recognize that kind-heartedness brings about better life situations. I am kind and compassionate with others and myself. I enjoy loving relationships. I attract healthy, harmonious relationships into my life. I allow love. I am grateful for the romantic relationship in my life.

Message from Pink Calcite

Heart-centered thoughts directed toward yourself automatically realign you to be able to receive and accept love from others. Place your awareness on your heart. Come to the realization that you deserve love and that you are love. It is up to you to cultivate and nurture the love that you are. Once you treat yourself with loving-kindness, you will experience happy relationships.

Additional Vibrational Matching Gemstones for Duck

Chrysoprase, magenta-dyed agate, pink tourmaline, relationship quartz crystal, rhodochrosite, rhodonite, rose quartz, ruby, tabular quartz, unakite, and watermelon tourmaline.

28. Eagle and Window Quartz

Do you see life from a higher perspective? Do you believe in the power of prayer and connection with God, Goddess, and Creator? Are you seeking greater understanding of your life and your life path?

Eagle totem is an ally that assists you in raising your view and your intelligence so that you can see life from a greater perspective. With a bit of prayer, contemplation, and introspection, you can gain insight and understanding, which offers you a potential for advance hindsight. They say, "Hindsight is 20-20," meaning that it's easy to understand and have a better perspective after the fact, but it is possible to foresee potential outcomes (and avoid them if necessary) when you have a wider perspective. Eagles fly at a high altitude, so Eagle energy helps you achieve greater heights and thereby gain a higher viewpoint.

When Eagle flies into your life, take the time to pray and send petitions for assistance to the heavenly realm. Calm the incessant chatter of your mind so that you can hear and receive Divine guidance. Be serene and regain your mental focus. Ask for understanding from a higher power in any area of your life. Once you ask, be mindful of signs, symbols, dreams, and messages that are sent to you to provide understanding and assistance. A higher aspect of yourself has the wisdom needed for most life situations. Eagle totem encourages you to spend time with elders. Ask them for their input to garner their wisdom. Take note of your insightfulness, and employ it when leading others.

Remember to ask for assistance from the heavenly realm if Eagle has come to you. Divine intervention is available, but you must ask for it. Sit in silence, and align your consciousness with the highest energy available.

Eagle's Vibrational Matching Gemstone: Window Quartz

Window quartz helps you see into the window of your soul. The stone of the solitary spiritual seeker, window quartz is a portal into your consciousness. Window quartz has an additional facet on the point that is a perfect diamond shape. Use this stone to practice self-observation, as if you are flying like Eagle above yourself. This higher observation technique is especially beneficial during meditation. Try open-eyed meditation, and gaze into the diamond-shaped face on the point, forming the intent to experience higher understanding.

Divine Influence

Call on Archangel Haniel to help bring clarity to your life's purpose and messages from the Divine and Archangel Michael to help you see life from a greater perspective.

Eagle's Location on the Wheel of Life

Eagle is located on the eastern quadrant, where clarity and perspective are found.

Contemplate This

Do you feel your connection with the sky above? Are you able to see the life from a greater perspective? Let your consciousness soar high, as you stay grounded. Allow your vision of your future to reach far and wide to align with the past and the present—for yourself and others. Recognize your leadership abilities, and use them to benefit your community. Leadership can be a solitary experience, so remember to recognize like-minded visionaries and enjoy time with them.

Message from Eagle

Take care of your vision, and use your spiritual vision to cultivate greater understanding. Be fearless and remember your magnificence. Be tenacious with your goals and dreams. Hold on to your dreams firmly, and visualize them as if they have already taken place. Seek out the company of those who are aligned with a higher vision. Cultivate the leader within you. Be the visionary, and activate positive change. Through self-knowledge, you have a greater capacity to become a good leader.

Eagle Affirmation

I am awakening every day in many ways. I enjoy seeking connection with my higher self and observing myself from a higher perspective. I have great clarity. I am a catalyst to awaken awareness of all beings. I am a visionary leader. I see clearly now and become aware of profound spiritual truths.

Message from Window Quartz

A search for higher spiritual truths may be underway. There is still so much more to learn in life and so much more room to grow mentally, spiritually, and emotionally. Observe your thoughts, patterns, and behaviors. Release those that are no longer useful, and realign with a higher consciousness. Allow for the evolution of your mind and your mental capacities. Stay attuned to the realizations you have. You always have so much more to learn through elevated observation.

Additional Vibrational Matching Gemstones for Eagle

Amethyst, apophyllite, citrine, danburite, gold tiger's eye, Herkimer diamond, golden calcite, indochinite tektite, kyanite, moldavite, sapphire, and selenite rose.

29. EARTHWORM AND STROMATOLITE

Do you enjoy going into your inner cave to uncover your true self? Are you rigid in your thinking and your way of interacting? Have you spent time in a garden lately?

Earthworm totem is an ally that helps you become more flexible in your views on life. The vibration of Earthworm invites you into your special journey of self-awareness. Because Earthworm has no skeletal structure, it is extremely flexible as it burrows through the earth. Earthworms are the ultimate composter's and gardener's friend. Their work is important, in that they aerate and fertilize the soil. They burrow into the ground and eat organic matter, excreting it in a way that plants can best use it. Earthworm guides you as you process, integrate, and digest what you find within your belief systems, so that your experiences become rich fertilizer as you progress along this Earth Walk, your life journey.

Earthworm offers support when you experience shamanic spiritual travel into the underworld of your consciousness, both your subconscious and unconscious mental and emotional bodies. The more you delve into knowing yourself, the better off you will be in your quest for self-realization, personal development, and spiritual awakening.

By going deep within yourself to know and understand the many layers of your consciousness, you will uncover and embrace your talents and the confidence stored within. These past events and experiences from this life and other lives have a cumulative effect on who you are today and feed your body, soul, and spirit.

Earthworm's Vibrational Matching Gemstone: Stromatolite

Stromatolites are among the oldest fossils on earth, considered to be more than 3 billion years old. The layers in stromatolites contain ancient records of life on Earth; therefore, this stone stores ancient wisdom. Meditate with it to download what you need to know or integrate into your knowledge base. Stromatolites also carry the energy of dislodging any stored information that is causing a repetitive pattern in your emotional consciousness. Stromatolites, along with Earthworm's energy, assist you when you are removing toxins from your physical body and aiming to replenish your stores of essential vital nutrients in your body. This combined energy is beneficial for the assimilation of vitamins and minerals.

Divine Influence

Call on Archangel Sandalphon to help light your way toward becoming a steward of the earth and to help you participate in a practice that heals the planet.

Earthworm's Location on the Wheel of Life

Earthworm is located on the northwest quadrant, where the vibration of ancient records and inner work reside.

Contemplate This

Are you ready to revisit old wounds or issues to bring them to the light? Do you believe in past lives? It's time to tunnel deep within to heal past lives or past situations that may still bother you. Through inner work, dislodge any stored information that is causing repetitive patterns in your emotional consciousness. There are many layers of your consciousness from this life as well, so be open to understanding and honoring all that you have within you.

Message from Earthworm

Take your time. Burrow into your consciousness, and allow realizations to liberate you from unconscious ties that might bind you to an unyielding demeanor toward others. Implement a lifelong practice of contemplation, meditation, and tranquility, moving at a slow but steady pace. Be diligent and focused in carrying out a daily practice of self-observation and self-love. Allow yourself to be grounded and nurtured. Do the inner work, and you will find a life of happiness within.

Earthworm Affirmation

With love, calm, and tolerance, I unearth understanding of karmic lessons from this lifetime and those in the past. My digestive processes are healthy and effective. I integrate life situations and emotions, which provide me valuable teachings. I release toxic thoughts that have seemingly been part of my consciousness forever, and now they are gone! I accept and embrace my true nature, which is filled with blessings and love.

Message from Stromatolite

Your talents, virtues, and morals are a composite of many lifetimes of experience. You have access to the records and ancient wisdom that are stored within you. During meditation, make it your intention to request guidance that is filled with wisdom and knowledge. Go deep within yourself, way below the surface, and find comfort and peace in your being. In doing the practice of inner work, you will find the spiritual fortitude and consciously create circumstances for the good of all with more dedication and force.

Additional Vibrational Matching Gemstones for Earthworm

Amber, aragonite, channeling quartz, chrysanthemum stone, green moss agate, Laser wand, orthoceras, record keeper quartz crystal, selenite, and tree agate..

30. ELEPHANT AND VARISCITE

Who is the wise woman in your life? Do you honor her? Are you blessed with a strong bond with family and friends? Do you feel and sense the energetic vibration of thoughts and feelings of those who are part of your tribe?

Elephant totem is an ally for when you are developing and cultivating a community held strong by women. When Elephant walks into your life, you are being called to notice and find a community in which women hold the power and vision of the structure. A matriarchal society, which is rare among humans these days, allows for care to all members of the community. Look to the energy of Elephant to help you make your own community, where women hold the vision and overview. Treasure the memories you make with your family, community, and tribe. Make an effort to be with those you love on a regular basis to keep the bonds of family strong.

Elephant's ability to communicate involves sound communication (acoustic vibrations), olfactory communication (an acute sense of smell), visual communication (seeing), and tactile communication (rubbing their bodies or touching each other). Elephant behavior teaches you to use all of your senses when conveying and receiving information. When you are deeply in touch with these senses, extraordinary bonds can be established, developed, and cultivated.

Elephant's Vibrational Matching Gemstone: Variscite

Variscite aligns you with the nurturing energy of the Divine Mother, as well as your own mother or the matriarch in your life. Variscite is also beneficial when you want to find the right way and words to communicate something important. Use this stone to find the truth within you and then the confidence to comfortably embody your truth. Variscite is an ally when you want to know or speak the truth. Let it be your reminder to act with integrity or attract people of integrity into your life.

Divine Influence

Call on Archangel Auriel to help align you with the Divine Feminine and the energy of the matriarchal society.

Elephant's Location on the Wheel of Life

Elephant is located on the eastern portion of the northeast quadrant, where the wisdom of our ancestors is made available.

Contemplate This

Do you trust your intuition? Are you sensitive to the vibrations around you? Do you have a very good sense of smell? Have you developed a strong circle of friends and family? You can access great power by believing your hunches and feelings about people and life situations. Use all your senses—vision, hearing, feeling, knowing, taste, and smell. Trust yourself and embrace the sacred circle of your community to enjoy companionship, love, and support. Spend time remembering memories for nurturance and comfort.

Message from Elephant

Develop and cultivate a deep family bond. Find your "village" of people beyond your family, and nurture those connections. Be receptive and a good listener as well as a good communicator. Pay attention to the subtle rumblings barely audible or noticeable to others. Sniff things out before you act. Check in to see how things feel to you. Trust your intuition, especially your sense of smell and the sensations you receive through touch or feel.

Elephant Affirmation

I trust myself fully. I welcome loyalty from my friends, family, and colleagues. I treasure memories and embrace lessons learned from life experiences. I am surrounded and supported by good people. My sense of smell is keen and alerts me when I need to pay attention. I use my intuition and follow my hunches. The women in my life are filled with wisdom, and I honor the guidance they provide me.

Message from Variscite

Be mindful of your connection with Mother Earth beneath your feet and Grandmother Moon above your head, bringing Heaven and Earth together with feminine energy. Teach and learn through storytelling. Listen for the nuances of the story and the intonation of the voice, as well as any body movements, in order to receive or impart the truth of the message being delivered. Honor the feelings and realizations you receive during the various moon cycles.

Additional Vibrational Matching Gemstones for Elephant

Angelite, amazonite, bloodstone, clear quartz crystal, girasol quartz, jade, laser wands, moonstone, opal, pink calcite, rhodochrosite, selenite, tabular quartz, and turquoise.

31. Elk and Brecciated Red Jasper

Do you find it beneficial to be part of a professional organization or community group? Are you in touch with your masculine side? Have you considered eating a vegetarian or vegan diet?

Elk totem is an ally for when you are seeking the camaraderie of brotherhood (or a sisterhood) of a fraternity or group. Elks feed and migrate together as a herd called a fraternity. Adult elks typically keep together with the same sex for the majority of the year—males with males and females with females and offspring. This characteristic signals a time in your life when it is beneficial for you to spend time with friends of the same gender as you.

When Elk migrates into your life, you can find comfort and great strength by eating with a group of people. The blessing of the community provides sustenance beyond the nutritional value of the food. Elks feed on vegetation, so when Elk becomes evident in your life, you may want to consider incorporating meatless meals into your diet.

Elk is an ally for strength, endurance, and sexual potency. Elk medicine has been revered since the times of the ancient Puebloans and other native tribes for the blankets produced from their fur. Elk grows a heavy winter coat and sheds this coat by early summer. This characteristic is symbolic of giving away what is no longer useful to you so that others may benefit. Elk's energy signals that this is beneficial time for you to clean your closets and give clothing that you no longer wear to those who would benefit from having them.

Elk's Vibrational Matching Gemstone: Brecciated Red Jasper

Brecciated red jasper is associated with the root chakra, the chakra of vitality, endurance, and sexual energy. Red jasper helps you put an end to procrastination. Use this stone when you have a task at hand that requires focus and mental endurance for successful completion. This is the stone of diligence. Use it to maintain a steadfast action to any goal. Red jasper reactivates your passion for living when you've been feeling apathetic, unemotional, or spiritually defunct. A stone of endurance, red jasper is useful when you are focusing on developing your physical power and strengthening your vital life force. This stone helps restore, regenerate, and rejuvenate your passion and libido.

Divine Influence

Call on Archangel Ariel to help enhance your health and vitality.

Elk's Location on the Wheel of Life

Elk is located on the northern portion of the northwest quadrant, where connection with elders and ancestors is made possible.

Contemplate This

How is your stamina? Do you feel healthy and strong? Do you let yourself relax and spend time with your family or group of friends? Renew yourself with the comfort of your favorite people. Spend some time with a companion of the same gender to balance your energy. Go through your closets and give away excess linens, blankets, and clothes so others can benefit from your excess. Exercise, like running or power walking, will help improve your endurance.

Message from Elk

Improve your endurance and overall health. Fellowship and friendly association with people who share the same interests are beneficial for your well-being. Recharge your energy centers, especially the root chakra, and renew your passion for living a vibrant life! Spend time with group of vegetarians and vegans to align yourself with the energy of plant-based nutrition as an option in your dietary plan. Make peace with the plant kingdom, and thank the plants for the sustenance and strength they provide. Activate your sexual and sensual energy.

Elk Affirmation

I am strong. My inner core is powerful. I am grateful for the support of my community. I am physically fit, mentally focused, and emotionally balanced. Vital life force flows vigorously through me, providing me with endurance. I live life with vim, vigor, and vitality. I enjoy passionate relationships that restore balance in my life. I have great sexual energy.

Message from Brecciated Red Jasper

Make an effort to stop procrastinating, and find the energy within to move forward. It is time to take action and complete what you have planned. Follow through, and take the necessary steps to see your projects to fruition. Have confidence in your ability to make things happen. Align with your tribe and accept the support of your comrades.

Additional Vibrational Matching Gemstones for Elk

Carnelian, citrine, clear quartz cluster, garnet, golden topaz, red jasper, ruby, ruby in fuchsite, ruby in zoisite, and sunstone.

32. Finch and Blue Calcite

Are you happy? Do you like to sing? Do you have a song in your heart that raises your spirits? Did you know that humming relieves stress? Have you found your joy?

Finch totem is an ally that assists when you need to find your voice and sing a joyful song. When Finch flies into your life, it brings vivacity and cheerfulness. This vibrant bird encourages you to have the courage and freedom to freely share what makes you happy and joyful. Finch is a perfect totem for feeling positive and optimistic. Its colorful plumage, along with the cheerful song it sings, attracts many bird lovers.

When colorful Finch flies into your life, it's time to focus on all that is good in your life. It is a reminder to release negative thinking and focus on what makes you truly happy. Turn on some music, and contemplate what you appreciate in your life. Pausing for a moment of gratitude while you sing a happy song will go a long way in creating a positive day.

Finches can learn to sing a tune by memorizing it. Call on Finch medicine when you need to recall information, and especially when you are learning a new tune to sing or play on a musical instrument. Finch is a good totem animal for musicians.

Finch reminds you to sing. Humming and singing relieve stress and invite a sense of calm and peace. Chanting and breathing exercises are beneficial for improving tranquility as well. When you sing or hum, you increase the oxygen in your body and relax your nervous system. Not only do you feel mentally and emotionally relaxed but also balance your heartbeat and blood pressure in the process. Humming also keeps your sinuses healthy by increasing airflow between the sinuses and nasal cavity.

Finch's Vibrational Matching Gemstone: Blue Calcite

Blue calcite encourages you to chant, sing, and play music. This stone makes you more aware of how you say things and what you say so that you can employ "word patrol," as necessary. As you move away from negative words to more positive expression, you will find that things in your life change to match your more positive approach. Blue calcite helps you to voice your feelings through conversation, song, or writing. It helps you change the manner in which you communicate your feelings. Let blue calcite align you with excellent communication skills that will help you align with your soul's purpose. Open your spiritual ears, and listen to the music of the sphere and hear the angels sing. Let their song open your heart and find joy and happiness.

Divine Influence

Call on Archangel Haniel to support your communication efforts and align you with Divine expression.

Finch's Location on the Wheel of Life

Finch is located on the eastern portion of the northeast quadrant, where illumination, clarity, and positive renewal are enjoyed.

Contemplate This

Are you dressing in the colors of the rainbow? Do you sing a happy song at least once a day? Make a daily practice of singing a song or humming along with music you hear. Allow the vibration of the color of your clothes, food, and décor to balance your life. Open yourself up to communication with the angelic realm and the realm of invisible helpers. Listen for the messages of joy, hope, and happiness in the lyrics of music.

Message from Finch

This is a time of celebration, happiness, congratulations, and excitement. Accept this good news, and find a reason to celebrate your life. If you feel you aren't satisfied with your life, search within yourself and uncover all the reasons to be grateful. Implement a daily practice of gratitude. In your mind, think of every little thing and every big thing you have a reason to be grateful for.

Finch Affirmation

I powerfully express myself with loving-kindness. Love vibrates through the sounds that come through me. Singing brings me happiness. There is so much to be grateful for. I feel calm and at peace. Color and sound help me find balance and happiness. I am grateful for all the blessings in my life. I am joyous, and life is good!

Message from Blue Calcite

Allow room in your life for the development of inner peace. Use peaceful energy to bring about enlightened activity, serenity, personal power, and transformation from anger. Listen for and hear the songs of the angels. Song and music help you remember your soul's purpose. Speak with loving-kindness. Make it your intention to let joy, happiness, and enthusiasm vibrate through the words, sounds, and song that come through you. Align with inner peace.

Additional Vibrational Matching Gemstones for Finch

Amazonite, angelite, blue lace agate, blue topaz, celestite, citrine, green aventurine, jade, kunzite, rose quartz, and turquoise.

33. FIREFLY AND APOPHYLLITE

Are you ready to be seen by others? Do you enjoy having time in the limelight? Have you taken time for inner reflection?

Firefly totem is an ally when you want to come out of the darkness and shine your light. It helps you feel confident and courageous. This nocturnal beetle teaches you that it is safe for you to shine your magnificence and be in the spotlight. Glow and sparkle to attract all that you need to be fulfilled and to help others have the confidence and courage to be all they can be.

Firefly as an ally helps when you need to spend time in meditation and contemplation. Fireflies hibernate—some for extended periods of time. This characteristic teaches you that it is important to go within for self-observation, inner examination, and deep reflective thought.

When Firefly lights your path, take time for inner reflection to expand your spiritual foundation and improve your inner light. Enjoy periods of light stretching and movement, contemplation, journaling, and guided meditation. Extended periods of silence are beneficial to create the space to empty your mind of incessant chatter and relax your nervous system. Leave your electronic devices behind, and spend some time journaling. Integrate grounded meditation experiences into your practices, and emerge with clarity and perspective.

Fireflies have a natural protective mechanism from predators: they taste bad due to a poisonous chemical in their bodies. This characteristic reminds you that you, too, have the innate ability to protect yourself and keep yourself safe and sound at all times. Through the thoughts, words, and emotions you broadcast, the light you emanate naturally protects you.

Firefly's Vibrational Matching Gemstone: Apophyllite

Apophyllite helps you focus your attention on having spiritual fortitude and self-confidence. Apophyllite and Firefly are allies that remind you of your brilliance and magnificence, thereby raising your spirit and increasing your self-confidence. Let the brilliant luminous light that you are evaporate out-of-balance watery emotions. Apophyllite is a stone of new beginnings and brings promise and optimism. Use it to help lift you from depressive feelings by bringing you the realization that happiness is always available to you and that it is up to you to embrace it. Experience a meditation with apophyllite placed on your forehead for a deeper meditative experience. It helps you release incessant chatter so that you can quiet your mind and find inner peace.

Divine Influence

Call on Archangel Uriel to help you realize the luminosity of your being and recognize the wisdom you hold within.

Firefly's Location on the Wheel of Life

Firefly is located on the eastern portion of the northeast quadrant, where the path of new beginnings is illuminated.

Contemplate This

Shed light on obstacles to reveal them and overcome them. Remember all of your good qualities and then maintain your focus on them. Self-confidence is necessary to improve your own life and be an instrument of peace and love to help all humanity. Imagine the golden flecks of light within your energy field shine brighter, offering you a step closer to enlightenment. Strengthen your courage to put promising ideas into action.

Message from Firefly

Remember that the luminosity of your being and inner light becomes a model for others so that they can find their light, too. Know that it is safe for you to be fabulous and magnificent! Your light offers both you and others more mental clarity. Stay focused on the love and light that you are with mindfulness and with positive thoughts.

Firefly Affirmation

My light shines brightly. I am self-confident and recognize my value and worth. Other people also recognize my value and worth. I shine the light of compassion, kindness, and love from my heart. My inner strength shines through in all I do. I am safe and sound. I am a luminous being of love and light.

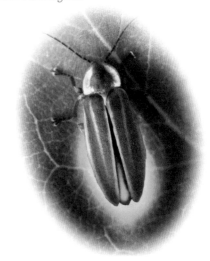

Message from Apophyllite

Do you need some brilliance and enthusiasm? You are ready to step into your power and be all that you were meant to be. You are aligned with the magnificence and the courage to show yourself in your fullest splendor! Develop your spiritual gifts. Recognize that you have a direct connection with the Divine. Activate that part of you that remembers your spiritual magnificence.

Additional Vibrational Matching Gemstones for Firefly

Citrine, clear quartz, golden calcite, golden topaz, labradorite, sunstone, tiger's eye, yellow jasper, and selenite.

34. FLAMINGO AND ROSE QUARTZ

Are you sociable? Do you desire the company of colorful, confident friends and colleagues? Are you looking for a monogamous relationship?

Flamingo totem is an ally for when you are ready to enjoy the company of good friends and large groups of like-minded people. Flamingo is also the perfect totem to call on to attract a monogamous life partner. These monogamous brightly colored pink birds enjoy wading in water, preening themselves, standing on one leg (for warmth), and spending time with their flock, which can go by a few names, a favorite being a flamboyance of flamingos. With Flamingo medicine in your life, activate the part of you that is flamboyant and full of vivaciousness.

When Flamingo wades into your life, perhaps it is time to consider spending a day at the shore's edge, walking in the water with friends or a beloved sweetheart. Flamingo's arrival in your life can give you a great excuse, if you need one, to go to the spa, enjoy a healthy meal, and spend a little time in the sun with your flock. The beautiful pink plumage is indicative of a diet rich in phytonutrients that absorb light for photosynthesis.

If Flamingo is one of your totems, you will do well to practice yoga, especially Tree Pose (Vriksasana). This pose mimics Flamingo's one-legged stance, reminding you to find balance in your life in a variety of ways, including spending time with friends, eating foods that keep your system in check, bathing in water, enjoying sociable interactions, and spending quality time with your significant other.

Flamingo's Vibrational Matching Gemstone: Rose Quartz

Rose quartz signifies the epitome of love. The combined energy of rose quartz and Flamingo help you improve your demeanor, attract and cultivate good friends, and cultivate a deeply loving relationship with a romantic partner. Rose quartz helps you attract more romance and love and can attract your soulmate if you haven't already found that person. The soothing pink color of rose quartz is perfect for situations when you need to feel comforted and surrounded by unconditional love. Use it when you need to amplify your own feelings of unconditional love for others as well. Rose quartz brings comfort and cultivates feelings of self-love. Use rose quartz to improve the relationship you have with yourself.

Divine Influence

Call on Archangel Chamuel to help you enjoy balanced and healthy relationships and the Angels of Romance and of Loving Relationships to help you improve all your relationships, especially the ones you have with your close-knit group.

Flamingo's Location on the Wheel of Life

Flamingo is located on the south path, where relationships are empowered and amplified.

Contemplate This

Rejuvenate your physical body and your emotions. Determine what makes you happy and then attract relationships that will provide loving companions or a mutually satisfying romantic relationship. Reactivate your passion for living. Health-promoting foods and sunlight are important for your well-being—mentally, emotionally, spiritually, and physically. Be with your sweetheart in relaxed atmospheres. Restore, regenerate, and rejuvenate your passion for life and living. Be flamboyant.

Message from Flamingo

The time has come to let your exuberance and confidence rise to the top and to shine your light. Be happy! Enjoy time with friends and family. Open up the part of you that is vibrant, gregarious, and vivacious, and hang out with your flock, which sparkles and is full of life. Birds of a feather flock together, so spend time with your special group and wear attention-grabbing colors.

Flamingo Affirmation

My actions are heart-centered, and I allow love in my life. I live life with vim, vigor, and vitality. My passion for living is dynamic. My inner core is powerful. I am physically fit, mentally focused, and emotionally balanced. Vital life force flows through me. I embrace my flamboyance with color, light, and joy. I am grateful for the romantic love in my life.

Message from Rose Quartz

It is time to activate your inner sparkle. If you are focused on romance right now, allow room for the development of a new romantic relationship or the rekindling of an existing one. Decide to create happiness and harmony. You'll start to see an increase in loyal and caring friends in your life as soon as you decide you are willing to accept love into your life.

Additional Vibrational Matching Gemstones for Flamingo

Danburite, emerald, garnet, green tourmaline, Herkimer diamond, kunzite, Mookaite jasper, pink opal, pink calcite, rhodochrosite, ruby, ruby in fuchsite, ruby in zoisite, and watermelon tourmaline.

35. Fox and Aragonite

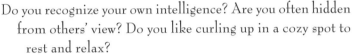

Do you recognize your own intelligence? Are you often hidden from others' view? Do you like curling up in a cozy spot to rest and relax?

Fox totem is an ally that helps you recognize your innate intelligence. The expression "sly as a fox" is an indication of the fox's ability to use its prior experiences to catch its prey. Foxes can be cunning and calculating in their behavior, which is associated with achieving their goal in an underhanded way. In nature, foxes must hunt for their food, and they do it by using their intelligence and camouflaging themselves to pounce on their prey.

When Fox trots into your life, observe your behavior and determine whether your actions are based on your capabilities and knowledge or if you are achieving your goals through deceit or scheming. Through self-observation, you can align your intellectual nature with the Divine and approach situations with authentic and ethical means. Know that you are an intelligent being and that you can lovingly accomplish whatever you put your mind to. Develop your inner genius.

Female foxes are called vixens and care for their young in a den. Male foxes are called dogs, tods, or reynards and are good providers, bringing the food to the entrance of the den to feed their young and the vixen. The word "vixen" has been used to indicate a sexually attractive as well as an assertive, sometimes bad-tempered woman. Women can benefit from vixen energy when they need to increase their personal power and ability to establish healthy boundaries. Use the energy of the vixen, the dog fox, and the den to encourage a strong family unit.

Fox's Vibrational Matching Gemstone: Aragonite

Crystalline aragonite carries within it the vibrations of caves. Aragonite encourages you to listen with your spiritual ears, to see with your spiritual eyes, and to use your Divine intelligence to tap into creative solutions to life challenges. Just as Fox must use its experience and crafty ways to hunt prey, you can use aragonite to open your consciousness and uncover innovative ways of obtaining your goals. With aragonite nearby, give your creative mind permission to experience a little chaos to allow new ideas to percolate and funnel into your awareness. This gem encourages skillful thinking, which opens your mind to a different way of looking at things. Aragonite clusters elicit creativity and encourage you to think outside the box.

Divine Influence

Call on the Angel of Creative Intelligence to help align you with ethically sound paths to achieve your goals.

Fox's Location on the Wheel of Life

Fox is located on the western portion of the northwest quadrant, where inner wisdom is cultivated.

Contemplate This

Is your assertive nature perceived as aggressive? Take the time to go within to find alternative solutions to achieve your goals. Calm your emotions in order to realign your perceptions and allow for objectivity and detachment. Open-mindedness releases the need to be aggressive. Use your memories and stores of inner knowledge as stepping stones on your future path. Allow your family and friends to provide you with care when you need it. Think outside the box, and create new circuits in the brain to help you arrive at solutions or new ideas.

Message from Fox

Balance your approach to getting ahead with compassion and kindness. Learn the benefits of taking time for introspection to gather inspiration. Go quietly within yourself to locate your center, get organized, and find imaginative paths to your dreams and goals. Connect with your inner wisdom, and recognize the value of past experiences.

Fox Affirmation

I am conscious of my intelligence. I can see things that others seem to miss. I stay focused on the task at hand, even when there is confusion around me. I solve problems with ease. It is easy for me to stay calm, even when I have many responsibilities. I integrate and process all that I perceive with ease.

Message from Aragonite

Create a nurturing environment—your den—to get in touch with feelings of loving-kindness in order to cultivate your ability to be assertive in loving ways. Believe in your magnificence, and embrace your power. Know that you are strong enough to set boundaries with others and lovingly assert yourself. Allow yourself to be who you truly are: a loving and magnificent being.

Additional Vibrational Matching Gemstones for Fox

Citrine, fluorite, green calcite, labradorite, lapis lazuli, moldavite, rhodochrosite, sapphire, septarian, and shell fossil.

36. Frog and Green-dyed Agate

Are you ready to leap forward? Do you need to cleanse away negative thoughts or energies that are holding you back? Do you believe you have good luck and great prosperity? Have you kissed any "frogs" lately?

Frog totem is an ally that helps you make significant leaps forward in your life, as well as in your soul's evolution. When Frog hops in, it may be alerting you to get ready to take action. Whether you are catapulting upward in your career or your spiritual practice, Frog symbolizes that you are ready. Metamorphosis is another aspect of this amphibian's medicine. The significance of the metamorphosis from tadpole to frog adds another layer to Frog's forward-leaping energy.

Frog is associated with water and rain, preferring to be in moist conditions. On a metaphysical level, water relates to your emotions. Unclutter your mind and emotions in order to lighten your energy for the big leap forward. For processing and clearing, try contemplation and/or meditation, journaling, forgiveness exercises, yoga or tai chi, cleansing baths, or spa treatments.

Frog is an indicator to bring your awareness to areas of your life that need cleansing. Perhaps you have to tie up some loose ends or clean out your closet, including the closet of your mind. Through focused spiritual practices, use the power of your intention to purify and cleanse. It is also advisable to take a moment to note if you are well hydrated. Frogs are very susceptible to dehydration; therefore, Frog medicine urges you to be sure to drink enough water daily. Frog also indicates good fortune and prosperity. Good fortune frogs, which are found in the ancient Chinese art of feng shui, symbolize wealth and good fortune. Also, look to Frog medicine to help with discernment when looking for your life partner. In ancient Egypt and Mesopotamia, frog symbolizes fertility. Frog is a good ally to have when you are ready to start a family.

Frog's Vibrational Matching Gemstone: Green-dyed Agate

Green-dyed agate helps you stay focused on your goal to cleanse away feelings that no longer serve you. Start by bringing clarity to the source of the emotional imbalance, which naturally releases its charge or effect on you because of your awareness of the source. Then use this stone with creative visualization to cut cords still clinging to you from past relationships or situations. Combined with your clear intention, use Frog medicine and green-dyed agate to release the charge associated with emotional buttons. Use green-dyed agate to align with your inner healer in order to overcome emotional imbalances or physical issues relating to proper water balance and nutrient absorption.

Divine Influence

Call on Archangel Raphael to help you connect with the healer within and heal your relationship with yourself and others.

Frog's Location on the Wheel of Life

Frog is located on the eastern portion of the southeast quadrant, where energy springs forward.

Contemplate This

Are you in the process of purifying your body, mind, or spirit? Is it time to transform situations that challenge you? Yes, it is time to cleanse and purify. Listen to the sounds of nature or make your own sounds and songs. Take time to take a walk in the rain, swim in the pool, or soak in a tub. You can change your life through the power of intention, using water and sound.

Message from Frog

Get ready to leap forward with joy and enthusiasm. It signals a powerful time for manifesting your heart's desire, including (but not limited to) business success, a new home, romance, or the birth of a child. You are ready for this, even if you don't feel you are ready. Take some action to prepare yourself for a sudden metamorphosis. Transform yourself, and live the life of your dreams!

Frog Affirmation

I gently release toxins and unnecessary clutter from my life. I have balanced emotions. I have a clean and clear space. I am blessed with peace-filled relationships. I drink the right amount of water daily for optimum health. I am fertile with great ideas and leap forward to bring them into reality.

Message from Green-dyed Agate

The process of reinventing yourself is a time for self-renewal and realignment. Take time to reflect on where you've been and where you are going. Through inward reflection, enjoy a wonderful sense of emotional balance. Understand the "mirrors" in your relationships to help see your relationship with yourself better. See through the various layers of your emotions, and be aligned with a higher aspect of yourself.

Additional Vibrational Matching Gemstones for Frog

Aquamarine, charoite, green aventurine, green tourmaline, emerald, enhydro-quartz crystals, elestial quartz crystals, larimar, and seraphinite.

37. GIRAFFE AND SMOKY QUARTZ POINT

Have you noticed that you are quite good at seeing what lies ahead? Have you tried to rise above situations to gain clarity? Are you comfortable sticking your neck out? Are you able to take the higher road in life situations?

Giraffe totem is an ally for you when you are seeking a vision or clarity on what lies ahead. Giraffe, the tallest animal, has excellent vision, as well as a good sense of hearing and sense of smell. These characteristics of Giraffe support knowing and trusting the bigger picture. Using all your senses, but especially vision, audio, and aromas, the path before you is clearer than it is for most.

Call on Giraffe to help you trust yourself so you have the courage to step forward on your path with confidence. These qualities come in handy when you might normally feel like you are taking a risk or "sticking your neck" out when making a decision. Giraffe's presence in your life assures you that your inner knowing and outer observations are serving you well.

Giraffe's coat serves as camouflage and is similar to the rosette patterns on Leopard. In fact, Greeks and Romans thought of the giraffe as a combination of Leopard and Camel. This suggests that you may also find more insight and deeper understandings from Camel and Leopard as well. Giraffes have a social structure considered a "fission-fusion society," where they are part of a larger group. There is a significant amount of space between individuals. Smaller groups within the larger group create associations of support for sleeping, social interaction, feeding, and breeding purposes. Giraffe is a good ally to help you find your position within your circle of friends and colleagues. It is also a good energy for aligning with a healthy amount of distance or detachment from those within the circle.

Giraffe's Vibrational Matching Gemstone: Smoky Quartz Point

Smoky quartz helps eliminate doubt and worry when you are faced with chaos and/or confusion. Use smoky quartz in situations where you intend to camouflage yourself to remain unnoticed until you can sort things out. Once the confusion clears, you can see, sense, and know which direction to focus on. This stone helps you feel safe and sound. With focused intent, smoky quartz helps amplify your feelings of security. Smoky quartz is an especially good protection tool. Grounding you and helping to clear out the constant chatter of the mind, smoky quartz is perfect companion for your meditation practice, which provides clarity in your life.

Divine Influence

Call on the Angel of Perspective to support your far-seeing visions and the Angel of Inner Knowing to help you trust your inner guidance.

Giraffe's Location on the Wheel of Life

Giraffe is on the east path, where clarity and the ability to see life from a greater perspective are experienced.

Contemplate This

Are you looking at something from only one angle? Do you need to rise above a situation to find truth and see with greater clarity? Are you fearful about your future? Stretch your mind and your vision to see life from a higher perspective. There are new and exciting experiences ahead. Try using your imagination to visualize positive scenarios. It is beneficial to spend time with your circle of friends while also maintaining a strong sense of self. Eliminate codependent situations, and be free to roam the planet, knowing that you have the support you need within your reach.

Message from Giraffe

Deepen your understanding of difficult situations and people to promote emotional balance. Gain mental clarity, and see life from a different viewpoint. Restore emotional balance as you sort out your feelings and gain perspective. Change the way you look at things. Take steps to gain a new perspective on life. The time has come to believe in your choices and know that they are good. Trust your ability to see things and read situations clearly.

Giraffe Affirmation

I easily maintain awareness of the intended outcome and release distractions. I perceive life from a higher perspective. I take time for reflection. Divine protection is all around me. My approach to life is from a higher perspective. I am in alignment with my intuitive vision of positive outcomes. I see my future filled with well-being and happiness.

Message from Smoky Quartz

Ward off negative thinking by becoming aware of your thoughts. Let go of your repetitive patterns. Focus on where you are going, and manifest your best life. If you feel that you've been scattered lately or you are feeling confused, find your connection and ground yourself. Stay focused on what is important in your life. Establish a circle of protection to keep you on course.

Additional Vibrational Matching Gemstones for Giraffe

Azurite-malachite, apophyllite, blue tiger's eye, Botswana agate, dioptase, dolomite, gold tiger's eye, labradorite, lapis lazuli, leopardskin jasper, and red tiger's eye.

38. Goat and Covellite

Are you a determined person? Is there something you are focused on and unwavering in your intention to achieve that goal? Are you ready to climb to great heights?

Goat totem is an ally when you need to be firm and committed regarding specific decisions or goals. Goat is a helpful energy when you want to step up your game and walk toward your dreams with a purposeful spirit. With Goat's vibe, you will uncover the part of you that not only walks toward high-reaching intentions but also climbs high to achieve and live your life purpose.

As pets, goats enjoy companionship with their human companion and will follow them around and keep weeds and grass trimmed (and your bushes and flowers eaten, too!). Goat is also a reminder to weed the garden of your mind and emotions. Weed out what no longer serves you, and embrace what does. Clear it out, just as Goat naturally clears land, weeds, and grass as part of its nourishment process.

When Goat gambols into your life, it is time to recognize your "herd" or companions and the warmth and enjoyment you provide one another. Goat is social and affectionate, fun, smart, and independent. Symbolically, Goat has a warm energy and relates to the warmth of community, which is symbolized by the mohair and fibers that are used in textiles. Because milk and cheese are another gift from Goat, your Goat ally amplifies your ability to produce the finances you need to meet your core needs. Have a meal with friends and take the time to love, laugh, and be merry.

Goat's Vibrational Matching Gemstone: Covellite

Covellite, a stone of great energy, provides support as a conduit to help you hold a vision. A calming stone, covellite promotes a positive outlook on life. It can help you ground and focus so that you can stay aligned with your goals and intentions. It is a good stone to keep close by when you are in the process of achieving your dreams. Use covellite and Goat as allies when you have stumbled upon an area of progress that is precarious. Embrace the dexterity of your mind, and jump over the hurdles that life offers, using them as opportunities to grow to even greater heights. Covellite helps when you are climbing to reach your objectives and on the precipice of something wonderful emerging. Covellite reminds you to keep moving forward, to not stop short, and to trust in the process.

Divine Influence

Call on Archangel Ariel to help you engage your core strength, good health, and great vitality in order to achieve your full potential.

Goat's Location on the Wheel of Life

Goat is located on the northwest quadrant, where abundance is magnified.

Contemplate This

Do you have herd mentality? Are you following along, or are you walking alongside your friends and companions? Take time to uncover your personal goals and intentions in order to focus on what you want to be and create in this lifetime. Advocate team mentality for the highest good of all. Enjoy the company of good friends and colleagues as you continue to climb to achieve your goals. Open your heart to enjoy the warmth and abundance in your life.

Message from Goat

Realize that it is up to you to consciously create circumstances to fulfill your dreams and destiny. Believe in the power of your imagination, and have a strong focus. Visualize your dreams as if they have already been realized. It is probably time to take action! Be determined and confident enough to make the necessary steps to live the life of your dreams.

Goat Affirmation

I'm self-motivated, strong, and determined to follow through on the next best thing and to be productive. I am strong, healthy, and unwavering in my body, mind, and spirit. I believe in the power of my imagination. I live life with vim, vigor, and vitality. My passion for living is heartfelt and dynamic.

Message from Covellite

Find your tribe, and cultivate good friends and colleagues. It takes time to develop and nurture strong bonds of friendship. Make an effort, and make the time to be with the people who are of like mind. Use your talents, and focus on establishing peace and fellowship. Open your heart to feel the warmth and love of your community.

Additional Vibrational Matching Gemstones for Goat

Ametrine, amethyst, aquamarine, blue chalcedony, chalcopyrite, golden sheen obsidian, fluorite, phantom quartz, pyrite, and red tiger's eye.

39. Goldfish and Gold Topaz

Do you believe that you are incredibly lucky? Are you aware of how you fit into the collective consciousness? Do you work well with others and attract loyal friends?

Goldfish totem is an ally when you are open and ready to receive abundant blessings, good health, great fortune, and awesome friends and coworkers. Goldfish are viewed as a good-luck charm or amulet. A pair of goldfish increases the abundance of love in relationships and marriage. Goldfish have been bred for color in China for thousands of years, with the primary color of orange or gold.

Goldfish can see and discern the four primary colors. Its color vision makes Goldfish a good totem if you work with color as part of your career, or if you are developing the ability to see or sense the auric field of others. Goldfish makes a good ally when you are focusing your attention on understanding color therapy, gemstone usage, and the chakra system. In fact, goldfish are good learners and can recognize individual humans. Consider your Goldfish totem as a guide to help you discern feelings and recall past interactions.

Goldfish have schooling mentality and behavior, which means they are mindful of their neighbors, including distance and flow. This characteristic of Goldfish symbolically represents mass consciousness or the collective consciousness. Goldfish reminds you to reflect and observe yourself and your reactions to those around you. Goldfish is an ally when you need to find your own way while at the same time work cooperatively with others for the good of the whole.

Goldfish's Vibrational Matching Gemstone: Gold Topaz

Gold topaz, a joy-filled gem, is good for mental clarity and reminds you that whatever you ardently believe and desire and passionately work toward will manifest. Gold topaz helps you relieve any feelings of inferiority or unworthiness. This radiant gem assists you when you decide you are ready to dissipate whatever challenge or negative emotion is blocking your way to happiness. Gold topaz is also helpful for maintaining mindfulness, acknowledging your magnificence, and recognizing that it is safe to be powerful in a loving way. Gold topaz helps you shine your light to reach your full potential. Use this stone as a focusing tool in order to remember your intention to accept prosperity, abundance, wealth, and good fortune into your life.

Divine Influence

Call on the Angel of Good Fortune, the Angel of Blessings, and the Angel of Health, Wealth, and Happiness to help light your path and support you in all your endeavors.

Goldfish's Location on the Wheel of Life

Goldfish is located on the south path, where perspective through transformation is found.

Contemplate This

Are your perceptions your own or influenced by the shared consciousness of those around you? Introspection and self-observation help you understand and discern your thoughts and feelings. Through this nonjudgmental form of contemplative thought, you can uncover if your thoughts are your own or heavily influenced by mass consciousness. Once clarity is obtained and you feel comfortable with the mentality of your group, be mindful of your part in cultivating friendships and peaceful interactions with them.

Message from Goldfish

This is your time to be peaceful and prosperous and enjoy professional success. Relax into your good fortune. Enjoy your wealth, and allow more abundance to flow into your life. Harmony abounds when you avoid confrontation or find ways to have healthy interactions with others when expressing your point of view. Respect boundaries, and anticipate respect in return. Pay attention. Good opportunities are available to you. You are incredibly lucky!

Goldfish Affirmation

I am so incredibly lucky! I have many blessings in my life. I am fortunate. I have excellent business skills. I earn an unlimited income doing what I love. Abundance and prosperity are constantly flowing in my life. I am a money magnet. I work well with others. I am a team player. I embrace joy, harmony, and inner peace on all levels.

Message from Gold Topaz

It takes confidence and courage to realize that you are worthy and deserve to have good luck, abundant blessings, and plenty of money to share. Open your mind to the idea of being a money magnet. Whatever you desire and imagine with passion must become a reality. Recognize that anything you put your mind to will become a reality in some form, but action is required, of course! Using passion, determination, and drive, allow magnified blessings to flow into your life.

Additional Vibrational Matching Gemstones for Goldfish

Citrine, golden calcite, fire agate, golden topaz, green aventurine, green goldstone, labradorite, red goldstone, jade, and sunstone.

40. GORILLA AND RED TIGER'S EYE

Do you need more rest? Do you enjoy a nap in the middle of the day? How well do you communicate with friends and family, even if they aren't nearby? Do you schedule time to play and relax?

Gorilla totem is an ally when you need to learn to rest, relax, play, and take the time to socialize. Gorillas spend the majority of their time resting and eating. They are early risers and enjoy a midday rest. While you may think that nests are for the birds, Gorillas sleep in nests on the ground (males) or in trees (females and youngsters). Sometimes, resting for Gorilla includes relaxed playtime with the members of their social group.

When Gorilla struts into your life, it signals a time for regeneration and rejuvenation through healthy diet and healthy social interaction in a restful way. Be like Gorilla, and enjoy more fruits and vegetables while you take time out from the daily grind. Consider a plant-based diet, with few or no animal products.

Gorilla's habitat is located in forests and rainforests, where vegetation is concentrated. To communicate with the members of its social and family group, Gorilla will beat its chest; this is known as chest drumming. Gorilla's presence signals a time to pull out your drum and beat it! According to *Sacred Drumming* by Steve Ash, drumming is beneficial for the nervous system, kidney and bladder function, and your ability to let go.

Gorilla's Vibrational Matching Gemstone: Red Tiger's Eye

Red tiger's eye is a useful grounding force in your spiritual practice. Use this stone to restore physical strength and well-being. The red energy of this tiger's eye supports the root chakra and strengthens your connection with the earth. This stone helps you maintain your focus on your core needs, which are always provided for you with the right intention: food, shelter, and water. Use red tiger's eye to align you with your core inner strength and fuel in order to live life to the fullest. Take time to play and socialize as you recognize the value of a life in balance. Red tiger's helps you get your energy centers recharged and then, once you've "fueled up," you will renew your body.

Divine Influence

Call on Archangel Ariel to help you with general health and vitality and the Angel of Sound Sleep and your Guardian Angel to encourage good rest.

Gorilla's Location on the Wheel of Life

Gorilla is located on the west path, where rest and inner work is done inside the home and hearth.

Contemplate This

When was the last time you gardened or just enjoyed the healing, nurturing power of nature? You may tend to love gardening, nature spirits, and working with the green vibration of Mother Earth. Mother Earth wants to spend more time with you, to feel your hands and feet upon her body, and to fill up your senses with her loving gifts. Investigate the use of nature's pharmacy, such as herbs and essential oils, for holistic health. Gift yourself with time to rejuvenate your physical body and your emotions.

Message from Gorilla

Rest, rest, and more rest! Schedule time to nap and have relaxed interaction with close friends and family. Eat more fruit to nourish and balance your body. Investigate the potential for more plant-based meals, and incorporate these options into your diet. Participate in a drumming circle as a form of a cleansing ritual as well as to restore balance in your body, mind, and spirit.

Gorilla Affirmation

The green energy of plants and trees restores my body, mind, and spirit. I spend time in nature. I enjoy the restorative energy of dense vegetation. The drumbeat rebalances my body, mind, and spirit. I am safe. My body is calm and relaxed. I sleep well and rejuvenate my body. Rest and relaxation are a regular part of my life.

Message from Red Tiger's Eye

Ground your spiritual practice by aligning with nature and shamanic drumming practices. Find the right combination of green leafy vegetables and fruits to nourish your physical body and strengthen your muscles and vital life force. Find the motivation and do the research to uncover the perfect balance of diet and rest in order to have a healthy and strong body.

Additional Vibrational Matching Gemstones for Gorilla

Amethyst, black onyx, blue calcite, chrysoprase, green moss agate, hematite, kyanite, red jasper, and ruby.

41. GRASSHOPPER AND CHALCOPYRITE

Is it time for you to make a powerful leap forward in your spiritual, personal, or professional life? Do you joyfully sing or express yourself with good news and happiness? Are you using your peripheral vision to see the bigger picture?

Grasshopper totem is an ally during times in your life when you are ready to reach greater heights and avoid unnecessary mistakes or threats. Grasshoppers have strong hind legs, which give them the power to catapult forward, usually to remove themselves from predators or threats. Symbolically, Grasshopper's leaping motion and all-round vision assists you in seeing things from many angles and perspectives. This characteristic lets you know when you need to take action for the highest good of all.

Grasshopper produces a shrill sound to communicate, which is sometimes called singing. They are rubbing their legs or other body parts to create the sound, which is more prevalent when all is well in their world. (They are quiet when adversity presents itself.) When Grasshopper leaps into your life, it teaches you to express yourself when life is good. The other side of this teaching is to avoid complaining too much when life is difficult.

Difficulties in life provide lessons from which you can grow and improve yourself. Grasshoppers go through an incomplete metamorphosis—a type of growth involving morphing to a larger size with each stage of growth. You, too, go through growth spurts on a mental and emotional level that may be barely perceptible to others, although you know you've made a leap forward with your personal and spiritual life.

Grasshopper's Vibrational Matching Gemstone: Chalcopyrite

Chalcopyrite is symbolic of great strength, prosperity, and mental clarity. Just as Grasshopper is a symbol of health, wealth, and happiness, chalcopyrite amplifies these qualities, creating a perfect set of allies. Chalcopyrite helps you locate the courage and strength that reside deep within you. This stone is beneficial for helping you overcome and discard any negativity impressed upon you and transforming that energy into fodder for personal growth. The brassy yellow of chalcopyrite lightens up your consciousness, bringing mental clarity. This stone helps you think clearly, stay focused on the task at hand, and remember what you are doing. Chalcopyrite supports you when you are engaging in strength training to build your muscles, especially when it involves outdoor activities.

Divine Influence

Call on Archangel Uriel and the Angel of Health, Wealth, and Happiness to co-create with others who support you.

Grasshopper's Location on the Wheel of Life

Grasshopper is located on the eastern portion of the northeastern quadrant, where wisdom, clarity, and financial abundance reside.

Contemplate This

Do you believe you are worthy of happiness and success? You are fertile with good ideas. You can conceive something magnificent. Have the courage to take action to make your dreams and ideas a reality. Increase your physical strength, and know that you have the fortitude to achieve anything! Employ your physical and intuitive sight to observe and assess situations. Focus on the good, and share those perceptions with others. Listen well and, likewise, make joyful communication through speaking and singing in order to express yourself when life is good. Focus on the good, and share those perceptions with others.

Message from Grasshopper

Mental cloudiness might be familiar to you right now. It's time for you to survey your surroundings and your options so you can take informed action. Recognize your inner strength—mentally, physically, emotionally, and spiritually. Step into your courage, and leap toward your dreams. Believe in yourself. It's time to rise and catapult higher in order to align with your magnificence. Be ready to accept prosperity into your life.

Grasshopper Affirmation

I am energized and enthusiastic. My endurance levels are strong. I've got "get up and go"! I move forward with focus and determination. I see life from a greater perspective. I am grateful for the abundance and prosperity in my life. I am open to angelic guidance offered through sounds, music, and song. Lyrics flow through me and touch my soul.

Message from Chalcopyrite

It's time to get things moving, to be self-motivated and take action. Activate the part of you that needs a push to move forward to take action on your projects, ideas, or business pursuits. Use your creative energy to manifest your heart's desire. Integrate new core beliefs into your mindset about money, wealth, and prosperity, and step away from limiting perceptions. Activate your "millionaire mind."

Additional Vibrational Matching Gemstones for Grasshopper

Amethyst, charoite, copper, Herkimer diamond, lapis lazuli, phantom quartz, pyrite, rutilated quartz, singing laser quartz wands, and vanadinite.

42. HAWK AND LABRADORITE

Are you able to look at life from a higher perspective? Have you made the effort to petition the heavenly realm for guidance and assistance? Do you desire a loyal life partner?

Hawk totem is an ally that encourages you to "fly" above your life or a particular situation for greater understanding and see all the potential outcomes. When Hawk swoops into your life, make an effort to uncover what you need to look at in great detail. Hawks have extraordinary vision, which includes ultraviolet-electromagnetic radiation. They are able to see approximately eight times better than humans. Invite Hawk to help you see your life with greater clarity. Use this vibration to notice what is barely perceptible to most people. With this foresight, your understanding will bring the courage to fly forward in the right direction.

Hawk is known to be one of the messenger birds: it brings messages and requests to Great Spirit, God, Goddess, or the Divine because of its ability to fly so high. With visual imagery, imagine your messages arriving in the heavenly realm on the wings of Hawk.

Hawk is aware of the right direction to go when migrating, using favorable winds to stay on course. Hawk medicine encourages you to feel the winds of change and find your right path. Fighting to go in a direction that isn't working is futile, so enlist the vibe of Hawk to help you see the right path, and you'll have the wind at your back to ease the journey.

Hawk is a good ally in order to encourage monogamy and a lifelong partner. Hawks mate for life in a monogamous relationship. Observe and reflect on what you want to manifest or revive within your future or current romantic relationship. Look at it from many angles and from a higher perspective.

Hawk's Vibrational Matching Gemstone: Labradorite

Labradorite is a gem for contemplation and amplifies your ability to perceive life through a wide-angle lens. Labradorite helps you reflect on your outer and inner light, which helps you recognize the varying effects that light, color, and sound have on your consciousness and spiritual practices. Gaze into this stone, allowing the light to refract off it, while you imagine or visualize the answers to whatever you seek arising in your awareness. This is a useful stone for meditation, lucid dreaming, psychic development, and spiritual awareness and expands the awareness of your heart and mind. Labradorite guides you toward understanding the "mirrors" in your relationships, helping you to better see your relationship with yourself.

Divine Influence

Call on Archangel Michael to help you see life from a greater perspective, Metatron to activate higher states of consciousness, and the Angel of Romantic Partnership to align with monogamy and longevity in relationships.

Hawk's Location on the Wheel of Life

Hawk is located on the eastern quadrant, where life is seen from a greater perspective.

Contemplate This

Rise above the situation at hand. Look beyond what you can integrate when you are enmeshed in a situation, and observe it from a broader perspective. Devote the necessary time to grasp the greater reality, and touch upon increased self-knowledge as well as tolerance for others. Prayer is a petition to invite the Divine to intercede for the highest good of all. Replace the energy you spend on worrying with a focused request for Divine intercession in your life.

Message from Hawk

It is good to pray and ask for help. Be open to the Divine flying into your life swiftly to reply to your requests. It is time to envision potential future realities and script out different scenarios on how you want your life to unfold (instead of focusing on what you don't want). Practice seeing your circumstances in a favorable way, and watch how you automatically make them evolve with your actions.

Hawk Affirmation

I see with higher perspective because of the benefits of hindsight. I see life from a positive perspective. I take the time for reflection. I observe how the world around me is a mirror of the world within me. I have mental clarity. I know and trust my inner truth. I believe in myself and what I see or perceive.

Message from Labradorite

Gaining clarity in some part of your life is necessary. Believe what you see or perceive. Acknowledge your inner visions and the ability to integrate the meaning of the reflections going on around you. Cultivate and nurture the loving relationships that are presently in your life, and change your mindset to think as "we" rather than "me" in order to attract or renew more love in your life.

Additional Vibrational Matching Gemstones for Hawk

Apophyllite, aragonite cluster, azurite-malachite, chevron amethyst, clear quartz, gold tiger's eye, hawk's eye aka blue tiger's eye, kunzite, lapis lazuli, optical calcite, and rose quartz.

43. HORSE AND MOSS-INCLUDED DOGTOOTH CALCITE

Are you a highly sensitive person? Are you consciously aware of everything that is going on around you? Do you feel balanced? How are you in group settings?

Horse totem is an ally to help you become extraordinarily cognizant of all that is occurring around you. Because they are prey animals, horses are overly aware of their surroundings. In fact, they have amazing vision and can see about 350 degrees. They have both monocular vision and binocular vision. With monocular vision, they can use both eyes separately because their eyes are on the side of their head. Horses also have binocular vision, which uses both eyes to see, increasing their field of view. Use Horse as an ally to increase your awareness and improve your situational awareness. Use your innate peripheral vision on a physical level (seeing with your eyes), and also use your peripheral vision mentally, emotionally, and spiritually. This encourages you to broaden your scope of understanding and realizations.

When Horse trots into your life, it signals a time to find your center so you can easily move forward at a moment's notice. Horses have a strong sense of balance as well as the ability to quickly make a decision to flee or further assess the situation. This characteristic reminds you to use the information you gathered using your hypersensitive nature to assess whether or not real danger is near. Align with Horse energy for endurance and the ability to take action and move forward.

Horses prefer to sleep with other horses nearby; they sleep better knowing that another horse is on security detail. Horses are herd animals, so they want to be with other horses. It is in their nature to be sociable and form relationships with other horses as well as humans. Let Horse support you in your social interactions with family and friends.

Horse's Vibrational Matching Gemstone: Moss-included Dogtooth Calcite

Dogtooth calcite is a stone of self-confidence. Dogtooth calcite with moss inclusions aids in nurturing the part of you that is extremely sensitive to the thoughts, feelings, physical challenges, and emotions of others. It is an excellent tool to help you focus on mental peace and serenity. The calcite family of minerals helps when you need to accept a change in your life and make determined action. This stone, with its mossy pattern, helps you remember to ground yourself. With grounding and focus, it is easier to accomplish your goals and move forward. With its earthy appearance, moss-included dogtooth calcite helps you reclaim your balance through nature. For example, imagine that a flow of emotional toxins is draining from the soles of your feet, and envision Mother Earth transforming the toxins into rich compost or fertilizer.

Divine Influence

Call on Archangel Raphael to help restore and maintain your balance and well-being and the Angel of Nature to feel protected outdoors.

Horse's Location on the Wheel of Life

Horse is located on the west path, where inner strength and intuitive knowing are available.

Contemplate This

Do you feel more comfortable with your family and friends around you? Become part of the herd, and experience the benefits of companionship from the group for social interaction and safety. Find comfort in people having your back, watching out for you. How do you feel when you take the time to walk in the grass, visit the water's edge, or embrace a tree? Give your emotional challenges to the earth through the use of imagery.

Message from Horse

Freedom and forward movement are the order of the day. It is time for you to move on or make it easy for someone else to do so. Be ready to take a journey. You may decide to take a journey within, or you can decide to journey into nature to restore your freedom and inner strength. Recognize the gifts of nature, and align with nature's pharmacy from animals and plants.

Horse Affirmation

I am willing to find new pathways to discover my inner power. I am determined to align with the forces of nature that feed my soul. It is easy for me to find freedom and make forward movement. I make a decision and take action effortlessly. I am determined to achieve my goals and dreams.

Message from Moss-included Dog Tooth Calcite

It's time to achieve the goal you've been working toward. Reach into the green energy of nature if you need a little boost in your motivation to take action. Enlist your innate courage to be all that you can be. Trust that you have the determination and endurance to reach the finish line. Practice is one of the keys to make it so.

Additional Vibrational Matching Gemstones for Horse

Carnelian, garnet, green moss agate, pyrite, red goldstone, red jasper, ruby, sunstone, and tree agate.

44. HUMMINGBIRD AND INFINITE

Do you know that you are fabulous, fortunate, and phenomenal? Do you need to make a shift in your perspective or change your attitude? Are you ready to live to your full potential?

Hummingbird totem is an ally when you are in need of shining your inner light, which has evolved from internal realizations. Hummingbird's beautiful iridescent feathers are one of the characteristics that align you with having the courage to embrace your potential and experience your extraordinary nature. Let the vibrant energy of hummingbird encourage you to shine your light brightly and be a wonderful contributor to all that is good in your community.

When Hummingbird hovers nearby, it is time to remember that you are unique and have a distinct way to perceive reality. Hummingbird has a way of flying that differs from any other type of bird, in that it can fly forward, backward, up, down, sideways, hover, and can rotate 180 degrees. This quality is a teaching from Hummingbird that you, too, can make adjustments to your manner of approaching life situations. Find unique ways to release pent-up feelings. A slight twist of your perspective can change your reality. A well-known quote by theoretical physicist Max Planck sums it up: "When you change the way you look at things, the things you look at change."

Hummingbird teaches you to be willing not only to see things differently but also to be seen differently. With light, color, and vibrancy, you can achieve great heights with great speed, just as this tiny but mighty bird does. Don't let the size of this bird fool you into thinking it is vulnerable. Hummingbirds are very effective at defending their territory in quite an aggressive way. You can call on Hummingbird to help you garner the courage to establish boundaries with great ease. Observe your emotions from different angles to decide and intend to remove the strong attachment to those emotions.

Hummingbird's Vibrational Matching Gemstone: Infinite

Infinite, a combination of serpentine and chrysotile, helps you think positively and stay focused on good outcomes. It is also helpful for visualizing ideas and beneficial results. Infinite partners well with Hummingbird to keep your mind focused on positive thoughts. This stone reminds you to be aware of negative thoughts so that you can immediately release them and replace them with positive thoughts. With infinite in hand, tap into another level of understanding, and see things from a greater perspective. The beneficial energy of infinite strengthens the vibe of seeing beauty and experiencing joy in virtually everything. Use infinite in conjunction with your gratitude practice, and remember to express gratitude for the beauty all around you.

Divine Influence

Call on Archangel Jophiel to help you become comfortable with your beauty and the Angel of Perspective to help you calmly change course when necessary.

Hummingbird's Location on the Wheel of Life

Hummingbird is located on the east path, where life is seen from varying perspectives.

Contemplate This

Are you living life with joy and enthusiasm? Do you know how to cultivate your plans and intentions? Are you easily distracted from what is best for your life and those you love? Step forward with clarity and focus. Maintain your awareness of what is important in your life. Engage in activities for healing and personal development. Recognize the blessings all around you.

Message from Hummingbird

Recognize that you see things from a different angle than most people do. Appreciate your ability to recognize solutions to challenges. Open up to a new reality in every moment. The reality you choose to perceive and embrace is up to you. Allow patterns and different perspectives to give you the insight and understanding needed to make necessary shifts to create a better life.

Hummingbird Affirmation

It is with clear intentions that I move forward—self-assured and confident. I connect with the right people at the right time. All of my hard work sweetens all areas of my life. I am blessed with good health, great prosperity, and fabulous friends and colleagues. Wherever I go and whatever I do, I find joy. I am grateful and fortunate for all that is good in my life!

Message from Infinite

You are lucky and aware of all of your blessings. Aim for the stars. You can and should expect the best from every positive action you take. You attract money, joy, happiness, and good fortune. With that as your intention, your life will transform! Recognize the blessings in your life, and practice gratitude. Decide to be filled with joy!

Additional Vibrational Matching Gemstones for Hummingbird

Apophyllite, chevron amethyst, dumortierite, green aventurine, jade, labradorite, lepidolite, moonstone, and peacock copper.

45. Jaguar and Axinite

Are you at the top of your game? Do you employ the full magnitude of your strength and power? Do you prefer to work alone? Are you good at seeing windows of opportunities and acting upon them?

Jaguar totem has been a symbol of strength and power since pre-Columbian days. Jaguar is at the top of the food chain. Jaguar is an ally to bring your strength and power to the surface in all aspects of your life. In business and the world of financial potential, Jaguar helps you observe the movements of business around you so that you can see opportunities when they arise. As an opportunistic, stalk-and-ambush hunter, Jaguar teaches you to be patient, observe, and be secretive or quiet about your intention and ideas in your career. When Jaguar saunters into your life, use your skills of keen observation for self-preservation as well as for personal gain. This solitary animal can support you if you have a tendency to prefer living and working alone.

Jaguar is a good ally for single mothers. Female jaguars reject the male partner after breeding for the safety of the infant cubs and because she prefers to parent them herself. Jaguar provides parental strength in raising a family as a single parent. Look deeper into your emotional body with Jaguar's support. Jaguars are felines that enjoy a swim and prefer to live near water. Use Jaguar medicine to empower you to embrace your feelings and accept them. Notice messages from the spirit world that provide signposts on your journey.

Mayan civilizations revered jaguars as companions in the spirit realm. They believed that Jaguar had the ability to bring messages from ancestors who have passed away. Many Mayan rulers or royalty carried the name B'alam, meaning jaguar. Jaguar may be your main totem if you have a strong connection with receiving communication from the spirit realm.

Jaguar's Vibrational Matching Gemstone: Axinite

Axinite helps you remember the teachings of your core spiritual essence. While you may not subscribe to the religious affiliation under which you were raised, you can use axinite to help examine your core spiritual foundations from this lifetime. Use the strong vibration of axinite to help renew your faith, and add to your spiritual basket by uncovering the spiritual teachings of ancient civilizations. Use this earth-colored stone when you feel challenged by scattered forces—from within and also from outside of yourself. Axinite grounds you so that you can accomplish your tasks with self-assuredness. Let order ensue by allowing this stone to help you deflect what might appear to be chaos. Axinite supports the intention to develop and maintain core strength and endurance you need for a healthy and prosperous life. This stone is also good for those who wish to have more energy in general.

Divine Influence

Call on Archangel Uriel to help you integrate higher wisdom and financial success, the Divine Mother to provide support for those who give strong foundations in the formative years, and Metatron to activate ascension and movement upward.

Jaguar's Location on the Wheel of Life

Jaguar is located on the north path, where we ascend to the next rotation of the wheel of life.

Contemplate This

Do you believe in the power of your emotions and personal observations? Embrace your feelings and accept them. Believe in yourself when you feel a certain way or receive an intuitive hit that provides clear guidance on your path. You are powerful beyond measure. Find your inner roar, and pay special heed to the workings of the world around you. Use the observations to feed your strength and confidence. Find your own brand of spirituality, one that is a fine blend of varying spiritual philosophies from around the world.

Message from Jaguar

Embrace your immense power, and allow it to shine. Live to your full potential. Listen, and use messages or signs received in many ways. Honor the messages that come from beyond the norm and in extraordinary ways. It is safe for you to be powerful in loving ways. Observe, and take action. Recognize your inner strength—mentally, physically, emotionally, and spiritually. Step into your courage. Follow your dreams. Believe in yourself.

Jaguar Affirmation

Power and strength are mine. It is safe for me to be powerful in loving ways. The transformation of challenges, negative patterns, and unhealthy habits occurs daily in my life. I release what is no longer for my highest good. I am confident. I embrace the wisdom of the Divine Mother. I live a life of success and fulfillment.

Message from Axinite

Recognize if chaos or confusion have taken over your life. Be aware if you are going in too many directions at once and feeling distracted. It's time to regroup and sustain laser focus. Do what it takes to strengthen your physical body, your mental body, and your emotional body. Be sure to feed yourself on all levels. Eat health-promoting foods to support strong muscles, teeth, and jaw.

Additional Vibrational Matching Gemstones for Jaguar

Cathedral quartz, cobaltoan calcite, fluorite, golden calcite, golden topaz, Herkimer diamond, hematite, leopardskin jasper, magenta-dyed agate, sapphire, tiger's eye, and tiger iron.

46. LADYBUG AND HELIODOR

Do you believe you are lucky? Are you taking the time to use your imagination and release your wishes to be fulfilled? Do you remember to pray for help and guidance?

Ladybug totem is an ally that keeps away pesky people and situations and, instead, encourages only blessings and well-being in your life. Ladybugs are a gardener's friend because they eat aphids, which can destroy plants. Farmers and gardeners often purposely release these beetles as a natural pest control to protect their crops and garden plants.

Ladybugs use natural self-defense in that they can coat their body with an unpleasant secretion that leaves a bad taste in the mouth of a predator. They can also play dead to distract predators. Ladybug reminds you to shield yourself from unwelcome negative energies. In this case, use your imagination to envelop yourself in the color red and add black spots or a black outer lining during times when you feel threatened.

On a personal note, I learned about Ladybug as a child from my mother. She was the first to inform me that this charming little insect is also known as Mary beetle or Our Lady's beetle. They got this name from a story dating back to the Middle Ages when food crops were being ravaged by insects. Farmers and villagers prayed to Mother Mary for help, and very soon, ladybugs arrived and ate the offending insects. Therefore, on a spiritual level, when Ladybug shows up in the garden of your life, it is a message to open your sacred heart and petition the blessings and help from Mother Mary or the Divine Feminine. When Ladybug flies into your life, know that you are blessed with good luck and all that is good.

Lady Bug's Vibrational Matching Gemstone: Heliodor

Heliodor, a yellow beryl, helps you maintain a positive outlook. Even when life seems overwhelming, let this gem be a reminder that, with a bit of clarity, you can make good decisions with confidence and courage. Use heliodor to cultivate a strong sense of self so that you can fulfill your purpose. This stone is a reminder of the miracle worker within you, which is in direct alignment with the energy of Mother Mary and her miracles. Heliodor is a reminder and an ally to be consciously aware of your thoughts so that you can discard those that are outdated and replace them with thoughts that focus on the life you want to live.

Divine Influence

Call on Blessed Mother Mary, the Angel of Good Fortune, and the Angel of Health, Wealth, and Happiness to help you with an illuminated path.

Ladybug's Location on the Wheel of Life

Ladybug is located on the southwest quadrant, where the transformation of challenging situations takes place.

Contemplate This

Do you believe that you are always safe and sound? Is your mind clear of negative thoughts? Are your emotions free from harmful feelings? Mindfulness is important in order to be able to dissipate contrary thoughts and emotions. As soon as you realize you have had a negative thought, immediately replace it with love and well-being. Visualize your goals. Believe that anything is possible! Imagine your life as if it already is filled with abundance, good health, happiness, and inner peace.

Message from Ladybug

Believe and know that you are divinely protected. Be the blessing in the lives of others. Believe in luck, good fortune, and prosperity. Connect with the spiritual practices of Mother Mary and all the angels. Use the angels and the Divine to assist you in creating a sphere of goodness and well-being around you. Focus your attention on creating a world filled with good fortune for yourself and your loved ones.

Ladybug Affirmation

I visualize my goals and aspirations effortlessly. My imagination is the key to my success. I envision my future and joyfully participate as it unfolds. I am so incredibly lucky! I have many blessings in my life. Abundance and prosperity are constantly flowing in my life. I am enveloped in a sphere of goodness and well-being.

Message from Heliodor

With a little focus and belief, good luck and beneficial results are always available to you. When negative thoughts arise, change your mind immediately by contemplating the opposite reality. Think positively and stay focused on good outcomes. Encourage daydreaming and visualizing ideas and beneficial outcomes. You have permission to make believe until you do believe!

Additional Vibrational Matching Gemstones for Ladybug

Black tourmaline, golden sheen obsidian, green aventurine, green moss agate, jade, magenta-dyed agate, red jasper, ruby, smoky quartz, and tree agate.

47. LEOPARD AND LEOPARDSKIN JASPER

Are you adaptable? Do you feel strong and have the ability to take on big projects or situations? Do you use strategy and make savvy decisions for the good of all?

Leopard totem is an ally that encourages you to be adaptable, strong, smart, and motivated. Leopards are strong creatures because they kill big prey and need to drag heavy carcasses up into trees. The rosette pattern in their fur offers you the vibration of camouflage, which lends energy to taking advantage of opportunities that arise. Leopard medicine is a symbol to be encouraged to think big. When Leopard visits, release small thinking and take chances by stepping up your game.

Leopards are known for their stealth, and therefore, humans or prey often aren't aware of their presence nearby. This characteristic can be used to support you when you need to take secretive or hidden action to avoid being seen or acknowledged by others. Leopard is a good ally in business or situations when you aren't ready to reveal an idea or invention yet. Due to Leopard's solitary nature, this quality signals that it is important to evaluate when it is better to work alone in certain circumstances.

Known to have excellent hearing and vision, Leopard is an ally for you when you need to hear and see what is barely perceptible. Just as leopards take the time to stalk their prey, you, too, can have the patience to see things through and listen well before you take action. With a little patience and some contemplation, you may notice that people aren't what they first appeared to be.

Leopard's Vibrational Matching Gemstone: Leopardskin Jasper

Leopardskin jasper grounds your spiritual practice through earth-centered spirituality. This mottled stone is beneficial for use in drumming circles or shamanic journeywork. This jasper grounds your spiritual practice and increases your flexibility in exploring different spiritual avenues. With self-observation as your intention, leopardskin jasper assists you in releasing emotional patterns. The rosettes, which are similar to Leopard's coat of fur, are an added energy that helps you observe yourself and your emotions. Doing so will open your awareness in order to uncover the source of repetitive patterns in your relationships, career, or any aspect of your life with gentleness and ease. Leopardskin jasper is also a stone of flexibility on a physical level, providing support for your muscles and tendons for increased strength and endurance.

Divine Influence

Call on the Angel of Physical Strength and the Angel of Inner Strength to help you go all the way and reach for the greater good of all and on the Angel of Opportunity to help you recognize opportunities and have the courage to take the leap forward.

Leopard's Location on the Wheel of Life

Leopard is located on the northeastern quadrant, where experience lends support to observations and adaptability.

Contemplate This

Are you adaptable? Do you pay attention to opportunities when they arise? Notice that a window or door has opened and take chances to experience something much greater than what you've experienced before. See opportunities as food for your soul and personal growth. Find the value in having challenges because they help you see hidden agendas or teachings. You have the strength and courage to tackle big situations or problems. Big rewards are available! Let yourself have the grand experiences.

Message from Leopard

Be willing to take advantage of opportunities and seize the moment. Take risks after you've evaluated the situation. Be willing to jump out of your seat and make things happen. Allow your ideas or projects to take form before you reveal it to the world. Flexibility is key. Adapt to the situation, and recognize that challenges are often opportunities for growth.

Leopard Affirmation

I am flexible and adaptable. I objectively observe circumstances and seize new opportunities as situations naturally shift and change in my life. I recognize and practice good timing in all that I experience. I am self-motivated. I bend and flex with the flow of life around me. There is no resistance, only willingness to go with the flow. I am strong!

Message from Leopardskin Jasper

Take note if people around you are showing you a different agenda or intention than was originally presented to you. Be clear with yourself if you are changing your mind and want to be a bit more secretive about your upcoming plans. Uncover your intentions, including those that are obvious and those you've hidden from yourself. Be strong and willing to look within. Also be willing to notice when people show you who they are and what their intentions are.

Additional Vibrational Matching Gemstones for Leopard

Bismuth, black obsidian, fluorite, golden sheen obsidian, iolite, phantom quartz, pyrite, snowflake obsidian, rutilated quartz, and tourmalinated quartz.

48. LION AND CITRINE

Do you take the time to observe situations before you take action? Do you prefer nocturnal life, such as socializing and other nighttime activities? Is sleeping during the day your normal mode? Do you have a strong family alliance?

Lion totem is an ally that helps you increase your situational awareness. Lions stalk their prey, and once they decide to take down an animal for food, they act swiftly and powerfully. Lion energy teaches you to observe your environment, integrate and understand all the facets of a situation, then, once you clearly know what action to take, take it quickly and with great confidence. Lion medicine encourages you to take on projects that might seem beyond your scope or greater than you initially think you can handle. (Lion often captures prey close to twice its own weight.) Be like Lion, and recognize that you have the power and fortitude to accomplish great things.

Lions are social. They live in groups called a pride, which consists of mostly females, their young, and a few males. The male lions, known for their full manes, are the security detail, protecting the fringes of the pride's territory. Lions spend most of the time resting—up to twenty hours a day. The remainder of the time is spent hunting or scavenging, which is most often a cooperative effort.

When Lion steps into your life, learn to be a team player. If you have a great idea that seems bigger than life, find the courage to take it on. Your willingness to do something big might just be the foundation for others to have a job or revenue to feed themselves and their family. Invite others to support your big vision, and they can benefit, too.

Lion's Vibrational Matching Gemstone: Citrine

Citrine helps you believe in yourself so that you can fulfill your dreams. There is no decision too magnificent. Citrine aligns you with your personal power and helps you shine your light with ease. Use citrine to clear the cobwebs and obstacles in your mind in order to achieve great heights. Citrine helps clear your mind, allowing you to realize the power of your intention and your thoughts. You can do anything! First, you have to have the mindset to believe it. Citrine activates self-confidence and joy. Citrine is perfect for relieving any feelings of inferiority or unworthiness. Citrine reminds you that whatever you ardently believe and desire and work passionately toward will manifest.

Divine Influence

Call on Archangel Michael to help you overcome your fears and the Angel of Self-Confidence to support you in achieving great things.

Lion's Location on the Wheel of Life

Lion is located on the northeast quadrant, where experience and practice bring confidence and courage.

Contemplate This

Make it a priority to pay attention to your personal life situations. Have the bravery to protect yourself on an emotional and physical level. Set boundaries with others. Notice everything that is going on around you. Take the time to gain clarity and clear your consciousness so that you know when it is time to take action. Have patience. Believe in your good ideas. You do have the ability to conceive something magnificent. Have the nerve to take action to make your dreams and ideas into a reality. Wait, watch, then do it!

Message from Lion

Sleep more. There is no project or situation too big. If something seems bigger than you, and you are drawn to tackle it, do it! Be willing to ask your circle of friends or family for their support. Find your courage and your power. Share your bounty, and be a productive member of your community. Invite friends over to your home for meals. Socializing is important for balance. Defend your space, both home and business.

Lion Affirmation

I have plenty of energy and plenty to share. I am vital and strong! I am determined. I am confident and courageous. I shine my light brightly. I honor and respect myself. I allow others to see my magnificence. Prosperity abounds in my life. Goodness multiplies. Whatever I desire, imagine, and passionately act upon becomes a reality. It is safe for me to be powerful!

Message from Citrine

Your inner critic may be telling you that you can't make changes in your life because you lack confidence in your abilities. Don't believe it. It's time to take action and be determined and confident enough to make the necessary changes to transform your life. Focus on what you do well to increase your self-esteem. Shine your light to reach your full potential!

Additional Vibrational Matching Gemstones for Lion

Ametrine, gold tiger's eye, golden sheen obsidian, golden topaz, rutilated quartz, and sunstone.

49. LIZARD AND HERKIMER DIAMOND

Do you adapt easily to situations? Can you find ways to avoid being noticed when needed? Are you aware that it is sometimes more powerful to do nothing? Are you willing to let go of something in order to grow?

Lizard totem is an ally that helps you deal with the ever-changing experience of life on Earth. Lizards have adapted quite well in a variety of ways to avoid being preyed on. Through varying techniques or illusions, Lizard adjusts to the current conditions to blend in or avoid detection. Lizard medicine is helpful to deflect negative energy and undesirable attention. Some lizards change their color to blend into the background and camouflage themselves. Some will play dead to discourage a predator and wait until the danger has passed. Others will drop their tail to get away from the attacker. Sometimes, interactions with others can feel like an attack.

Release and sacrifice is symbolic of situations when you feel like you have to drop something, such as a job or a former friend, for self-preservation. Lizards leave behind their wiggling tail as a distraction to save themselves from the predator. Let this characteristic teach you to use distraction techniques to keep others from seeing you or some aspect of yourself that is private. Magicians use distraction for sleight of hand, and parents use distraction to realign a child's behavior. Distraction and camouflage is why Lizard medicine is often related to illusions.

The tail of the lizard does regrow, and this translates to your life in that you have the opportunity for significant growth in your personal development when you release something else. That is when your ability to modify your behaviors or perceptions provides you the support to realize the long-term benefits. Adaptability and ease are the keys to going through the process with grace.

Patience is an important attribute of Lizard. Lizards are sometimes passive in their hunting techniques. When Lizard shows up in your life, it could signal a time to just watch all that is going on, protect your space, and wait for the right time to take action.

Lizard's Vibrational Matching Gemstone: Herkimer Diamond

The Herkimer diamond is a good ally for clarity and memory in the dreamtime experiences. It is an energizing crystal in the quartz family that is used for dream recall, though it isn't a first choice for sound sleep. It is the number-one tool to use for lucid dreaming, shamanic journeywork, and vision seeking. Herkimer diamond heightens your awareness to help you shine light on a situation. Use this stone to improve your spiritual sight and clairvoyance.

Divine Influence

Call on Archangel Gabriel to help you understand your dreams and visions, Metatron to awaken higher consciousness, and Archangel Raziel to see through illusions.

Lizard's Location on the Wheel of Life

Lizard is located on the northwest quadrant, where inner work, dream work, and wisdom is realized.

Contemplate This

Are you able to recall your dreams? Dreams can be your internal psychologist or your spiritual advisor. Take the time before going to sleep to form an intention to remember your dreams upon waking. Record your dreams upon waking. Dreams are powerful tools for self-healing, personal awareness, and spiritual growth. Go deeper into your consciousness and awareness of situations around you in your waking life—at work, in social circles, and in your home. Patiently observe the illusions you create and the illusions created by others.

Message from Lizard

Determine if you are caught up in illusions. Look deeper into situations to uncover the truth or hidden aspects. Go within, retreat, and take time for contemplation. Visions from within yourself are available. Stop and reflect. Be willing to change and adjust to modifications in your life. Being amenable and accommodating while still being alert and aware is beneficial in the long run.

Lizard Affirmation

I easily adapt to my changing environment. I see through the falsities of a situation to get to the truth. Change is good. I assist people who are challenged by changes. I embrace transitions as they exist within life. Illusions fall away in front of me. I see through appearances and bravely follow my intuition without hesitation. I realize the impermanent nature of all life. I process and integrate information into my being with great ease.

Message from Herkimer Diamond

Make a decision to be clear and connected so that truth in all situations is provided to you. Believe yourself. When a dream, vision, or intuitive insight continuously comes to your awareness, look deeper into its meaning and how you can apply the message in your life. Recognize that you have the ability to continuously be fed clarity and understanding in all areas of your life.

Additional Vibrational Matching Gemstones for Lizard

Amethyst, black obsidian, dioptase, howlite, iolite, labradorite, lapis lazuli, moonstone, peridot, pietersite, and window quartz crystal.

50. MOCKINGBIRD AND AMAZONITE

Have you uncovered your truth? Are you speaking this truth? Do you recognize the many variations of opportunities and possibilities available to you?

Mockingbird totem is an ally that helps you find your truth, live your truth, and speak your truth. With Mockingbird's energy, learn the many variations on the theme, much like the variations of melodies within songs. This songbird has quite the repertoire of songs. Be like Mockingbird, and find the many ways you can use your talents and skills to be who you truly are. Mockingbird helps you when you want to find your voice.

When Mockingbird sings its way into your life, observe yourself to determine if you are mimicking someone else's way of doing things or if you are finding your unique path. Through self-awareness, Mockingbird makes you aware of the ways of being you admire in others. Model yourself on the qualities you want to emulate. Go beyond their personal achievements, and follow your heart to your unique brand or image.

Check in with yourself to be sure that you are in alignment with your personal truth. Take time to notice if others are copying you. Although copying is said to be the greatest form of flattery, watch out. You may need to defend your territory. Mockingbirds aggressively defend their territory. They can be found observing from a high perch. These characteristics teach you to observe and be watchful. While you may need to defend your copyrighted materials, an assertive approach is often more congenial than an aggressive one.

Mockingbird's Vibrational Matching Gemstone: Amazonite

Amazonite is the ultimate go-to stone for communication and speaking your truth. Use amazonite when you need to speak the truth. Let it be your reminder to act with integrity and hold the thought or intention of honesty. With this stone in hand, you are better able to discern the truth and set the boundaries with those who are not coming from a place of genuineness and integrity. Amazonite's energy offers a direct connection to the heavenly realm and makes you receptive to its assistance. Angels must be invited to help you, so ask your angels for help in any area of your life. It is a perfect vibrational match for hearing the sounds and songs of the angelic realm, which bring divine guidance.

Divine Influence

Call on Archangel Haniel to help connect you with your truth.

Mockingbird's Location on the Wheel of Life

Mockingbird is located on the east path, where Divine intervention and clarity are cultivated.

Contemplate This

Be aware of Divine timing and Divine orchestration at play in your life. See life from a higher perspective. Wouldn't you like God and the angels to orchestrate your life with you? Decide what you want, make a plan, take action, and be mindful of the signs and symbols the angels have placed along your path. Attract people of integrity into your life. Listen, and hear your melody and follow your sacred path.

Message from Mockingbird

When you listen, you can hear the song of the angels. Be ready to receive healing energy from the music of the spheres. Your song and manner of expression are within you. Find your specific tune—your way of being—and live your truth with joy and passion. Allow sound and music to help you remember why you are here on Earth at this time. Through meditation, recall your sacred agreements, which guide you to fulfill your life purpose.

Mockingbird Affirmation

I live my truth. I easily and honestly communicate what is on my mind. I speak eloquently. I am heard. My courage helps me communicate with ease. I stand up for myself. I say what I need to say. I surround myself with people who easily speak their truth. I set boundaries. It is easy for me to be powerful in loving ways.

Message from Amazonite

Recognize if you are holding something back that you need to say. Perhaps the truth about a certain matter needs to be spoken. Honesty is very important, so dare to speak up with grace and eloquence. Remember there are many ways to say what you need to say. When your words come from a loving and compassionate place, they have the power to heal or improve a situation.

Additional Vibrational Matching Gemstones for Mockingbird

Angelite, apatite, aquamarine, blue calcite, brucite, celestite, dioptase, iolite, larimar, sapphire, turquoise, and vanadinite.

51. Monkey and Golden Sheen Obsidian

Do you let yourself show your funny, clever, and dramatic nature? Are you gregarious, playful, sociable, and a bit dramatic? How connected are you with your tribe?

Monkey totem is an ally that helps you step into your power as a loving, joyful, outgoing being. When Monkey swings into your life on its tail, you are being encouraged to live life passionately with laughter and fun-loving comrades and friends. It's important for you to be a vital part of your family and community. Monkey teaches you to embrace your emotions and let yourself experience the full gamut of feelings. Practice vocalizing among people who you know already love you. Let Monkey be your ally to attract people who encourage you to be gregarious and playful in all situations. With Monkey's energy on your side, you are empowered to feel comfortable showing your true emphatic and sometimes dramatic nature to your tribe. Let yourself be a bit mischievous in a positive way! Like Monkey and its tail, put yourself out there and swing forward. If you need to, go ahead and "hang upside down" to gain perspective and find balance.

Monkey's energy is often used as an analogy when discussing the incessant chatter of the mind. The expression "monkey mind" refers to the never-ending thoughts rolling around in your consciousness. When Monkey swings into your life, make note of your mental state. Do you have a busy monkey mind, or are you just busy and sociable in a balanced way? Focus on the opposite state of consciousness by moving into a quiet, aware state. Through quiet awareness, you are more able to accept your feelings and thoughts as a calm observer.

Monkey's Vibrational Matching Gemstone: Golden Sheen Obsidian

Golden sheen obsidian, a naturally occurring volcanic glass, shows golden bubbles within it that occur during the cooling process. This characteristic is symbolic of the shimmer and shine you have within you. Through inner reflection, you can use your insights for the good of yourself and your community. Golden sheen obsidian is a good tool to enter deeper meditative states, releasing the monkey mind so that you can tap into higher levels of intelligence. With a clear mind and a bit of monkey's joyful and clever nature, you can use the energy to find balance on an emotional level. Monkeys are emotional or dramatic by nature, and golden sheen obsidian can help you find the balance.

Divine Influence

Call on Archangel Zaphkiel to support your efforts to be mindful and Archangel Muriel to help rebalance your emotions.

Monkey's Location on the Wheel of Life

Monkey is located on the southwest quadrant, where balanced emotions through inner reflection are found.

Contemplate This

What kind of drama is playing out around you? Keep your emotions in balance, and maintain a strong sense of self to avoid being drawn into someone's energy where emotions may be off-kilter. Detach from drama by being observant in order to gain a greater understanding of people and situations. Be sociable, and also take time to tune in to realign your consciousness with love and well-being. Quiet your mind, and listen to the wisdom within.

Message from Monkey

Find balance in your life through play, work, rest, exercise, and laughter. Nurture yourself and attract nurturing people into your life. Be attentive to the types of people you allow to play with your emotions. Focus on drawing in those filled with joy and respect. Laughter and play are keys to a balanced emotional state. Activate your childlike nature and be carefree.

Monkey Affirmation

I love life. I live in the present moment and enjoy the company of my friends, family, and colleagues. I am mindful of the energetic connections between others and myself. It is easy for me to maintain mindfulness and single-pointed focus. I am discerning about the people I allow into my circle. I am mindful of being in peaceful places to support my loving vibration.

Message from Golden Sheen Obsidian

You can be a charismatic part of your tribe. Have the courage to allow the dramatic part of your nature to bubble up. Have fun and remember that life is meant to be loving, joyful, and filled with supportive, fun friends and family. Be sociable. Increase your motivation in all aspects of your life. Sharpen your mental aptitude, and embrace your intelligence. Add verve and vigor to your spiritual practice, too.

Additional Vibrational Matching Gemstones for Monkey

Black tourmaline, brown agate, blue goldstone, carnelian, clear quartz cluster, green goldstone, red goldstone, orange calcite, rhodonite, selenite, and turquoise.

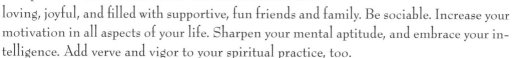

52. MOOSE AND BLUE TIGER'S EYE

Do you prefer a solitary life? Are you a peaceful person? Does it take a lot to get you agitated? Do you rarely feel the need to assert yourself?

Moose totem is an ally for you as your personality and your presence mature into a state of peace. Moose are peaceful, quiet, solitary animals. They are rarely aggressive and will react only if threatened. Moose medicine encourages you to step away from and eliminate situations where you will feel threatened. Use the energy of Moose to help you connect with gentleness, inner wisdom, and spiritual fulfillment. Moose's presence in your life indicates that there are times that peaceful power is necessary. Stay strong with getting your way. There are times when it is appropriate to be headstrong and unyielding to assert your authority.

When Moose comes into your life, keep your head high and raise your sight to a higher level. Align with the part of you that remembers your spiritual heritage and lineage. Male moose have distinguishable antlers that are broad and flat with a velvet-like covering. The antlers are heavy and can weigh up to forty pounds. This requires them to keep their head up the majority of the time. Symbolically, Moose calls you to raise your head and keep your sights on a higher spiritual wisdom. Moose calls you to remember to access your spiritual authority.

Moose's antlers are associated with virility and fertility. They fall off after breeding season to conserve energy for wintertime. The antlers regrow in the spring. This characteristic is a reminder of the changing seasons and the cyclical nature of life. Impermanence is natural, as is the ability for regeneration and rejuvenation.

Moose's Vibrational Matching Gemstone: Blue Tiger's Eye

Blue tiger's eye aligns you with the cosmic forces that provide inspirational messages to guide you in your life. Blue tiger's eye is an ally to help you begin to grasp the significance of the ever-turning wheel or cycles of life. Use it to understand karma, retribution, and the spiritual consequences and benefits of action or lack of action. Blue tiger's eye helps ground you and calms your mental chatter. This is beneficial as it allows you to have the clarity to move in the right direction. Carrying the vibration of sight, this stone promotes seeing life with your head held high so that you can approach life from a higher perspective.

Divine Influence

Call on Archangel Jophiel for help with inner wisdom, Metatron to understand higher states of consciousness and the path of your soul's evolution, and Archangel Uriel for illumination and peace.

Moose's Location on the Wheel of Life

Moose is located on the northeast quadrant, where wisdom leads into the renewal cycles of the wheel.

Contemplate This

Are you searching for answers to life's big questions and want to learn how to be at peace? Integrate grounded meditation experiences into your practices. Spend time alone to allow for insightful realizations. Maintain a focus that keeps you looking ahead. Notice what is right in front of you. Strengthen your connection with the moon and the movement of the celestial realm to help align you with the cycles of life. Recognize the cyclical nature of life. Embrace the seasons of life.

Message from Moose

Spend time alone in nature to find peace and calm. Take the necessary steps to shift your focus from that which troubles you to that which brings you joy. Remove yourself from stressful situations, and reduce stress in general. Learn to communicate your emotions and feelings. Recognize that life flows in circles and all cycles shift and change. Open pathways in your consciousness to accept the challenge of cultivating spiritual fortitude and spiritual authority.

Moose Affirmation

I am at peace. All is well in my life. It's easy for me to see beyond the obvious. I accurately read between the lines and hear what isn't being said. I embrace the circle of life and all the cycles that shift and change. I am grateful for the deeper insights and awareness that are available to me. I feel safe and know I am divinely protected.

Message from Blue Tiger's Eye

Notice whether you are looking at something from only one angle. If necessary, rise above a situation to find truth and see with greater clarity. It is time to take steps to gain a new perspective on life. The time has come to believe in your choices and know that they are good. Trust your ability to see things and read situations clearly.

Additional Vibrational Matching Gemstones for Moose

Apophyllite, bismuth, blue lace agate, cathedral quartz, charoite, chrysanthemum stone, garnet, magenta-dyed agate, morganite, prasiolite, selenite, and sugilite.

53. Moth and Moonstone

Do you prefer the nighttime over daytime? Do you use your sense of smell for direction and purpose? Have you paid attention to your dreams—both waking and sleeping dreams? Moth totem is an ally that helps you find your way around by using your senses, especially your sense of smell. This ally helps you connect with and examine the recesses of your mind. Use Moth's energy to shine a light on your intuitive senses. Moths are primarily nocturnal and gather nectar in the dark, guided by their ability to detect odor molecules. These characteristics of Moth are symbolic of your connection with the sweetness of life (the nectar), which may or may not be obvious. If Moth is one of your totems, your ability to pick up scents as well as clairolfaction (the ability to intuitively pick up a smell that doesn't physically exist) will be a guiding force in your journey in life. Notice if the scent or aromas of a person or place is inviting or repulsive. Take note, and act accordingly.

When Moth flies into your life, follow the directions you have been given in the dreamtime. Moths remind you to pay attention to your dreams by taking time to remember them and interpreting the symbols in your dreams. The symbols are gifts to help guide you on your journey here on Earth. When you have a dream that feels prophetic, believe yourself, observe, and use the information provided to move forward.

A notable characteristic of Moth behavior is their ability to camouflage themselves to avoid predators. Moth's wing coloration and patterns match the patterns of the trees, bark, or leaves of their setting in nature and are considered iconic examples of camouflage. Research has shown that moths actively look for the perfect spot that will make them invisible to predators. This distinctive quality is an ally when you need to avoid being noticed by someone who makes you uncomfortable or who behaves inappropriately toward you. Moth can help you disguise yourself until you can remove yourself from a situation.

Moth's Vibrational Matching Gemstone: Moonstone

Moonstone helps you awaken your intuition and strengthen your confidence so that you can trust your intuitive hunches. Moonstone also promotes dreaming, which provides tools for self-knowledge and help bring mental clarity. With moonstone under your pillow, interpret the messages of the dreamtime to restore mental balance. Moonstone encourages you to trust your intuition and step into your personal power. Moonstone, also known as hecatolite, is associated with the ancient Greek moon goddess, Hecate. This is a good stone to use when you are discovering how the 13 moon cycles affect you and learning what each of the nocturnal celestial movements are teaching.

Divine Influence

Call on the Angel of Inner Reflection, the Angel of Intuition, and the Angel of the Dreamtime for guidance toward self-understanding.

Moth's Location on the Wheel of Life

Moth is located on the northeast quadrant, where connection is made with the wisdom of the cycles of life.

Contemplate This

Do you remember your dreams? Do your senses bring you where you need to be? Are you connected with the lunar cycles? Let your dreams become messages to help you develop your personality and spirituality. You've spent enough time figuring things out. Let yourself emerge, using the knowledge spun within your consciousness. Believe in your intuitive insights and impressions. Put together the clues received in the dreamtime to gain insight, understanding, and directions for your life purpose.

Message from Moth

Follow your senses. Detect clues that help you find the sweetness of life. Dreams provide tools for self-knowledge and help bring mental clarity. Relax amid the negative ions of the great outdoors, and know all is well. Gaze at the moon, connect with its cycles, and allow yourself to receive the spiritual benefits from its vibrations. Deepen telepathic, psychometric, and visionary intuition, along with all six senses.

Moth Affirmation

The rainbow of light and positive energy expands my consciousness. My dreams are emerging to guide me on my path. I pay attention to my dreams and easily interpret them. I am aligned with the movement of the moon. I take the time for reflection. I observe how the world around me is a mirror of the world within me.

Message from Moonstone

Take time to interpret your dreams. Note the feelings, scents, and nuances and the symbolic representations throughout the dream. Distinguish between the psychological processing of your consciousness and the intuitive guidance being presented. Notice inner visions and lucid dreams that flow through your consciousness in your wakened state and have a dream feel to them.

Additional Vibrational Matching Gemstones for Moth

Blue tiger's eye, honey calcite, hiddenite, girasol quartz, howlite, labradorite, magnesite, phantom quartz, snowflake and obsidian.

54. Mouse and Yellow Jasper

Are you a nocturnal being? Can you see or hear what is not obvious to all? Are you able to find your way through potentially complex situations?

Mouse totem is an ally that opens your mind to previously unnoticed avenues of understanding and knowledge, and also a great pathfinder. Use the energy of Mouse to help you transcend current situations by being a trailblazer who finds alternative solutions and different routes to achieve goals. A mouse's sense of hearing and sense of smell are its two sharpest senses; thus, Mouse can help you sharpen your skills of clairaudience (the ability to hear messages from within) and clairolfaction (the ability to intuitively pick up a smell that doesn't physically exist).

When Mouse scurries into your life, be aware of what is going on around you. Note the scents in the vicinity, and use them as clues about which direction to take with current situations. Pay attention to the minute details of life. Let Mouse energy help you closely examine which path is the best. Mice are nocturnal creatures, so pay attention to your dreams, feelings that are under the surface, as well as things that aren't obvious to most people.

Mouse is a popular character in fiction. The list of fictional mice in literature, folklore, myth, television shows, and video games is long and varied, but the best known is Mickey Mouse, created by Walt Disney in 1928. Mouse is widely personified, and its vibration raises our ability to communicate with all beings—from mice to elephants, and beyond. Treat Mouse as an ally in opening your consciousness so that you can understand your animal companions and telepathically connect with all beings, even if that is not normally possible.

Mouse's Vibrational Matching Gemstone: Yellow Jasper

Yellow jasper helps you gain access to the part of your consciousness that is connected to the information and knowledge available from the unseen world, including intuition and the Akashic records. Let this jasper assist you as you tunnel into the part of you that is mentally clear, revealing untraditional approaches to the task at hand. Align with the realization that you can experience interspecies communication to hear and know messages from other realms of consciousness. Yellow jasper enhances mental clarity. Hold on to a piece of yellow jasper and visualize your mind clearing so that you can more accurately see the situation at hand. Trust your intuition to activate your ability to "see" using your ears and nose.

Divine Influence

Call on Archangel Gabriel for help with trusting your inner knowing, interpreting dreams, and clairaudient guidance.

Mouse's Location on the Wheel of Life

Mouse is located on the west path, where understanding comes from within.

Contemplate This

Are you paying attention to details? Do you tend to overscrutinize things? Consider reorganizing and rearranging your home so that you can see on all levels; you might be missing something that is right in front of you. It's time to pay attention to the minutiae of your life. With focus, you have the opportunity to see other areas of your life with greater clarity.

Message from Mouse

Trust your intuition. Listen to your inner voice. The small voice within, coupled with other clues such as scent, provides you with the insightful direction you need to find your way through any given situation. Take one step at a time, and know that the answers you need will be revealed as you work through things systematically and methodically. Follow your nose in order to illuminate your path, help sort out feelings, and recognize the best direction to travel.

Mouse Affirmation

I am extraordinarily perceptive and discerning in all areas of my life. I am consciously aware of everything going on around me. I comprehend the details of every-thing set before me. I am organized. I quiet my mind and tap into alternative pathways to my goals. I am aligned with inner knowing. I create a cozy nest in which to live and learn.

Message from Yellow Jasper

Take time to sort out all the details of what's going on around you and within you. Make an effort to gain some clarity around which direction you want to head in. Take a grounded approach, and gather realistic solutions by taking the necessary time to examine yourself and the situation through quiet contemplation.

Additional Vibrational Matching Gemstones for Mouse

Amethyst, bismuth, blue chalcedony, celestite, Dalmatian jasper, Herkimer diamond, fluorite, larimar, scolecite, and selenite.

55. OSTRICH AND APATITE

Are you good at discerning when it is best to step away from a situation? Do you avoid an argument and agree to things even if it doesn't suit you? Do you pay attention to your surroundings and what's happening around you?

Ostrich totem is an ally that helps you recognize when it is best to step away from negative situations as fast as possible, when avoiding an issue is worse than confronting the situation, and when it is best to lie low and wait it out to see if the negative situation resolves on its own.

Ostriches can run up to 40 miles per hour when threatened, and running is usually their best option in order to stay safe. Ostrich teaches that there are times when it is appropriate to avoid arguments rather than lash out. Pause, reflect, and observe if the issue will resolve itself on its own through self-observation and awareness. If you must confront the situation, be sure that you have all you need readily available to deal with the situation, such as information, tact, and assertiveness.

It is commonly believed that ostriches bury their heads in the sand; in truth, they lie down and keep their head and neck flat to the ground and look just like a mound of soil. Ostrich teaches that, in some circumstances, it is best to blend in with your surroundings; this is healthy avoidance of unnecessary aggravation.

Ostrich's eyesight is extraordinary. When Ostrich walks into your life, activate your intuitive abilities to help with protection and situational awareness. Use your spiritual eyes for intuitive peripheral knowing and your intuitive senses—hearing, smelling, tasting, and sensing—for overall well-being.

Ostrich's Vibrational Matching Gemstone: Apatite

The teal color of apatite matches the energy of activation and usage of all six clairs—clairvoyance, clairaudience, claircognizance, clairsentience, clairolfaction, and clairgustation (see the glossary on page 215.) Apatite is one of the stones of endurance and good health. Use it to develop the fortitude to attract people of integrity into your life. Hold the thought or intention of honesty in all aspects of your life. Use apatite and Ostrich as allies to aid you when you realize it is most important to rise above situations and allow healing to take place where once confrontation existed. Find inner strength and connection to higher realms of consciousness and Divine will.

Divine Influence

Call on Archangel Michael to help protect you and resolve disagreements with a fair and just outcome for all involved.

Ostrich's Location on the Wheel of Life

Ostrich is located on the east path, where the ability to see the higher resolution is learned.

Contemplate This

Have you noticed your words coming across the wrong way? Have your communications been misunderstood? Avoid making inaccurate assumptions that might lead to hurt feelings. Discern the truth, and set boundaries with those around you who are not coming from a place of genuineness and integrity. Honesty is always important, so have the courage and grace to speak up. Notice when you've said enough or retreat (doing and saying nothing) is more powerful than taking action. When your words come from a loving and compassionate place, they have the power to heal or improve a situation.

Message from Ostrich

Have the courage to act and make your dreams and ideas a reality. Perhaps you've avoided looking at an emotional issue. Take a moment to rest and reflect and find the root cause of emotional patterns. On an emotional level, deal with the source of the aggravation, and avoid running away from the challenges presented. Find creative peaceful solutions to change perplexing situations.

Ostrich Affirmation

It's easy for me to transform and transmute challenging situations. I use my intuition and follow my hunches. I am aligned with higher wisdom. My body is perfect. I am the ideal weight for my height, build, and genetics. I am quick on my feet. I am speedy in all that I do. I avoid confrontation when it will benefit all involved. My digestive processes are healthy. I easily absorb and process all that goes on around me.

Message from Apatite

It is beneficial to process emotional aggravation that manifests as indigestion, heartburn, or an upset stomach, as it helps you to look more objectively at what feelings, people, places, and situations are causing you agitation. Remove challenges, or stay away from interacting with those who have been causing you distress. Transform challenging situations, and call on Ostrich and the help of celestial beings to orchestrate peaceful resolutions.

Additional Vibrational Matching Gemstones for Ostrich

Amethyst, apatite, black tourmaline, citrine, citron chrysoprase, chrysocolla, golden calcite, green calcite, peridot, prehnite, red jasper, ruby, and turquoise.

56. OTTER AND SILVER TOPAZ

Is your life balanced with laughter and joy? Are you spending enough time on personal care and grooming? Have you spent time playing lately?

Otter totem is an ally that helps you to balance responsibilities and playtime. While otters are known for their playful nature, playtime happens after Otter has met its basic needs—food, shelter, and grooming. Otters in captivity play more often than those in the wild because humans meet their basic needs; they don't need to hunt for food or a safe place to sleep. When Otter playfully swims into your life, you are being encouraged to complete your responsibilities in a timely manner so you have plenty of opportunity to play and relax.

For otters, grooming can take anywhere from a quarter to half of the day. They must groom their fur to keep it at its best for insulation. They aerate their fur by beating it to remove water. This animal makes a good totem for hair stylists or anyone who enjoys spending a lot of time on their personal hygiene. Otters are very flexible and have loose-fitting skin. Otter medicine reminds you to take the time you need to coif and/or stretch. Yoga and other practices that include stretching are a good match for someone with Otter as a totem animal.

Otter encourages you to wake up your inner child and remember how fun life can be. Invite others to play with you. Frolic in the water. Because otters spend a considerable amount of time in the water, Otter energy also relates to finding balance in your emotional body as well as between work and play.

Otter's Vibrational Matching Gemstone: Silver Topaz

Silver topaz activates the part of you that is able to see the good in all people and all situations. Silver topaz increases your ability to find the positive no matter what. By using the power of visualization, you can get your tasks and responsibilities taken care of and use the remaining time to enjoy life. Open your mind to imagine potential realities as you script your life. Find the silver lining in all you do. Silver topaz and the energy of Otter support you when you need to emphasize the positive or optimistic perspective in all life situations.

Divine Influence

Call on Archangel Muriel and the Angel of Balanced Emotions to help balance your life and emotions and the Angel of Fun and Play to help you more thoroughly enjoy life.

Otter's Location on the Wheel of Life

Otter is located on the south path, where self-care and balance take precedence.

Contemplate This

Do you stay focused on getting your work done? Are you fully aware of your daily activities? Find ways to fulfill your responsibilities so that you have plenty of time to spare. Be present so that you can appreciate your tasks and find pleasure in your recreational activities. Allow work to feel like play, and observe yourself to be sure you are consciously enjoying your leisure time.

Message from Otter

Get all of your work done so that you have time to play. It's important to take time to relish life, away from responsibilities. A rigid mentality gets in the way of happiness and the energy to have fun! Be flexible in your daily life so that you can enjoy your time on this planet.

Otter Affirmation

I find balance in my life through play, work, rest, exercise, and laughter. My creative energy is alive. I easily nurture myself. My visualizations focus on positive outcomes. I spend time at the water's edge to regain my balance. I attract nurturing, happy people into my life. There is always a silver lining, and I am able to see the good even when others cannot.

Message from Silver Topaz

There is always a silver lining within any challenge. Open your consciousness in order to see the good even when others can't. Stay calm amid your many responsibilities. Decide that you will always have plenty of time to do the things you want and need to do. Align with your inner knowing that you have clarity, organization, and the ability to creatively arrive at solutions to potential problems when needed.

Additional Vibrational Matching Gemstones for Otter

Aragonite, aquamarine, citrine, chalcedony, cobaltoan calcite, gold tiger's eye, golden calcite, golden topaz, larimar, magenta-dyed agate, moonstone, pink tourmaline, and unakite.

57. OWL AND INDICOLITE

Do you enjoy the pursuit of wisdom and knowledge? How strong are your spiritual sight and physical eyesight? Are you able to see or know what others do not?

Owl totem is an ally that helps you see, hear, and know what needs to be known by interpreting the messages from both the physical and spirit worlds. Owl allows you to "see in the dark" and "read between the lines." When Owl swoops into your life, it signals a time to pay attention to what is going on behind the scenes. Owl alerts you that there is more to notice than you might see at a glance.

In mythology, Owl is a companion of Athena (Greek) and Minerva (Roman). By either name, these are the goddesses of wisdom. Athena is also known as Pallas. It is said that Athena's owl sat on her blind side so that she would always see or know the truth. In many cultures, owls are known as symbols for spiritual and intellectual wisdom.

Owl helps you align with the intuitive gift of clairaudience (the ability to hear that which isn't said) and clairvoyance (seeing what isn't obvious to all) by picking up thoughts through telepathy—heart-to-heart and mind-to-mind connection. Owl is a reminder to pay attention to your still, small voice within. This totem helps you resolve frustration or anger by understanding other people's point of view. Hidden agendas can be revealed to you with guidance from Owl. See the truth, know the truth, and experience the truth through Owl's presence in your life.

Owl's Vibrational Matching Gemstone: Indicolite

With its royal associations, indicolite is a stone of wise leadership. Indicolite's energy cultivates wisdom, which brings loyalty and integrity in your words, thoughts, and actions. Indicolite helps you train your mind for single-pointed focus, so it makes a good meditation tool to help direct the mind to contemplate and understand underlying truth. Use it to reduce confusion and gain clarity and understanding. With its ability to sharpen mental capacity, this stone is helpful for better comprehension of written material, especially difficult scholarly texts, including spoken discourses. Indicolite has an oracular energy, so use it when you want to sharpen your intuition. Indicolite and the energy of Owl support both intellectual and spiritual pursuits.

Divine Influence

Call on Archangel Michael to help you see life from a greater perspective and know the truth in all matters.

Owl's Location on the Wheel of Life

Owl is located on the eastern quadrant, where perspective and clarity are gained.

Contemplate This

Are you able to hear what isn't being spoken aloud? Can you read between the lines? Do you know what hasn't been revealed? When you are certain that someone is telling the truth or not, don't second-guess yourself; believe yourself. Studying and learning are good habits for your overall well-being. You are wise. Engage in illuminating activities, such as meditation, contemplation, and reflection, to better understand the true nature of reality, which will further illuminate spiritual truths for you.

Message from Owl

It is time to align with your inner mystic. Look beneath the surface in both the spiritual and the mundane worlds. Be the spiritual seeker, and find deeper truths. Tune in to your innate ability to see, sense, feel, and know the truth. Follow your intuition. Promote clarity in your dreams, and remember them. Interpret your dreams, so that they can provide you with guidance and knowledge.

Owl Affirmation

Hidden intentions, masks, and illusions are disclosed. Knowledge and wisdom regarding secrets are revealed to me when needed. It's easy for me to see the unseen and hear the unsaid. I acknowledge and trust my intuition. It is my intention to improve my spiritual sight and clairvoyant capabilities. I have a clear view of the truth.

Message from Indicolite

Maintain a sense of calm, and tap into your divine intelligence and innate wisdom. Stay focused, and sort out thoughts in a peaceful manner. Make a clear decision to release fears and step forward with determination to be a champion of the truth. Take the time to meditate so you are clear and calm and, therefore, better able to follow your internal guidance system. Recognize that sage wisdom is available within you.

Additional Vibrational Matching Gemstones for Owl

Cathedral quartz, channeling quartz, clear quartz, golden sheen obsidian, kyanite, lapis lazuli, moonstone, record keeper quartz, sapphire, selenite, and sodalite.

58. PANTHER AND TIME LINK QUARTZ

Do you prefer to spend time alone? Would you rather not be noticed? Do you spend time in the inner world as a solitary spiritual practitioner?

Panther totem (or jaguar or leopard depending on the geographic location) is an ally for when you prefer to be alone and detached from social interactions. The big cats are solitary predators. They live, hunt, and travel alone—except during mating season—and female panthers raise their cubs alone.

Panthers are nocturnal animals that live in dense vegetation so that their dark fur serves as camouflage. They eat, hunt, and travel at night. In a shamanic sense, Panther is a totem for shape shifting, which gives a shaman the ability to transform himself or herself into other physical forms for the purposes of orchestrating Divine intervention in the mystical world. Panther medicine enables you to activate a "cloak of invisibility" (that is, be energetically less obvious to others) for those times when you just want to observe situations and prefer not to be noticed.

When Panther skulks into your life, it is time to find balance between spending time alone and fostering a connection with others. Develop trust and humility. While the journey from one-dimensional reality to another is a solitary one, it is beneficial to find a balance in your conversational abilities with others. After all, you are not alone; you are living in a world filled with people. Panther is a good totem to align with when you are ready to transition and spiral into the next level of consciousness or rebirth.

Panther's Vibrational Matching Gemstone: Time Link Quartz

Time link quartz crystal is a portal to the unlimited source of No Mind, the Great Mystery, the Great Void from which all things come forth. Use this crystal, a quartz point with a seventh facet that is a parallelogram, in contemplation and meditation to go deep within to the place of nothingness. In the nothingness, you will find all that exists. The time link crystal is a perfect meditation companion to help you quiet your mind. It helps take you through a timeline of your thoughts so that you can sort out what you need to keep in your consciousness, front and center, and what you can release. A time link crystal opens your mind to the unlimited potential future realities from which you can choose. Every future moment depends on your present thoughts and state of consciousness.

Divine Influence

Call on Archangel Michael to help guide you on your spiritual journey on Earth and help you connect with the mystic within.

Panther's Location on the Wheel of Life

Panther is located on the northeastern quadrant, where transition into the next level of consciousness occurs.

Contemplate This

Are you aware of your past lives, potential future realities, and parallel lives? Have you aligned with the magnitude of your personal power? To better understand the present moment investigate the past, and notice how it might affect your future. Invite the wisdom and knowledge of the Great Mystery into your life. Open your mind in order to realize that you choose from unlimited potential future realities.

Message from Panther

You may have released your need for companionship and relationships in your social and professional life and developed a preference for working alone. The fact remains that you have incarnated on this planet, and you are not alone. Make an effort to increase your tolerance of coworkers who might not be as fast or as smart as you are. Explore the inner sanctums of your consciousness as you empty your mind of the usual chatter to understand why you have chosen to walk a solitary path.

Panther Affirmation

I am powerful beyond measure. I am patient, kind, and tolerant. I am strong and healthy. I imagine potential future realities. I manifest my reality with my thoughts, words, and actions. I have unlimited potential. Wisdom and knowing are mine. Mystical awareness is my primary goal. I find balance being alone as well as interacting with friends and family.

Message from Time Link Quartz

Questions like "Why is this happening to me?" or "What did I do to deserve this?" may be familiar at this time. You may be caught in a pattern in which you experience the same situation over and over, with the only difference being the people who play a role in the scenario. Now is a good time to look into regression therapy or guided imagery meditation. Through regression, you can begin to uncover the original source of the issue(s) currently affecting you.

Additional Vibrational Matching Gemstones for Panther

Ammonite, black obsidian, blue topaz, cathedral quartz, jet, kyanite, malachite, lapis lazuli, rutilated quartz, and silver topaz.

59. PARROT AND BI-COLOR TOURMALINE

Are you filled with joy and enthusiasm? Do you enjoy wearing many colors in vibrant tones? Are you inspired by mentors and use them as a model for your behavior or work?

Parrot totem is an ally when you are working with color—in art, in gemstones, in clothing, in décor—in all aspects of life. Parrot's energy helps you remember to sparkle and shine. Look to Parrot to increase your self-esteem and willingness to be seen and heard. Parrots are intelligent and encourage you to uncover your own innate intelligence.

Parrots have the ability to mimic the human voice. This behavior is a message for you to find your voice and vibrantly express yourself in living color. For inspiration, observe and model the behavior of those you admire. Instead of copying or mimicking them, develop similar qualities and be equally brilliant and fabulous.

Parrots mate for life. The vibration of their monogamy assists you with increasing loyalty and devotion with your existing romantic partner. If you are single, call on this energy to align you with the perfect life partner, one with whom you can enjoy love, commitment, and reliability.

According to fossil records and molecular studies, parrots have been evolving for up to 70 million years! Therefore, Parrot can help you tap into the Akashic records and other ancient records stored within your own consciousness. When Parrot squawks into your life, be open to advancing your ability to know and understand all that has occurred in the past, all that is happening in the present, and all that is a potential future reality.

Parrot's Vibrational Matching Gemstone: Bi-color Tourmaline

Bi-color tourmaline increases your awareness of your thoughts, and whether they are positive or not. As you become aware of these thoughts (also called thought forms or mental energy), bi-color tourmaline can help you focus on what you want. It can help release any energy preventing you from attaining your goals by helping you restructure your thoughts into positive statements. Use this stone with the intention of receiving inspiration.

Divine Influence

Call on the Angel of Communication and Archangel Gabriel to help you cultivate healthy communication in all aspects of your life.

Parrot's Location on the Wheel of Life

Parrot is located on the east path, where higher perspective and insights are gained.

Contemplate This

Are you drawn to specific colors? Do you find benefit from crystal alignments? A crystal alignment is the practice of laying stones on and around your body to experience a deeper meditation or a healing. Crystal healing is a good way to balance your energy. Embrace the colors of the rainbow when making choices regarding food, clothing, and other items. Spend some time in the sun. Observe the benefits of what others are doing as a form of inspiration and then find your own way of being and doing.

Message from Parrot

Acknowledge your magnificence and focus on what you do well to increase your self-esteem. Trust that it is safe to be powerful, fabulous, colorful, and magnificent. Shine your light to reach your full potential. Express yourself. Speak up. Show up for life with vibrancy, joy, and enthusiasm. Observe people you admire, and use them as a model to inspire you. Spend time in nature, and get sufficient sunlight to maintain a healthy body, mind, and spirit.

Parrot Affirmation

I enjoy working and playing with color and crystals. Colorful gemstones help me rebalance my energy. I model the behaviors of successful people in order to further my own success. I honor and respect myself for who I am and what I can do. I am grateful for my life partner. I am loyal and faithful. It's easy for me to speak up for myself. I shine my light brightly and acknowledge my magnificence.

Message from Bi-color Tourmaline

A loyal dedicated life partner who is filled with joy and happiness might be on your radar. You may desire more attention and affection than you've been receiving. Nurture yourself, and treat yourself the way you want others to treat you. Improve your demeanor in order to attract devoted friends or a life partner. To bring more romance into your life, first learn how to enjoy your own company. Determine what makes you happy. Rev up your self-acceptance, and increase your willingness to allow more love into your life.

Additional Vibrational Matching Gemstones for Parrot

Angelite, blue lace agate, chalcopyrite, green moss agate, green tourmaline, larimar, peacock copper, peridot, turquoise, and watermelon tourmaline.

60. Peacock and Blue-dyed Agate

Are you comfortable revealing your full splendor? Do you find that you have a tendency to intimidate people with your magnificence? Are you interested in attracting a mate?

Peacock totem is an ally that assists you in becoming more comfortable with showing your splendor and magnificence to others without intimidating them. Peacock aligns you with your source of self-esteem. Use this energy to help you be seen in the world—in your family, your community, or on the world stage. When Peacock majestically appears in your life, be mindful of the manner in which you display your talents and beauty. Avoid showing off, but don't be afraid to use your impressive abilities.

Peacock is a good ally when you are in the process of looking for a romantic partner and encourages you to be confident in your appearance. Peacock, the brilliant bird with those amazing "multi-eyed" tail feathers, is actually the name of the male bird—though both male and female are commonly referred to as peacocks. The female is a brown, muted-colored bird called a peafowl or peahen.

When courting a peafowl, the peacock raises his brightly colored tail feathers to attract her, reminding you to display your most attractive qualities in order to attract the best into your life. The peacock's tail, which makes him appear quite large, is also used as a defense—a reminder to be mindful of how your magnificence might make others uncomfortable.

Peacock's crest links this totem to the crown chakra and spiritual royalty—the place within your consciousness that aligns you with the Divine. In Hinduism, Peacock symbolizes Divine knowledge, pride, and beauty. Peacock has associations with several Hindu gods and goddesses, as well as with the Buddhist deity Kuan Yin, Goddess of Compassion. Mercy, compassion, prosperity, royalty, love, and peace are all qualities associated with Peacock. In Buddhism, peacock feathers are used in purification ceremonies. In the Greco-Roman culture, as an ally to Juno, Peacock protected against material harm due to the "evil eyes" on its tail feathers. Call upon Peacock medicine when you want more compassion, clarity, and protection.

Peacock's Vibrational Matching Gemstone: Blue-dyed Agate

Blue-dyed agate heightens your ability to be a clear conduit for messages and inspiration. Use blue-dyed agate to sharpen your intuition and to find the strength to trust your inner guidance system. It opens your heart despite aggravating or demeaning situations created by you or others. Use blue-dyed agate to look, with understanding and compassion, at what took place in your past. Gaze into yourself, and see how your inner beauty is mirrored around you. Blue-dyed agate is an ally to improve the flow of ideas and creativity and increase faith in yourself. Pay attention to the signs and symbols around you. They give you clues and make your life easier.

Divine Influence

Call on Archangel Michael to shine his brilliant electric blue ray for your protection, fair play, and alignment with the Divine.

Peacock's Location on the Wheel of Life

Peacock is located on the east path, where the ability to see things from varying perspectives improves.

Contemplate This

Are you interested in the mystical? Do you feel a connection with spiritual symbolism, visions, and the Divine? Open your spiritual eyes to see with greater insight. Tap into your clairvoyant abilities, and be aware of visions and messages perceived through your physical sight. Be watchful and alert in order to maintain a safe and sacred center for yourself and others. Remember that you are always divinely protected. Take the time to make your own rituals to help you align with your inner mystic.

Message from Peacock

Activate your creative energy with the brilliant vibration of electric blue energy in order to help you see things from a new and colorful perspective. Now is the time to be open up to fresh new ideas, new people, and great happiness as you release worn-out life situations and perspectives on life. Be open to new opportunities, and enjoy riding the wave of change! Be a clear channel, and allow wisdom to flow through you. Believe in yourself.

Peacock Affirmation

Light illuminates my path to see circumstances from a place of wisdom. I am kind, loyal, and compassionate. I purify my consciousness regularly. My physical and spiritual sight provides me with visions for understanding. I am highly intuitive. I have advance hindsight because I see life from a higher perspective. I am safe. I have a balanced mental perspective.

Message from Blue-dyed Agate

Get in touch with your magnificence, and live your life in full splendor. Find ways to bring more joy into your life. It's time to be aware of the source of your emotional challenges or perceived blocks so that you can release them. Align with your inner radiance, and shine your light brightly. Have confidence in your ability to tap into universal knowledge and wisdom.

Additional Vibrational Matching Gemstones for Peacock

Angelite, celestite, citrine, clear quartz, copper, howlite, iolite, kyanite, lapis lazuli, sodalite, peacock copper, sapphire, rhodochrosite, and selenite rose.

61. PENGUIN AND MAGENTA-DYED AGATE

Are you seeking more emotional balance in your body? Can you clearly see what's going on around you even when your emotions are running high? Are you a loyal life partner?

Penguin totem is an ally that prepares you for joining with a loyal and dedicated mate and aligning with the energy of being a parent. Just as penguins walk long distances for the sake of breeding, turn to Penguin medicine to support you when you have to go the distance in any area of your life—especially as a parent, in a creative project, or with a business endeavor.

Penguins spend about half their time in water and the other half on land. This energy is symbolic of your need to balance your emotions with healthy detachment. Even though penguins are birds, they are flightless. However, they do "fly" underwater, using their wings as flippers. Penguin's ability to see underwater supports you in understanding the depth of your emotions, and its buoyancy is a reminder to stabilize yourself even when your emotions are causing turbulent "waters" for you or those around you.

When Penguin waddles into your life, take a moment to decide if you might benefit from a fast (no food) or a cleansing diet for a period of time. Either of these practices can help you clear your energetic and mental space and allow room for ideas and inspirations currently incubating in your consciousness. If fasting or a cleansing diet isn't what your body needs right now, consider spending some time immersed in water at the beach, a lake, a swimming pool, or even a bathtub.

Penguin's Vibrational Matching Gemstone: Magenta-dyed Agate

Magenta-dyed agate helps you balance your emotions, thereby increasing your emotional maturity. The color magenta is a reminder of the Divine Mother within, who hears and knows the truth and accepts you unconditionally. The Divine Mother—or the Divine Parent—is an archetypal energy that embodies loyalty, dedication, compassion, nurturing, and great wisdom. Use magenta-dyed agate as a reminder to practice self-care, and recognize when to grant yourself permission to embrace nurturing activities and rest. This brilliant pink stone encourages passion and fortitude in order to establish healthy boundaries to care for yourself and those you love. Balance emotions, and improve confidence within relationships, and use magenta-dyed agate to remember to let go of expectations or assumptions so that disappointment is less likely.

Divine Influence

Call on the Angel of the Sea to support you in taking time to enjoy bodies of water, the Angel of Parents to maintain your patience and support your lifelong job of parenting, and Archangel Chamuel to strengthen your ties with your significant other or co-parent.

Penguin's Location on the Wheel of Life

Penguin is located on the southwest quadrant, where love, loyalty, and emotional stability are integrated.

Contemplate This

Are you seeking unconditional love? Do you want others to demonstrate their love for you? Do you know that you are well loved by many people? You have a natural ability to love and be loved. Allow this love in and become its receptacle. Accept the part of you that is able to hold a vision, and imagine a better way of life for all beings. Take time to swim, float, or spend time in any body of water to restore balance.

Message from Penguin

Dedication is the key to nurturing your creative endeavors. Give birth to your dreams by dedicating yourself to going the distance. Parent your creations by recognizing that it takes time, effort, loyalty, and dedication to nurture your dreams—whether a child, a creative project, or a business endeavor. Perseverance over the long haul is required.

Penguin Affirmation

I am in touch with my emotions. It is easy for me to relax into the ebb and flow of life. I am balanced, whole, and complete. I am love. I am willing to receive love. Blessings flow into my life. I am compassionate and kind. I am dedicated and loyal. I am able to help others by vibrating love through my presence.

Message from Magenta-dyed Agate

Open your heart center to allow love to enter. Many sensual feelings naturally arise when the heart center opens. With this stone in hand, use the breath and discipline to harness the sensual energy for the higher good of all. Awaken your awareness of your spiritual purpose. Focus on attracting your perfect life mate and, if applicable, being a devoted parent.

Additional Vibrational Matching Gemstones for Penguin

Aquamarine, bloodstone, green calcite, green tourmaline, kunzite, larimar, pink calcite, pink tourmaline, relationship quartz crystal, rhodochrosite, rose quartz, ruby in zoisite, and unakite.

62. PIG AND SUGILITE

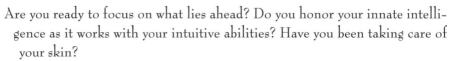

Are you ready to focus on what lies ahead? Do you honor your innate intelligence as it works with your intuitive abilities? Have you been taking care of your skin?

Pig totem is an ally for forward movement. Pigs are food driven and use their snout in search of sustenance. They eat in a unique manner, using their hooves to scratch in a backward motion to uncover their food. Pig, therefore, is a symbol of progress. They cannot move their necks and look backward the way we do, so they cannot see behind them without completely turning around. This is a reminder to keep moving forward and not look back.

Pigs roll in mud primarily to protect their skin from the sun and insects. Pig medicine, thus, reminds you to take care of your skin by being mindful of ultraviolet rays and protecting yourself from biting insects. Contrary to popular belief, a distinctive characteristic of pigs is their cleanliness. Pigs really aren't dirty creatures; they just like spa treatments!

Pigs are intelligent creatures. When Pig shows up in your life, honor your intelligence. Know that Pig is supporting you in all areas where your memory and intelligence are being put to the test. Pig also teaches you about healthy detachment. As pets, pigs require less attention than many other pets. This energy of detachment can help you when you need to stop being clingy in a relationship.

Because pigs are nearsighted, they have a well-developed sense of smell and hearing. These qualities enhance the intuitive senses of clairolfaction and clairaudience. With clairolfaction, you notice smells (both physical and nonphysical) that provide you with important insight into a situation. When clairaudience is primed, you have the intuitive ability to receive auditory guidance (both physical and nonphysical). This is the inner voice of intuition.

Pig's Vibrational Matching Gemstone: Sugilite

Sugilite helps you let go of the past and move forward in a positive way. Use this stone in harmony with Pig medicine to deflect negative thoughts stemming from your past. The transmutational power of purple within sugilite transforms negative belief systems from the past, gently guiding you toward more beneficial belief systems. Use this stone to develop a true understanding of detachment. It can help you develop healthy relationships through the realization of the impermanent nature of reality. The indigo blue energy of sugilite calms relentless inner chatter and invites peace and calmness in the mind so you can move forward with ease. Sugilite supports your intuitive abilities and expands your awareness so that everything makes sense. It provides the foundation for a grounded spiritual practice.

Divine Influence

Call on the Angel of Intelligence to help guide your forward movement and Archangel Raziel to help you embrace the gifts of clairolfaction and clairaudience.

Pig's Location on the Wheel of Life

Pig is located on the east doorway, where the new cycle around the earth-centered walk begins.

Contemplate This

Have you noticed that you have a small voice within that brings you intuitive insights? Do you believe yourself when you hear the guidance? Do you have a conscious reaction to odors and aromas? Have you noticed that when you don't listen or pay attention to your olfactory alert, you regret it? The time has come to allow your heightened sense of smell to be a guidepost on your path. The same goes for your heightened awareness of your inner voice. Listen to the messages you are receiving and believe yourself!

Message from Pig

If you have grabbed onto a thought, memory, or life experience and have been chewing it over ever since, it is time to release it. Let go of thoughts about the past (whether it was five minutes ago or five years ago) so that you can find inner peace and true happiness in the moment. Imagine the bright future ahead of you, and move forward peacefully and calmly.

Pig Affirmation

I move forward with grace. My intuition is strong. I am an intelligent being with the ability to focus on complex tasks. I enjoy learning new things. I create the perfect space to learn. I pay attention to the messages I receive through aromas and inner voice. I use my intuition and follow my hunches.

Message from Sugilite

Surround yourself with people who recognize your talents, intelligence, creativity, kindness, and thoughtfulness. Allow your intuitive nature to meld with your intelligence, combining your knowledge with spiritual wisdom. Cultivate tools to love and be loved without neediness on your part or the other person's. Develop a true understanding of detachment.

Additional Vibrational Matching Gemstones for Pig

Amethyst, carnelian, fluorite, golden topaz, hiddenite, indochinite tektite, labradorite, moldavite, red calcite, red jasper, and selenite.

63. PORCUPINE AND PURPLE-DYED AGATE

Do you feel vulnerable? Do you feel like you need to defend or protect yourself? Are you keeping company with people you respect and admire? Porcupine totem is an ally for when you feel the need to constantly be on the defensive. Call on Porcupine's vibe to help you discern between needing to be mindful of who you are around and sharing what is on your mind. This ally helps you differentiate between paranoia and justified protection. Once you've established whether you need protection, take action to ensure your safety. Porcupine teaches you to use your protective defenses only when real danger is present or when you are susceptible to emotional attack or harm.

When Porcupine scurries into your life, take the time to discern if defensive responses are really necessary. Ask yourself if it is a valid perception or a case of paranoia. Make the sincere effort to surround yourself with trustworthy people, and envelop yourself in a sphere of goodness and well-being. Porcupine invites you to develop trust. Note whether the people around you do what they say they will do. Develop your communication skills to cultivate relationships. Discern who you let into your circle of friends or on your team at work.

Porcupine is an ally that helps you transform negative thoughts or beliefs by awakening your awareness to the incessant chatter of your mind. Draw out dark, negative emotions that are holding you back from living a happy life. Uncover the deeper, hidden reason for your negative actions or reactions toward others. Find the source of the emotional problem so that you can heal the drama and the trauma.

Porcupine's Vibrational Matching Gemstone: Purple-dyed Agate

Purple-dyed agate helps you transform and transmute challenging situations. With purple-dyed agate in hand, open your heart, mind, and emotions to seeing and knowing the truth about people and situations. Knowledge and understanding are keys to guide you toward taking the appropriate action regarding situations and people who may mistake your good nature for being defenseless or weak. Together, purple-dyed agate and Porcupine's good energy help you recognize when you need to take special care to remove whatever is not for your highest good. Purple-dyed agate carries the transformative power to remove people, places, or things from your life that upset you emotionally. With this stone, you can lovingly release people from your life who keep hurting your feelings. This agate is useful to let go of feelings of insecurity, depression, and lack of confidence.

Divine Influence

Call on Archangel Michael to help you know that you are always divinely protected and the Angel of Protection to walk with you as your guardian so you can feel safe and sound.

Porcupine's Location on the Wheel of Life

Porcupine is located on the south path, where transformation takes place.

Contemplate This

Are you telling everyone all of your personal business? Be mindful about who you let into your inner circle. Pay attention to how much personal information you reveal to certain people. Notice whether any people or situations are causing you discomfort, and step away. Believe people when they show their true personality or if you find out what they say about you when you aren't around. Make the necessary changes to adjust your life so that you are healthy, happy, and fully supported by loving family and friends. Remember to enjoy life and to play!

Message from Porcupine

Constantly being on the defensive can be draining. You might often feel like you need protection. Ask yourself if your defensive behavior is justified. If it is, then stop being around people, places, and situations that make you feel and act defensively. Adjust your attitude to create a happier life. Make a clear intention that you only want loving and supportive vibrations around you wherever you are. Create peaceful space and energy around you so that you don't have to defend yourself.

Porcupine Affirmation

I am discerning about the people I allow into my circle. I am mindful of being around people who support my fun and loving vibration. I set boundaries with ease and grace. I know when to stay and when to step away. I enjoy life. It's easy for me to transform challenging situations. I am grateful for my circle of loving friends, family, and colleagues.

Message from Purple-dyed Agate

Clear mental energy associated with jealousy, negative self-talk, confusing mental chatter, and general chaos. Think outside the box, and find different ways to approach a problem or any mind-bending challenge. Make the necessary changes to adjust your life so that you can be healthy, happy, and fully supported by loving family and friends. Ground your spiritual practice in everyday life, and as you do so, you will be surrounded by an aura of peace and protection.

Additional Vibrational Matching Gemstones for Porcupine

Amethyst, black kyanite, black obsidian arrowheads, black tourmaline, golden sheen obsidian, hematite, jet, lapis lazuli, shungite, and tourmalinated quartz.

64. Praying Mantis and Mookaite Jasper

Are you experiencing significant changes in your life? Do you notice that things are so dramatically different that your life seems unrecognizable? Are you listening to your inner voice in order to have a clearer understanding of your potential future?

Praying Mantis totem is an ally that will help you transform your life when you listen closely. This ally teaches you the value of using color in your wardrobe to help with your life. Just as a praying mantis uses color changes to camouflage or conceal itself for protection, you too can use color to help protect yourself during transformational times in your life.

When Praying Mantis jumps into your life, observe transformational leaps in your consciousness and personal development. A praying mantis molts its skin with every growth spurt, approximately seven times in its life. As you go through life experiences that are dramatic or profound, take note of how that change brings with it emotional, cathartic relief. Let the energy of Praying Mantis help you shed the layers of your consciousness to create transformation in your life.

Praying Mantis also symbolizes the experience of hearing, sensing, or knowing when it is important to make a change in direction in your life. This insect has stereovision—big compound eyes and three additional eyes in the center of its head. This many-eyed quality supports your clairvoyant abilities. Praying mantis also has an ear in the middle of its stomach that registers echolocation calls, offering them protection from bats as predators. This characteristic supports your ability to trust your inner knowing for self-preservation and protection.

Praying Mantis's Vibrational Matching Gemstone: Mookaite Jasper

Mookaite jasper offers stabilizing and grounding support during periods of growth to integrate the teachings of past emotional lessons. Mookaite jasper is a grounding force that helps you stay in the present moment. With clear intention, great focus, and dedicated action toward your goals, you can achieve anything you put your mind to. Use this stone to help you make leaps in your personal development and self-awareness. Unlimited potential in spiritual growth into dimensions not yet explored is available to you. Employ this jasper to realize what you need to understand for your soul to evolve and for you to further develop your personality.

Divine Influence

Call on Archangel Raphael and his healing power to support transformation and transmutation of challenging situations on all levels—mentally, emotionally, physically, and spiritually.

Praying Mantis's Location on the Wheel of Life

Praying Mantis is located on the south path, where transformation from one way of being into another is available.

Contemplate This

Are you going through a growth spurt in your life? Take a look at where you've been, and realize that there is so much more you can do and learn in order to grow. Release past patterns, and heal those issues once and for all. Tap into who you truly are and where you are headed. Realize that you have much more to learn in life and will encounter many opportunities that offer you room for growth. Let all your senses and your peripheral psychic sight guide you on your path.

Message from Praying Mantis

You may be experiencing major changes in your life that are challenging your emotional state. Trust in the process of change, and acknowledge and honor your feelings. Take the time to balance your physical, mental, emotional, and spiritual energy. Uncover inner awareness to understand yourself as you grow and learn with each life passage. You have all the information you need to see your life clearly. Process and integrate each growth spurt you experience and then move forward.

Praying Mantis Affirmation

I embrace the hard-earned lessons of the past to catapult me into a bright and positive future. I love to learn new things every day in all areas of my life. Opportunities constantly present themselves to me. I recognize opportunities and take immediate action. I process and integrate information into my being with great ease.

Message from Mookaite Jasper

Use the colors of the rainbow to support you with each transformational experience—red for vitality and protection, orange for action and creativity, yellow for confidence and courage, green and pink for loving-kindness, blue for ease in expression, purple for alignment with intuitive gifts, and white for clarity of purpose. Install positive thought forms, or mental energy, in the emotional body immediately after an emotional release.

Additional Vibrational Matching Gemstones for Praying Mantis

Blue calcite, green calcite, indochinite tektite, Isis quartz crystal, phantom quartz crystal, optical calcite, orange calcite, pink calcite, and red calcite.

65. Rabbit and Botswana Agate

Are you conscious of the cycles of the moon—especially the new moon and the full moon? Do you recognize that you are the creator of your life experiences? When was the last time you stopped and retreated for renewal and insight?

Rabbit totem is an ally whose support is threefold: during times of renewal and new beginnings; when you must face your fears; and times of introspection, gestation, and creative realizations.

Rabbits freeze or pause when they perceive danger nearby in an effort to deflect attention away from themselves and blend into the background. I was told by Ted Andrews, author of *Animal-Speak*, that when you see Rabbit in your path, it means you should wait a full moon cycle (28 days) before making a decision or taking action. This represents the need for introspection before taking action, which often provides a better understanding of a situation. Rabbit supports you in developing a deeper understanding of things by using introspection and contemplation to heal perceptions that cause fears and phobias.

Rabbits are plentiful in the spring during the time of birth and new beginnings. When Rabbit hops into your life, this is a time to observe opportunities that are presenting themselves and hop closer to those that appear most promising. Rabbit urges you to take a look at your creative ideas and assess your productivity. You probably have a running list of things you would like to do someday. The fertile nature of Rabbit encourages you to get to work and give birth to some of those great ideas or projects and see them through to fruition.

Rabbit's Vibrational Matching Gemstone: Botswana Agate

Botswana agate keeps you grounded and receptive to spiritual wisdom and knowledge in order to heal your fears and phobias. On a vibrational level, Botswana agate holds a creative vibe, good for connecting with artistic ideas and pursuits. Together, Botswana agate and Rabbit assist you in recognizing the patterns in your life and within so that you can heal fears. Being conscious of repetitive patterns is beneficial. The tool of self-observation helps clarify what shifts you might choose to make. If you are stuck down a rabbit hole of limiting beliefs, you can hop out.

Divine Influence

Call on Archangel Auriel to help realign your consciousness so that you can finally let go of conscious and subconscious fears.

Rabbit's Location on the Wheel of Life

Rabbit is located on the west path, where personal truth is found within.

Contemplate This

Are you fertile with great ideas? Observe your surroundings with alertness and focus. Be aware of the cycles of life, and notice the changes in the cycle of the moon. Align yourself with these cyclical energies for deeper understanding of yourself through the cycles of life. Be aware that the movement of things around you affects you personally, so keep an eye on everything that is going on.

Message from Rabbit

Relax and do nothing so that you can see a situation from a different perspective. Pause to examine yourself within. What you need to realize, understand, remember, or know is buried deep within you. Allow yourself the freedom to hop forward and away from fears based on past experiences. Be grateful for the years of experience that have molded you into who you are today, and let that knowledge shift your ability to perceive prolific future possibilities.

Rabbit Affirmation

I pause and reflect on the patterns revealed to me. Different perspectives give me insight and understanding. It is easy for me to give birth to ideas. There are infinite possibilities available to all beings. My creative endeavors come to fruition. I easily hop forward with renewed clarity. I find balance within the cycles of life.

Message from Botswana Agate

Unearth what is buried deep within your consciousness. Notice if you have stagnant beliefs that block your exit from the rabbit hole. If something is petrifying you, examine and face the source of the fear. Step outside yourself, and observe ancient patterns that have been in your ancestral history for many generations. All the knowledge and wisdom you need is available within the recesses of your mind. Bring embedded feelings in your subconscious to the surface in order to remove unnecessary limits on your potential.

Additional Vibrational Matching Gemstones for Rabbit

Cobaltoan calcite, carnelian, girasol quartz, moonstone, petrified wood, opal, pink calcite, rhodochrosite, and selenite.

66. RACCOON AND BLACK TOURMALINE

Can you understand things better when you can touch them? Have you found that you know the truth that is often hidden or masked? Are you a highly sensitive person?

Raccoon totem is an ally for when you need to uncover the truth. The "mask" is one of the predominant physical features of Raccoon. This mask symbolizes your ability to discern what is really going on beneath it all, with regard to yourself and others. Interactions with others reveal their true intentions when Raccoon energy is present in your life. You can unearth any hidden agendas or secondary intentions, and similarly, determine if you are masking your true intentions. Are your interactions transparent and authentic?

When Raccoon walks into your life, trust your five senses as well as your feelings and innate intelligence. Raccoons are nocturnal, and their eyesight is more attuned to nighttime than daylight. Basically color blind, these intelligent creatures rely on their sense of touch to remember how to do certain tasks. Raccoon's vibe supports tasks that require polished skills and agility with your hands. You'll find that your ability to remember how to do a task is easier with this ally in mind.

The hypersensitivity of Raccoon is an ally for those who are highly sensitive. It helps empathic people distinguish between what is relevant and what is not in the midst of what isn't clearly seen or obvious, and offers comfort to individuals who feel these subtle vibrations. Raccoon encourages you to acknowledge and trust your perception of the vibes around you. Believe yourself.

Raccoon's Vibrational Matching Gemstone: Black Tourmaline

Black tourmaline provides a layer of protection and understanding of the interconnectedness with all life. Work with this gemstone with the intention to keep unwelcome energies from interfering with your ability to sense the truth. It is a buffer during times when you are extremely sensitive to the thoughts, feelings, physical challenges, and the emotions of others. Let black tourmaline be your ally to deflect negativity or undesirable vibes so you can feel safe and sound. Use black tourmaline when you need to discern which thoughts or feelings are your own and which thoughts and feelings belong to others. Knowing this clearly will help you relax into your space and reinforces your intuitive abilities.

Divine Influence

Call on the Angel of Intelligence to help you complete complex tasks and Archangel Zaphkiel to help deepen your understanding of problems and increase mindfulness.

Raccoon's Location on the Wheel of Life

Raccoon is located on the east path, where seeing, sensing, and knowing the truth is possible.

Contemplate This

Do you hide your worries behind a smiling face to avoid revealing your challenges? Are you able to see, sense, feel, or know when others are hiding something that needs to be clearly revealed? Be transparent. Live your truth, and attract trustworthy, authentic people into your life. Remember that you are an intelligent being, and you are able to focus on complex tasks and situations. Your memory serves you well. Recognize that you are smart and can always learn new things.

Message from Raccoon

Open your ears and other senses right down to your physical nerve endings to be able to hear and grasp what others are communicating. Turn to your memory to solve problems and when you need to work through complex tasks and situations. Uncover previously hidden information in your storehouse of knowledge, and bring it into light. When you resolve situations, commit the solution to memory so that you can recall it when you need to the information or insights in the future.

Raccoon Affirmation

I perceive life from a higher perspective. I take the time for reflection. I observe how the world around me is a mirror of the world within me. I am focused. I see, sense, feel, and know the truth. I follow my intuition and my senses. I am aligned with the healing powers of inner peace and empathy.

Message from Black Tourmaline

Get in touch with your connection to all life, both the seen and unseen. Tap into your innate ability to intuit whatever you need whenever you need it. Acknowledge your intuition, and trust your awareness of your own feelings as well as the feelings of others. Find the support you need to get through the cycle of getting to know previously hidden aspects of yourself. Recognize features and characteristics that were eclipsed behind old preconceived notions.

Additional Vibrational Matching Gemstones for Raccoon

Amazonite, amethyst druzy, angelite, apophyllite, fluorite, hiddenite, labradorite, lapis lazuli, petrified wood, selenite, and trilobites.

67. RAM (BIGHORN SHEEP) AND GARNET

Do you believe in your ability to overcome great obstacles? Are you ready to climb to great heights with ease and grace? Are you in touch with your inner strength?

Ram totem is an ally for you when you need extra strength and endurance to overcome problems or situations that require you to rise above the ordinary to see the challenge through to successful resolution.

Rams are male sheep, in this case, bighorn sheep with large curling horns. While rams resolve arguments or conflict by ramming their heads into each other, this characteristic does not suggest you should use brutal force to resolve an issue; rather, it encourages you to use your higher mind and consciousness for successful resolution of an issue. Ram reminds you to look at why you are experiencing challenges in your life. A ram's powerful horns also symbolize using higher consciousness in alignment with the Divine.

When Ram climbs into your life, it is a sign to once more rethink what you have already integrated before finally absorbing it into your plan or your life. Just as Ram regurgitates partially digested food and chews on the cud as a regular process of its digestion, it is beneficial to use this characteristic as an analogy to think and rethink through something more completely before final implementation.

Sometimes, people exhibit ram-type behavior to get their way. Notice if you or someone in your life is using this tactic, and make the appropriate adjustments to react with higher intelligence and loving-kindness, regardless of how your feelings are affected.

Ram is a good ally for business dealings and financial success. The ram's ability to climb high on rocky mountains adds energy to your ability to reach great heights with the work you do in the world for either personal gain or philanthropic pursuits. Align with this totem when you need strength and endurance to reach your goals.

Ram's Vibrational Matching Gemstone: Garnet

Garnet keeps you focused and determined, when used with conscious intent. Carrying the vibration of passion and fortitude, this red gem helps you follow through on your goals and manifest your desires. When you need to stop procrastinating and get motivated, turn to garnet. Use this stone with the intention to make significant strides in your life and climb to great heights. This stone of successful endeavors is good to have nearby when you are drawing on your internal strength, vitality, and endurance. Garnet also helps you maintain emotional balance to prevent anger and frustration. This stone reminds you to honor yourself and charges you to set up healthy boundaries with others. Use garnet when you simply want to state your case and claim your space.

Divine Influence

Call on Archangel Ariel to help enhance endurance, courage, good health, and strong physical structure.

Ram's Location on the Wheel of Life

Ram is located on the eastern portion of the northeastern quadrant, where life experience brings inner strength.

Contemplate This

Are you butting heads with others? Find a way to examine your actions and reactions as objectively as possible. Things aren't always as they seem. Sometimes, disagreements are conjured up to justify making a change in plans. Not all people are equipped with the mental or emotional fortitude necessary to part ways amicably. Always take the higher road, even when the higher road requires strength and courage. Access the kinder, gentler part of yourself, and practice being compassionate in a loving way.

Message from Ram

Think things through . . . and then think them through again. As you finalize and integrate realizations and a plan of action, be open to receiving further insights. Take action. Do it now. Tomorrow never comes. Be a leader in your community, and remember that everyone is their own leader in the group. Support people when it is their turn to lead the way.

Ram Affirmation

I have plenty of energy and plenty to share. I am vital and strong! It is easy for me to take action and complete tasks. I live a full, passionate life. I am determined. All my needs are met. I am healthy to the core of my being. I am grateful for my financial success.

Message from Garnet

Live your life with passion, and focus on achieving your goals with determination. You probably have plenty of energy and some to spare. You are committed to yourself and others. You are self-empowered, making it is easy for you to take charge of a situation and make things happen. Assert yourself, and do what it takes to make your move and know that strength is inherent within you. Vitality and passion are key ingredients for your success.

Additional Vibrational Matching Gemstones for Ram

Ammonite, carnelian, carborundum, emerald, orbicular jasper, red calcite, red jasper, pyrite, and ruby.

68. RAVEN AND MOQUI MARBLES

Do you believe in good luck omens? Are you able to see into the future? Are you open to prophetic experiences? Is it time to clear away something that is no longer for your highest good?

Ravens are harbingers of good luck and are considered messengers of the gods of the mortal world. In mythology, Odin, a Norse god, had two ravens that served as his ears and his eyes, telling him everything that had happened and everything that would happen in order for him to gain the wisdom needed to save the world. Raven is also found in Greek mythology in association with Apollo, the god of prophecy. Raven is a helpful totem when you need extra ears and eyes to know what's going on in circumstances where you can't quite see or hear for yourself.

When Raven flies into your life, you have the opportunity to glimpse potential future realities. Every thought you've had until now has created your current reality, and every thought you will have creates your future. With Raven as your ally, you can cultivate the gift of prophecy and use it to garner wisdom and benefit all beings.

Ravens are dedicated to the disposal of the dead. They are scavengers that pick at the decaying flesh of dead animals, keeping the environment clean from bacteria and fungi. Raven is an excellent ally if you are dealing with the deterioration or decline of some part of your life. Raven's vibration can help you consciously release whatever is dead or dying within your mind and body before it has a chance to decay. When you learn Raven's lesson, you liberate yourself and improve your health and well-being.

Raven's Vibrational Matching Gemstone: Moqui Marbles

Found in the Four Corners region of the southwestern United States, Moqui marbles are naturally forming spheres of sandstone and iron. Moqui marbles are associated with shamanic transformational work to help you delve into the parts of yourself that are preventing you from feeling fully alive and free to be who you are. Let this mineral aid in removing the stagnant energy. Use it during meditation and inner journey work. On another note, Moqui means "dear departed ones" in the Hopi language. Hopi legend says that the ancestors visit from the other side and play with these marbles at night to show that they are happy in the afterlife. Moqui marbles can help you remember lessons learned from your ancestors.

Divine Influence

Call on Archangel Raziel to help you embrace the gifts of clairvoyance, prophecy, revelation, and the great mysteries.

Raven's Location on the Wheel of Life

Raven is located on the north path, where the ancestors and all those who have walked on this path before us offer insight.

Contemplate This

Are you still revisiting the past? Are you annoyed by emotional remnants of a situation? Are you in touch with your ancestors through memories or visitations in dreams and visions? Strengthen your connection with the core of your being, and embrace any issues you may find there. Recognize that less-than-positive life experiences often provide you with the emotionally mature backbone required for dealing with other situations. Learn from those experiences, and put the teachings into your emotional toolbox, providing wisdom to draw on another day.

Message from Raven

Become conscious of when it is time to end situations at work or in relationships that are deteriorating due to a lack of love and attention. Clear away emotional debris in your mind, body, and spirit. If it is no longer healthy for you, release it and refill that space with good fortune, health, wealth, and happiness. Open your spiritual ears to hear what isn't being said. Open your spiritual eyes to see what is hidden from your view.

Raven Affirmation

I am tapped into the spiritual laws, and apply them to my life. I relate easily to others and align with their vibration. I hear, see, and understand messages from Spirit. Prophetic visions and dreams bring clarity for potential future realities. Blessings are found within my current opportunities. I recognize when it is time to put an end to toxic situations.

Message from Moqui Marbles

The veil between worlds is very thin. Your ancestors are found in the earth you walk on, the water you drink, and the food you eat. Open to the wisdom of those who have come before you and walked this Earth Walk. Believe in your ability to translate the messages you hear and see coming from other worlds and departed friends and relatives for the purpose of expanded awareness and understanding.

Additional Vibrational Matching Gemstones for Raven

Axinite, bismuth, celestite, channeling quartz crystal, elestial quartz crystal, hematite, iolite, Isis quartz crystal, lapis lazuli, morganite, pietersite, and phantom quartz.

69. RHINOCEROS AND CATHEDRAL QUARTZ POINT

Are you territorial? Do you find it challenging to set boundaries? Have you considered a plant-based diet? Do you need a little time off just to eat or sleep, or go to a spa?

Rhinoceros totem is an ally for you when you need to find balance in your community, which is best done by establishing healthy boundaries with your neighbors and friends. Rhinoceroses aren't so subtle in the way they establish their territories, though you do not have to be as blatant as they are.

One of the distinguishing characteristics of rhinoceroses is their highly prized horns. This horn is filled with keratin and other valued nutrients. Unfortunately, many rhinos are killed to obtain the horns, and measures have been put in place to save them from poaching by removing the horns before poachers can get to them. This characteristic is teaching you to place your treasures in a safe place and protect yourself from people who may want to use you for the parts of you that are highly valued.

Rhinoceroses enjoy grazing on grasses the majority of the day, taking breaks during the hottest parts of the day to sleep or take a mud bath. When Rhinoceros rumbles into your life, it signals that it would be beneficial to eat more plant-based meals, rest, and enjoy some spa or bath treatments to restore your body, mind, and spirit. Detach from your "herd" to regenerate and rejuvenate with plant-based nutrients and sunlight.

Rhinoceros's Vibrational Matching Gemstone: Cathedral Quartz

The many spires and multiple terminations in cathedral quartz assist in the manifestation of your physical goals. Just as rhinoceroses utilize light absorbed into their horns, align with the higher level of consciousness to remember you are a being of light. Cathedral quartz is your ally and a reminder to spiral higher and absorb spiritual nutrition that is invaluable through meditation, contemplation, and prayer. The spires of this stone are your reminder to maintain a focus on channeling light to absorb all that is good and ground it through your physical, mental, emotional, and spiritual bodies. Use this stone to help you remember to keep your mind open to the many opportunities and perspectives available to you.

Divine Influence

Call on the Angel of Setting Boundaries and the Angel of Inner Strength to help you increase confidence and courage and Archangel Michael to be Divinely protected.

Rhinoceros' Location on the Wheel of Life

Rhinoceros is located on the northwest quadrant, where inner wisdom and protection are available.

Contemplate This

Do you need to establish clear boundaries? Surround yourself with a protective shield that will deflect any negative energy that comes your way. Ancient wisdom resides within you, and when you subconsciously tap into it, can keep you protected and transform your life. The color of the soil and the energy of mud is a useful tool for grounding your awareness by connecting with the earth. Tap into how it feels to have your feet and your hands in Mother Earth.

Message from Rhinoceros

Visualize yourself rising to connect with the cosmic consciousness, while your body is firmly established in the present moment. Feel your connection with Mother Earth through your feet, and step out barefoot into the soil. When something is "as clear as mud," visualize your mind clearing and your body enjoying Earth's nutrients. Determine whether you need to set boundaries with someone in your midst.

Rhinoceros Affirmation

I have the courage to set boundaries with love and grace. I am protected. I am connected with the sacred energy of the trees, plants, shrubs, vines, and smaller vegetation. I embrace the sunshine as well as the rain. I am in balance with all life. I make the time to rest, regroup, and rejuvenate. I enjoy dark-green leafy vegetables and other iron-rich foods.

Message from Cathedral Quartz Point

You are ready to align with the Divine. You are an amazing being of light, and it's time to be a light worker. Acknowledge your own direct connection with higher wisdom and knowledge. Find the shining light within you, and step away from the useless act of playing small. Expand your energy and establish a boundary of light and well-being.

Additional Vibrational Matching Gemstones for Rhinoceros

Axinite, brown agate, citrine, golden calcite, golden topaz, green moss agate, rutilated quartz, septarian, tree agate, and yellow jasper.

70. Sandpiper and Andalusite

Do you maintain focus on what's important? Do you need a period of rest or relief from something difficult or unpleasant? Are you ready to allow yourself the time and space to balance your life?

Sandpiper totem is an ally for you when you have meticulous work to accomplish. A sandpiper's quick and consistent pecking just below the surface symbolically represents going deeper into your awareness for fulfillment mentally, emotionally, and spiritually. With Sandpiper on your side, you have an ally to help you keep your nose to the grindstone and stay focused on the task at hand. These tasks include emotional and spiritual tasks for personal improvement. With meticulous focus, you can achieve what you need to in order to support yourself in all aspects of your life.

Spend time by the water's edge. Walk along the shoreline and contemplate your life. Use the time to integrate and digest all that has been transpiring. Go within to find what is just beneath the surface of your emotions. When Sandpiper runs into your life, make plans with your favorite group of friends to have a meal together. Be open to exploring your emotions with your close-knit group. Letting yourself open up and discussing how you are feeling with those close to you can be extremely nurturing and fulfilling. These meaningful interactions are food for your soul.

Sandpiper's Vibrational Matching Gemstone: Andulasite

The grounding elements of andalusite aid in maintaining focus. With the cross, or X, in its center, andalusite helps you align with earth-centered spirituality and determination. It is especially useful when staying on target with your task is especially challenging. It is a stone for those who jump from one great idea to another yet are seemingly unable to complete anything. Just as a sandpiper quickly darts from one spot to another and still achieves the goal of feeding itself, this stone brings the vibrational energy to stay on course. Gaze at the cross running through the stone to find focus. Andalusite enhances the healing power of the negative ions of the great outdoors to balance your emotions. If you are feeling out of sorts go outside, where you can be renewed. Take the journey to the center of yourself, and find balance in nature.

Divine Influence

Call on Archangel Muriel to help balance your emotions and Archangel Uriel and Archangel Thuriel to strengthen your connection with nature as a grounding and natural force for personal well-being

Sandpiper's Location on the Wheel of Life

Sandpiper is located on the eastern portion of the northeast quadrant, where balance is found through life experiences and mindful inner reflection.

Contemplate This

Are you aware that you can do many things to improve yourself on a personal level? Through focused self-observation, explore what lies just below the surface in your mental and emotional bodies. Through inner reflection and outer observation, you can deepen your understanding of your actions and reactions. While this is a gain for your personal development, keep in mind that you are not alone but in a constant interaction with others. Try not to take things personally. You are only responsible for your own meticulous mindful interactions and actions. Maintain a focus on loving-kindness.

Message from Sandpiper

Spend time by a body of water, or dine with good friends. A respite is always good for rest and relaxation to digest and integrate your life. Find comfort and support from difficulties or unpleasant situations from your closest friends. A day by the beach, lake, or spa is beneficial for emotional balance. Be a supportive friend, and assist your good buddies with their lives.

Sandpiper Affirmation

My emotions are balanced. I am able to observe my reactions to others in an objective and loving way. Love allows me to awaken my consciousness. I understand the underlying cause of challenging situations. I easily refocus my efforts away from distractions. I have a grounded connection with Mother Earth. I am free of emotional baggage. I am aware of my feelings.

Message from the Andalusite

When you are in search of a deeper spiritual connection, this is a time to find that connection in nature. Go outdoors and commune with the birds and the bees. Listen for the soft voice of the fairies speaking to you and for the messages being communicated by the trees, plants, and animals. You may need some time by a body of water. Put your attention on aligning with Mother Earth.

Additional Vibrational Matching Gemstones for Sandpiper

Aquamarine, aragonite, chlorite phantom quartz, elestial quartz crystals, green moss agate, larimar, orange calcite, peridot, smoky quartz, and unakite.

71. SEAGULL AND AQUAMARINE

Have you considered using other people's resources, the ones they no longer need? Is it time to go through your closets (literally and emotionally) to get rid of things that you no longer need or use? Do you need to secure your valuables to keep them safe from those who might take them?

Seagull totem is an ally for you when you are ready to release unnecessary clutter in your life. Seagulls are known kleptoparasites, meaning that they "steal" from others. Their perceived thievery is actually a boon for ecological balance. Historically, seagulls have been known to help farmers and gardeners rid their crops of harmful insects. When Seagull swoops into your life, it signals that it's time to closely observe both your outer and inner worlds. A friend or colleague may be available to help you restore balance in your life, to reuse and recycle. It has been said, "One person's trash is another person's treasure."

Use this vibration as an ally to clear out closets and pass on the goods to someone who can use them. Letting go of what you don't need is a powerful and valuable way of cleaning out your emotional and mental wasteland. Observe the thoughts and emotions you associate with the object, and use the object as a tool for personal transformation. Determine the extent of your awareness, and strive to further awaken your consciousness.

Seagull's appearance in your life may also indicate that people or situations are preparing to take something that belongs to you. Cover your bases, and make sure that your personal and intellectual property is well protected. With conscious awareness, you can avoid this type of challenge.

Seagull's Vibrational Matching Gemstone: Aquamarine

Aquamarine connects you with sea creatures. It is a good self-development tool, one that helps with spiritual awakening. This blue-green translucent gem helps you clearly see the truth of a situation. Use this stone with the intention of developing and opening a telepathic channel with the ocean and all its sea life, allowing you to hear, feel, and know thoughts and emotions without verbalization. Water, as represented by aquamarine, assists in regaining emotional balance and releasing emotionally charged thoughts. With this semiprecious stone in hand, allow tears to flow to wash away sadness or other emotional hurts.

Divine influence

Call on your Guardian Angel to help you see and understand what you need to release that blocks your growth and Archangel Muriel to help you weed out emotions and let them go.

Seagull's Location in the Wheel of Life

Seagull is located on the east path, where life can be observed from a higher perspective.

Contemplate This

Might it be time to "stalk" your mind and emotions in order to pick out the pesky thoughts and feelings that no longer serve you? Emotional and mental stalking is another level of self-observation; it is when you go farther into your consciousness in order to uncover the source of issues or challenges. Make something positive out of emotions and thoughts that are clogging your mind, and use them as fodder for healthy personal growth. Remove the hooks in your personality that cause repetitive patterns.

Message from Seagull

There are times in your life when you feel that something dear has been stolen from you. Recognize that the removal of people or situations is often predestined as a way of allowing you to have a better life and reach your full potential. Only in hindsight will you recognize the benefits that come from removing these people or situations. Give it some time, and you'll understand why certain things occurred.

Seagull Affirmation

I see and understand my life from a higher perspective. I use the experiences from the lessons I have learned to improve myself. I am willing to release what no longer serves my highest good. It's easy for me to let go of unnecessary items and beliefs so that I can fulfill my highest potential. Understanding and realizations come to me with each passing day.

Message from Aquamarine

Be the best you can be, and live your life with integrity. Practice being honest with yourself and in your interactions with others. Strive for personal excellence. Observe yourself, and figure out how to be the best you can be. Be impeccable with your word. Use experiences to provide foundational insights. It takes time and hindsight to see that silver lining, but rest assured, it does exist.

Additional Vibrational Matching Gemstones for Seagull

Amazonite, ametrine, blue lace agate, celestite, epidote, larimar, moldavite, peridot, rhodochrosite, and unakite.

72. SEA LION AND CELESTITE

Are you a social person? Do you enjoy being in the company of a group of friends? Do you feel comfortable expressing yourself?

Sea Lion totem is an ally for you when you are seeking the companionship of groups of friends. Sea Lion's energy lends assistance to help you establish a strong social community of like-minded people. Sea Lion is gregarious, social, and communicative, and expresses itself with gusto. Use this good energy to help you overcome fears of talking in front of groups or simply express yourself in a group setting. Sea lions are extraordinarily chummy and will cuddle up with their fellow sea lions, even lying on top of each other, as part of a closely knit group. They swim together and laze together.

When Sea Lion swims into your life, it signals a time for you to find your herd or tribe. Spend time hanging out with your close-knit group. If you need to find one, join a congregation or a group that meets regularly as a way of creating cohesion and support in your life.

Sea lions are territorial and aggressive. They use their vocalization skills to bark out their clearly defined territory, typically during breeding season. Sea Lion's ability to "speak up" in order to establish boundaries can help you when you need to do the same. Call on Sea Lion's energy to help you establish boundaries, especially when you are in the process of creating or developing a product. Instead of aggression, use tact and good communication skills.

Sea lions use their whiskers to sense food and objects in the deep, dark ocean, making Sea Lion a good ally for you if you are empathic and pick up feelings of those around you. Trust your senses, even during those times when you can't clearly "see" what you are feeling.

Sea Lion's Vibrational Matching Gemstone: Celestite

Celestite helps you find your voice and speak your truth. Use celestite to help you speak up but also to remember to listen to what others have to say. Celestite's light-blue energy manages communication that might initially be perceived as aggressive so that the expression is assertive instead—the pale-blue energy tones things down when you really want to assert yourself verbally. This heavenly blue gem is a perfect companion to help you get over fears of speaking in groups or in front of large numbers of people. Celestite invokes Divine inspiration, so that you always seem to find the right words and share them at the right time.

Divine Influence

Call on Archangel Camael to help you shift feelings of aggression and Archangel Haniel to help you communicate in a peaceful yet powerful way.

Sea Lion's location in the Wheel of Life

Sea Lion is located on the western portion of the northwest quadrant, where feelings and the inner voice are to be trusted.

Contemplate This

Do you take time to cultivate your place in social groups? Do you enjoy the company of others and find comfort in being part of a community? Turn to the support of a cohesive, extended family, and experience the value of stress reduction. Band together with like-minded people for personal enjoyment as well as support. Clearly set boundaries in order to find a balance between the group and your own personal space. Find your voice, and speak your truth. Trust your feelings, as they help you navigate through life.

Message from Sea Lion

Build relationships with people who are warm, outgoing, and friendly. Spend quality time with your tribe. A group of friends provides well-being and reduces stress on a psychological level. Avoid isolating yourself, and be an active part of the community. Find enrichment within a community setting and your place within that group. You can attract good friends who listen to you and understand you. Relax into the ebb and flow of life.

Sea Lion Affirmation

I easily and honestly communicate what is on my mind. I speak eloquently. I am heard. My courage helps me communicate with ease. I stand up for myself. I speak up when I need to set a boundary. I say what I need to say. I surround myself with people who speak their truth. I listen and truly hear what others are saying.

Message from Celestite

You will feel much better after spending time at the shore with friends and family. Arrange to be together with your good buddies, preferably by the ocean. Connect with the healing, salty energy of the seawater and your circle of friends. The supportive energy and cleansing properties of the ocean support your health, both physically and emotionally.

Additional Vibrational Matching Gemstones for Sea Lion

Azurite-malachite, carnelian, chrysoprase, chrysocolla, garnet, golden calcite, golden topaz, lapis lazuli, and ruby.

73. SKUNK AND PIETERSITE

Do you live a solitary life? Do you make such a stink about things not going your way that it scares people away? Do you have a heightened sense of smell?

Skunk totem is an ally for you if you prefer to live a solitary life. Skunks are loners and minimize interaction with fellow skunks. Use Skunk as a teaching tool to become aware of the ways in which you act and react that cause people to stay away from you—they don't want to be subjected to the stink of your words and actions. Skunk gives plenty of warning before it uses its dreadful-smelling anal scent glands for defense. Skunk can help you take the action needed to warn people that you might blow soon.

When Skunk shows up in your life, it could indicate that you have to defend yourself and your space. It also indicates that you could be mindful of minimizing food waste. Skunks are scavengers and will eat the leftovers of humans and other animals. If you are especially thoughtful about using up food so that it won't go to waste, Skunk is probably one of your totems. Scavengers are beneficial for the environment.

Skunk's poor vision is balanced by its excellent sense of smell and hearing. Tap into your intuitive abilities of clairaudience (the ability to hear messages from within) and clairolfaction (the ability to intuitively pick up a smell that doesn't physically exist). Amplify your awareness of scents and sounds around you for guidance and protection.

Skunk's Vibrational Matching Gemstone: Pietersite

Pietersite serves as a grounding force while you take spiritual steps to develop your third eye and intuitive nature. Its iridescence and swirling fibrous segments combined with the stabilizing force of this stone increases your ability to bring forth inspired self-awareness. This is a good stone to enhance the sensory gifts of clairolfaction and clairaudience. Pietersite has the quality of chatoyancy—from the French oeil de chat, or cat's eye, meaning a gemstone that is changeable in color and has an undulating band of light; it helps you go within in order to reflect but also to notice reflections coming from the outside. This stone provides an avenue for self-reflection and doing inner work. Use it to shine light on the knowledge and wisdom within you. Pietersite is an ally for contemplation. Gaze into this stone, allowing the light to refract off it, while you imagine or visualize that the answers to what you seek are rising in your awareness.

Divine Influence

Call on the Angel of Meditation and Contemplation to help you understand the inner workings of your consciousness and Archangel Zaphkiel to help you be mindful of how you interact with others.

Skunk's Location in the Wheel of Life

Skunk is located on the western portion of the northwest quadrant, where the energy of going within and seeking solitude is found.

Contemplate This

Do you understand that there are benefits to a solitary life? Time alone is useful for meditation, prayer, inventing products, writing books to entertain or offer self-help, or to engage in nonprofit service. Self-employment is reclusive. Consider working for yourself if you prefer solitude. There are plenty of things you can do to entertain yourself recreationally that don't require interaction with others. It is beneficial to spend time with others, but you can decide how often and how long you choose to be with a particular person or people.

Message from Skunk

Spend time in your inner world. Take time to meditate and pray. Listen to your inner voice. The inner world provides you with many clues to help you create inventions or writings that help many people. Pay attention to odors and scents in businesses and homes. Their smell offers clues to their reliability and your safety. Be mindful of food waste. Reduce waste, and share unused food with animals in your backyard.

Skunk Affirmation

I am at peace. All is well in my life. I am grateful for my ability to stay focused on what is truly important. I am a steward of the earth. It is easy for me to "think green." I reduce the amount of waste produced in my household. I reuse and recycle everything I can.

Message from Pietersite

Muster up the courage to set boundaries. Retreat to peaceful environments, and practice meditation. Take the time for some inner reflection. Have confidence in your intuitive senses. Contemplate what is truly important. Focus your intention on understanding the inner workings of your heart and how you relate to others. Make the necessary adjustments to realign your material and physical worlds as well as your mental, emotional, and spiritual aspects.

Additional Vibrational Matching Gemstones for Skunk

Amethyst, azurite, blue-dyed agate, chlorite phantom quartz, green most agate, kyanite, labradorite, moonstone, optical calcite, selenite, and tree agate.

74. Snake and Black Obsidian Arrowhead

Is your life in a transformative state? Are the layers of your consciousness peeling away? Do you need to heal aspects of yourself—physically, mentally, emotionally, and/or spiritually?

Snake totem is an ally to assist you when you are in the process of awakening your awareness of the parts of you that need healing. The transformative power of Snake supports you when you need to go below surface emotions or perceptions. Just as Snake molts an outer layer of skin, you have the opportunity to peel away anything that is worn out in your life. When Snake releases its worn-out layer of skin, it also rids itself of parasites. When Snake slithers into your life, examine all the situations, whether created by others or by you, to determine if it is time for you to slough off pesky people or belief systems. Transform the negative into the positive.

Snake is very sensitive to vibrations and scents. Using their strong sense of smell, they interpret airborne particles to provide direction and help them capture prey. Snake advises you to be conscious of all types of odors, including those that are pleasantly fragrant as well as odorous people or places. Snake helps you improve your intuitive sense of clairolfaction (the ability to intuitively pick up a smell that doesn't physically exist) and your ability to interpret all types of scents in your environment to provide directional clues for the journey on your path.

Snake's presence in your life indicates an opportunity for realization and awakening within your consciousness. It is time to accept transformation in your life. Release unyielding patterns. Snake is a spiritual metaphor related to healing and the transformational realizations of awakened kundalini. Snake medicine is a supportive aid if you are studying the Tree of Life or Kabbalah, or learning about kundalini, or life force. When you activate kundalini energy (a sleeping, dormant force naturally coiled at the base of the spine), you have a powerful opportunity to unleash your full potential.

Snake's Vibrational Matching Gemstone: Black Obsidian Arrowhead

Black obsidian is a natural glass formed during the cooling of volcanic lava. Volcanic glass is associated with emotions that are buried deep within you. This stone reminds you that negative emotions can wreak havoc in your life by broadcasting an unconscious program that perpetuates negative patterns. Gemstones formed into arrowheads are a reminder that there are always signs pointing you in the right direction so you can get to the "point" or the heart of the matter. Use black obsidian arrowhead as a tool for focus while you search the darker recesses of your emotional body.

Divine Influence

Call on the Angel of Transformation for support as you work through the changes in your life and Angel of Awakening to help bring realizations and revelations.

Snake's Location on the Wheel of Life

Snake is located on the south path, where transformation and transmutation of challenges in relationship with one's self, others, and all life takes place.

Contemplate This

Is it time to transform a challenging situation? Do you need to shed layers of emotions and disappointment? Are you completing a chapter of your life? It's time to finalize the release of that which is old and worn. Awaken memories, and contemplate how these memories are currently affecting your life. Acknowledge repetitive patterns, and make a clear decision to remove the obstacles that keep these patterns in motion. Let go of the past, and open your heart and mind to start anew. New opportunities and beginnings await you.Be open and embrace them.

Message from Snake

Quiet reflection is the key to comprehending what you need to uncover in order to grow. Subtle vibrations are available to help you find your way. Peel away the layers of your feelings to transform your emotions. You have the ability to uncoil the layers of your consciousness in order to awaken and grow through perceived challenges. One of the gifts of maturing is the transmutation of uncomfortable situations into fodder for spiritual growth and healing. The evolution of your spirit depends on these experiences.

Snake Affirmation

It is safe for me to feel my feelings. I easily interpret subtle vibrations and scents to show me my path. It is easy for me to transform and transmute challenging life situations. A new cycle offers a new and happy promise. I awaken my consciousness. Awareness and self-understanding bring spiritual growth.

Message from Black Obsidian Arrowhead

If your mind is carrying around toxic memories, it's time to take the necessary steps to clean up these thoughts and emotions and rid yourself of damaging energy. Look deeply inside, and you will see a reflection of all that is going on around you. Prioritize your intentions, and focus on one thing at a time. Use your powers of intuition to find the guidance you require.

Additional Vibrational Matching Gemstones for Snake

Amethyst, apophyllite, golden sheen obsidian, jet, selenite, snowflake obsidian, and unakite.

75. Spider and Picasso Stone

Do you realize that you are the one who creates your world? Are you consciously creating the circumstances around you? Have you taken the necessary action to make your dreams come true?

Spider totem is an ally for writers. It has been said that the first letters of the alphabet or the written word were inspired by the various designs found in the webs of spiders. Writing is one of the tools for creating reality. Writing it down makes it happen—or at least starts the process. Spider supports you in embracing your power as the one who creates your daily life.

Spider medicine brings the energy of a weaver and creator of dreams. Call on Spider when you feel like a victim of circumstances. Stop and write down whatever is confusing you and leading you to believe that others control your life. Next, write down exactly what you do want, and all the steps it will take to get there.

Spider Woman is a vital part of the Hopi creation cosmology. In various stories in the oral traditions, Spider Woman demonstrates that she can bring clay to life, including her own two sons as depicted in the *Book of the Hopi* by Frank Waters. Spider is a reminder that it is through thought, focus, intention, action, and cultivation that you can surrender your fears and live your life purposefully. To create your reality, action is necessary to make it happen. Creative visualization is only one of the tools to own your world and create the life of your dreams. You must take the steps to weave your dreams into reality.

Spider's Vibrational Matching Gemstone: Picasso Stone

Picasso stone helps you get up and get moving. If you perceive blocks, real or imagined, use Picasso stone as a tool for transforming your emotions and achieve life-enhancing self-transformation. The grounding qualities of Picasso stone help you sort out the many choices available to you. When mental confusion arises, contemplate the lines mapped within this stone. Use it as a tool for focus. Just as Spider must build and rebuild her web, you, too, must hold a clear vision of what you want in your web and what you want it to look like. If a piece of your world becomes tangled, both Picasso stone and Spider medicine can help you untangle the confusion so that you can rebuild.

Divine Influence

Call on Archangel Gabriel to help guide you to the path within your consciousness to know your direction and your truth.

Spider's Location on the Wheel of Life

Spider is located on the west path, where dreams are born.

Contemplate This

Have you seen the writing on the wall? Do you need to express yourself through the written word? Are you aware of how your thoughts create your world? You are the weaver, and you are the woven. You are the dreamer, and you are the dream. Accept that you have the power to define your destiny, fate, and reality through your focus and imagination. Take action and then wait patiently for all you need to come to you. Build the arena in which you create your world.

Message from Spider

Daydream, and use your imagination. Contemplate and write down your dreams, visions, and goals. The more you focus on what you want your life to be like, the better your chances of creating your reality. Whether you want to hone your ability to focus on eating a healthy diet or manifest driving a certain type of vehicle, visualization and imagining your intention as if it already exists is the first step to accomplishing your goals.

Spider Affirmation

I observe patterns and symbols and easily interpret their meanings. Writing and creating bring greater understanding. My imagination is active. I have great creative ideas that I easily bring into reality. I believe in the power of my imagination and have strong visualization skills. I visualize my dreams as if they have been realized. Creativity flows through me in myriad ways.

Message from Picasso Stone

Open your mind and soul to experience your path of enlightenment and the secrets of the creative vacuum. Ask that direction and guidance be revealed to you daily. Make it your intention to clearly see your way and experience a purpose-driven life, with your wishes and dreams fulfilled. Be the painter of your own canvas in order to map out the various experiences you wish to have in this lifetime.

Additional Vibrational Matching Gemstones for Spider

Aquamarine, Botswana agate, bloodstone, carnelian, covellite, girasol quartz, golden topaz, heliodor, labradorite, rainbow moonstone, red goldstone, and yellow jasper.

76. Squirrel and Tree Agate

Are you prepared for unforeseen circumstances? Have you put money into savings accounts and solid investments for the future? Are you mindful of how your actions will affect future generations?

Squirrel totem is an ally that reminds you to prepare for whatever the future may bring. When Squirrel scurries into your life, preparedness is on the agenda. This may be the time to top off your gas tank and start gathering the items you need to face a looming storm or other challenging situation. Squirrel encourages you to be ready for almost anything. This ally helps you remember to save money and keep some cash in your wallet for emergencies. Perhaps Squirrel is showing up to make sure you fill your pantry with nonperishable food for a time of need.

While you want to be prepared for various situations by squirreling away items to support your basic needs, doing so requires a fine balancing act. Be mindful that you aren't accumulating more than you need and become a hoarder. If you have more than you need and your closets are cluttered with stuff you will probably never use, set aside time to go through everything and donate or recycle what's no longer useful.

Squirrel's diet mostly consists of seeds, nuts, fruits, and vegetation. If Squirrel continuously shows up in your life, observe if your diet needs an adjustment. Incorporate some plant-based food sources into your diet, adding more fruits, vegetables, seeds, and nuts to your daily meals to balance out other food choices that aren't as beneficial.

Squirrel's Vibrational Matching Gemstone: Tree Agate

Tree agate reminds you to sway with the winds of change so that you can readily and easily adapt to new things and situations. This is a good stone for earth-centered spiritual pursuits and rituals and shamanic journeywork. Tree agate amplifies your ability to gather knowledge and wisdom from the universal consciousness. It also helps you more readily access the vast information stored within your own mind. Imagine that the crown of your head is like the branches of a tree reaching out for and absorbing information, while you stay rooted in the earth. Like Squirrel, keep this information stored in your consciousness so that you can access it when you need it. It will be there ready for your use.

Divine Influence

Call on Archangel Uriel to help you understand your responsibility as a steward of the earth, and on Archangel Sandalphon to help guide you toward becoming a steward for earth healing.

Squirrel's Location on the Wheel of Life

Squirrel is located on the western portion of the southwest quadrant, where future preparations are made.

Contemplate This

Are you taking the steps to be a caretaker of the earth? Do you compost? How good are you about recycling and reusing? Preparation for the future isn't just about squirreling things away to have enough food or supplies. It also includes taking steps to be sure that the next seven generations have a planet with trees and oxygen. Spend time in nature and contemplate what action you can take to prepare your soul and spirit for your evolution and revolutions around the wheel of life.

Message from Squirrel

Climb to new heights to experience life from various perspectives. Take the time to contemplate what you need to do to prepare for your future on a physical, mental, emotional, and spiritual level. Enjoy healthy green foods and drinks to fortify your body. Open yourself to the spiritual wisdom of the plant kingdom and the devic forces of the plants and trees.

Squirrel Affirmation

I am prepared for the future. I am organized. I spend time in nature. I am a steward of the earth. I have an intimate connection with Mother Earth and tools for natural healing. I leave our planet a better place and in better condition than before I arrived. I gather knowledge and wisdom.

Message from Tree Agate

Align with the vibration of nature and all that is part of the natural world around you. Tap into your "greenprint" to help you engineer new ways of planetary stewardship. Be inspired, and find out how you can implement more green building and green living. Observe the negative emotional challenges of your past so that you can use it as fertilizer or foundational nutrition for your future experiences.

Additional Vibrational Matching Gemstones for Squirrel

Clear quartz, elestial quartz crystals, chlorite phantom quartz, green moss agate, moss-included dogtooth calcite, moldavite, indochinite tektite, peacock copper, and selenite.

77. Starfish and Chrysanthemum Stone

Do you overanalyze everything? Are you currently experiencing analysis paralysis and are unable to make a decision as a result? Do you feel like you can't let go and that you must control everything?

Starfish totem is an ally that offers support for clearing away leftover emotional debris. A starfish's mouth is located on the underside of its body. It grazes the ocean floor and feeds on debris. Starfish do not have a centralized brain and are therefore unable to plan their actions. Starfish are not fish but echinoderms, which are closely related to sea urchins and sand dollars. Also known as sea stars, these starry creatures have no ears or eyes. When Starfish rides a wave into your life, it signals a time for you to stop trying to control and analyze everything. Instead, go with the flow and allow the current of life to take you where you need to go for nourishment and fulfillment. Put your analyses to rest, and trust your feelings and your intuition.

Starfish locate their prey through their sense of smell. This characteristic reminds you to pay attention to your own sense of smell—both the mundane (your ordinary sense of smell) and the extraordinary (clairolfaction). Pay attention to your reactions and feelings from the odors or scents you experience emanating from people, places, and situations. When a foul smell arises don't ignore it, especially if no one else can smell it. The scent serves as an alert, encouraging you to notice what is going on around you. Be like Starfish, and feel your way through the experience.

Starfish's Vibrational Matching Gemstone: Chrysanthemum Stone

Chrysanthemum stone supports you when you need to go with the flow and embrace challenging emotions. The flowerlike sprays of celestite and calcite crystals in this rock represent the Divine spark within each of us. Use this stone as a reminder that the Divine is within you, now and always. Tap into the universal wisdom available within the recesses of your consciousness to remember that you are one with All That Is. Use this stone to stay grounded when you communicate with the angels. This stone is also beneficial to strengthen your connection with the moon, the ocean tides, and the movement of the celestial starry realm and to help align you with the cycles of life.

Divine Influence

Call on the Angel of Emotional Balance to help you release emotional turmoil, regain balance, and relax, knowing that all is well.

Starfish's Location on the Wheel of Life

Starfish is located on the northeast quadrant, where knowledge and wisdom are integrated.

Contemplate This

Are you flexible and adaptable? Do you relax into life situations, or are you trying to control everything and everyone around you? Objectively observe circumstances, and seize new opportunities as situations naturally shift and change in your life. Bend and flex with the flow of life around you. Release the need to overanalyze everything. Just be with your current experiences, and let go of resistance. Be willing to go with the flow.

Message from Starfish

Feel, smell, and taste your way through life at this time. Let go of the need to think things through. There is a time and place for thinking and analyzing, but now is not the time for that. Now is the time to feel your feelings. Digest and let go of emotions that are just emotional debris. Experience the currents of life and where they take you when you relax into your happy life.

Starfish Affirmation

I easily tap into universal wisdom. I am one with the knowledge of my ancestors. I am aligned with the movement of the moon, sun, and stars. I am grounded and focused. The Divine spark resides within me. I go with the flow and allow myself to feel my feelings. Through awareness and self-understanding, I release past hurts and challenges.

Message from Chrysanthemum Stone

Find the beauty within the vast array of your emotions. Uncover your true feelings. Follow the flow inward, and examine the source of the feelings. Use the information you uncover from going within as a tool for growth and self-development. Embrace the light within, and accept your feelings and emotions just as they are in the moment. Integrate the realizations so that you emerge with a clearly lit path for self-realization.

Additional Vibrational Matching Gemstones for Starfish

Aquamarine, blue topaz, brucite, elestial quartz crystals, howlite, larimar, moonstone, smoky quartz, and unakite.

78. Swan and Green Kyanite

Do you feel awkward or poised? Are you aware of how beautiful you are? Are you balanced in body, mind, and spirit?

Swan totem is an ally that helps you live harmoniously and at home in your spiritual consciousness, even as you are walking on this earthly physical plane. Recognize that there is much more to you than you usually acknowledge. Cultivate your connection with all aspects of your mental, emotional, spiritual, and physical being. As a waterfowl, Swan's connection with water invites you to dive into your emotions, transform them, and express them with grace.

When Swan glides into your life, let it help you attract a healthy romantic relationship as well as supportive loving friendships and ethical business colleagues. Develop and cultivate a personal practice of kindness, compassion, and tolerance—for yourself and all beings.

Permit Swan's grace to support you when you are consciously transforming into the best version of yourself. With mindfulness, create a spiritual makeover. What you once perceived as the ugly part of yourself (the ugly duckling) is beautiful and powerful when you embrace it. Connect with your light (energy) body, and illuminate your soul as you connect with your higher self. Draw insight from all the incoming and outgoing wisdom, vibrations, and communication from the spiritual realms, and travel between worlds.

Swan's Vibrational Matching Gemstone: Green Kyanite

Green kyanite, a heart chakra stone, is a reminder that love is the answer to everything. This stone, combined with Swan medicine, helps you radiate love in a wide radius around your being. The heart chakra is the center of your consciousness, and love is who you truly are. Imagine that all you are, all you do, and all you attract is love. Where there is love there is grace, and grace is a gift of Divine assistance for personal regeneration. Embrace the part of you that is holy and sacred. Be in touch with this part of yourself, and invite Swan to support you from a place of purity and goodness as you stay in touch with your sacred heart.

Divine Influence

Call on Archangel Gabriel to help you interpret your dreams and guide you to become a Divine channel for God's love and Archangel Seraphiel to help you reawaken peace and personal grace within.

Swan's Location on the Wheel of Life

Swan is located on the southwest quadrant, where the lessons of self-image and body transformation are learned, and on the northeast quadrant, where ancestral karma is released.

Contemplate This

Do you recognize your beauty and power? Are you in touch with your inner mystic? Do you remember your dreams? Place your attention on yourself, and be aware of how beautiful and powerful you are. Be comfortable with that. Go within, and become a seeker of spiritual wisdom. Make an effort to remember your dreams, write them down, and interpret their meaning. Dispel illusions, and surrender, accept, and be transformed.

Message from Swan

It may be time to say good-bye to an aspect of yourself or to someone in your life. Be willing to let go of a negative self-image. It's time to surrender to a higher state of grace and wisdom. Use your intuition as you move forward, and let negative emotions glide away. Step into the part of yourself that is aligned with simple elegance, freedom, and overflowing blessings.

Swan Affirmation

I am beautiful! It is safe for me to be powerful in graceful ways. I am balanced. My body is calm and relaxed. I look within and find spiritual truth and wisdom. I am connected with my elegance and flow with the tides. I am very grateful that I remember my dreams and interpret them. Spiritual growth is a daily part of my life. I am aligned with the Divine.

Message from Green Kyanite

Align the spiritual being within you with the higher realms of consciousness. Enhance your connection with wisdom, purity, and grace. Open your heart to harmoniously work with the higher realms. Every day in every way you have the opportunity to maintain mindfulness to step forward in grace. Make it your intention to remember your dreams so that you can learn from them.

Additional Vibrational Matching Gemstones for Swan

Amethyst, danburite, girasol quartz, howlite, kunzite, magenta-dyed agate, moonstone, morganite, pink calcite, pink tourmaline, rose quartz, scolecite, and selenite.

79. Tiger and Gold Tiger's Eye

Are you the head of your home or business? Do you embrace the part of you that is dynamic and powerful? Are you in tune with everything that is happening around you?

Tiger totem is an ally to help you improve your senses—olfactory and sight. Tigers have exceptionally good eyesight and a strong sense of smell. They live a solitary life in their vast territory and mark it with their scent. Tiger reminds you to take notice of the aromas and odors wherever you go in order to interpret information regarding authenticity and the safety of the setting. Use your peripheral vision consciously to maintain situational awareness.

Tiger medicine helps you own your world with confidence and courage. When it comes down to it, it is up to you to take responsibility for your life. You come into this world alone, and you leave this world alone. The largest member of the cat family, tigers are accustomed to ruling the immense lands that make up their world. Other than humans, they have no predators. Tiger is frequently found on flags and brands as a symbol of power and leadership in their domain. When Tiger visits you, it is a confirmation of your leadership abilities and the power to make things happen. There are many ways to lead—the most effective are to lead by example, listen to your colleagues, and do your share of the workload. Focus on your vision, and work with your team using passion, integrity, and patience.

Tiger enjoys regular swims and its den needs to feel like home. Tiger medicine encourages you to establish your home and/or office and equip them all the amenities you need to feel comfortable. With Tiger as a totem, you will find it advantageous to have access to a pool or a place to swim, a den, and a fairly large space around your home or yard.

Tiger's Vibrational Matching Gemstone: Gold Tiger's Eye

Gold tiger's eye helps you improve mental clarity and your innate ability to use all your senses in order to integrate what's going on around you. This stone is a good companion when you want to remain grounded and focused on goals and dreams and accomplishing them on your own. Gold tiger's eye can help you feel self-empowered and reduce the need for approval from others, and is beneficial for those in leadership positions. Hold gold tiger's eye with the intention in mind to know and follow your personal truth. The golden tones remind you to expand your outlook and open your mind to unlimited possibilities. This stone enlivens your imagination and spiritual potential. Use this tiger's eye to increase vital life force and receive nourishment from the sun.

Divine Influence

Call on Archangel Michael for support in powerful, far-seeing leadership.

Tiger's Location on the Wheel of Life

Tiger is located on the eastern portion of the northeast quadrant, where wisdom and clarity meet.

Contemplate This

Are you observant and mindful of your surroundings? Put your finger on the pulse of your environment, and stay aware. Train your mind for single-pointed focus, and see with clarity. Improve your mental advantage, and increase your attention to detail. Engage in illuminating activities such as meditation, contemplation, and reflection to better understand the true nature of reality. Invite the illumination of spiritual truths. Pledge an allegiance to your heart while maintaining a leadership role or strong position in your circle.

Message from Tiger

It is okay to feel comfortable being the singular force in your world. Believe in your vision for your future. You have the power and resources to make it happen. Be brave, and present yourself to the world as a leader in your field. Clearly show yourself through defined intentions. Be in the flow, accept yourself, and establish your territory. Remain objective about your emotions and reactions to life experiences.

Tiger Affirmation

I am balanced, aligned, healthy, and strong. It is easy for me to stand in the center of my power and emanate love. I am in tune with the center of my personal power. I can achieve anything I put my mind to. I am safe. I have constant protection surrounding me. I have the courage and self-confidence to create my world. I am always in the right place at the right time.

Message from Gold Tiger's Eye

You are a visionary. Step into your power to share a positive vision for the future. Be in a place of allowing, and enjoy what life has in store for you. Allow powerful and dynamic divinity into your spiritual practice. Use your inherent abilities to hear, see, and know. Accept these natural gifts in your daily life, and trust your higher guidance.

Additional Vibrational Matching Gemstones for Tiger

Blue lace agate, celestite, citrine, golden topaz, iolite, lapis lazuli, moldavite, pyrite, sapphire, and selenite rose.

80. TURKEY AND GROSSULAR GREEN GARNET

When you cook, do you do so in a state of gratitude? Are you aware of how many people were instrumental in making it possible for you to put a meal on your table? Do you feel the shower of blessings constantly flowing in your life?

Turkey totem is an ally for when you have an abundance of food available to you. It is the perfect totem for cooks and chefs. Turkey is symbolic of giving of oneself to benefit many. As early settlers of North America established their homesteads, Turkey provided them with delicious nourishment. This bird has since been associated with the Thanksgiving holiday in the United States. In this way, Turkey teaches you to give of yourself while maintaining an air of gratitude. One way to practice gratitude is to prepare food mindfully. Maintaining a state of gratitude, think about the person who fed the animal or tended the crop, cleaned the space, provided water, packaged the meat or produce, loaded the truck, drove the truck, delivered the food to the store, stocked the shelves, did the accounting, paid the bills, washed the floors, priced the products . . . and so on.

When Turkey gobbles its way into your life, remember to maintain a regular practice of gratitude for the abundance and prosperity in your life. Be the blessing in other people's lives as well. Realize that love, wealth, and plentitude are a natural state of being, and embrace them. Turkey is a reminder to be grateful for the many people, places, and situations in your life. Now is the time to put your attention on all that is good.

Turkey's Vibrational Matching Gemstone: Grossular Green Garnet

Grossular green garnet is a stone of blessings, good energy, vital life force, and good health. The message of this stone is to focus on your blessings and all that is good in your life. This stone improves your energy level and enhances your physical endurance. It adds chi, or life force, to the body, mind, and spirit. Green garnet is a reminder to clear your thoughts while you eat by sorting out which are of value to you. As you eliminate confusion, understand that you can clear away the need for emotional eating by creating healthy thought forms and conversations around mealtime. Pay attention to the food you are putting into your body as well. Wholesome food, thoughts, and conversation can make things easier to process and accept.

Divine Influence

Call on Archangel Uriel to amplify the shower of blessings in your life and illuminate your body, mind, and spirit with a sense of gratitude.

Turkey's Location on the Wheel of Life

Turkey is located on the western portion of the northwest quadrant, where the harvest is abundant and bountiful.

Contemplate This

When was the last time you paused to count your blessings? Do you recognize the value of expressing gratitude and being thankful? Are you able to both give and receive? Practice gratitude daily for the obvious and not-so-obvious blessings in your life. Think outside your own experience, and keep in mind that there are many people in the world without regular access to food and water. This can help you be more conscious of taking the time to honor the sacredness of your food and clean running water.

Message from Turkey

Practice gratitude while you cook by consciously being present with the food you are preparing. Be aware that many people, places, and situations had a hand in getting that meal to your table. Accept the nourishing energy of gratitude and blessings. Open your heart, and be willing to receive as well as give. Offer a gift to someone you appreciate and feel grateful for.

Turkey Affirmation

With focused intention, I draw upon the gifts of the law of attraction. I have many blessings in my life. Abundance and prosperity are constantly flowing in my life. I enjoy writing in my gratitude journal. I have gratitude for all the blessings still to come. My heart is open to give and receive. All my needs are met. I pause for a moment of gratitude!

Message from Grossular Green Garnet

Take steps to improve your endurance and overall health by using visualization and practicing gratitude. Recharge your energy centers, and renew your passion for living a vibrant life! Imagine that you are healthy and vital, and believe it. Eat health-promoting foods, but also stay focused on gratitude and the blessings in your life. Bless your food when you sit down to eat it.

Additional Vibrational Matching Gemstones for Turkey

Apatite, golden calcite, dioptase, green aventurine, green calcite, green chrysoprase, jade, peridot, petalite, rutilated quartz, and serpentine.

81. TURTLE AND PRASIOLITE

How connected are you to Mother Earth? Are you aware of the earth energy beneath the soles of your feet? Do you act in a peaceful manner? Do you feel safe and protected?

Turtle totem is an ally that aids you in connecting with the cycles of the moon above you and the earth beneath your feet. There are 13 segments on the inner part of the shell of most turtles. There are 13 moons each year, one cycle every 28 days. These 13 segments on Turtle's shell are reminders to become aware of your relationship with the cycles of life.

When Turtle makes its slow entrance into your life, you are being reminded to maintain a connection with feminine energy, receiving intuitive insights while simultaneously staying grounded and focused on your earthly experience. Turtle is a sign to go within. Spend some silent time inside your own "shell" for quiet reflection. The practice of contemplation and inner connection brings transcendent strength.

Due to Turtle's connection with the moon and her cycles, this totem helps those with the desire to steadily increase their intuitive skills. The receptive quality of the moon is aligned with the feminine vibration, which is receptive and intuitive by nature. Call on Turtle medicine to "be" instead of "do." In the state of being, realizations arise to guide you on your path toward a balanced and stable experience.

Turtle's Vibrational Matching Gemstone: Prasiolite

Prasiolite, a green variety of quartz, is an excellent tool to improve your ability to stay focused and follow through on a task to completion at a steady pace. Use prasiolite when you feel stuck and need to make a shift in order to move forward. It helps you find inner strength and endurance. This stone is especially useful when you have long hours of mental activity ahead of you, because it increases your mental strength and determination. Prasiolite opens pathways in your consciousness to help you accept the challenge of spiritual fortitude. With endurance and determination on your side, you have the opportunity to amplify your ability to sit in meditative states for longer periods.

Divine Influence

Call on the Angel of Meditation and the Angel of Contemplation to help guide you inward to experience deeper states of consciousness.

Turtle's Location on the Wheel of Life

Turtle is located on the western portion of the northwest quadrant, where the energy of going within to find balance and strength is located.

Contemplate This

Do you stay the course and follow through on a task until completion? Are you able to recognize the value of the cyclical nature of life? Do you feel at home in your skin? Hasten slowly, and maintain a steady focus on your goals. Spiritual practice is just that—practice. Practice meditation, practice being silent, practice going within. Connect with the cycles of the moon and the planets, and embrace the natural ebb and flow of life.

Message from Turtle

Check in with yourself to observe your meditation practice. Determine if you are spending enough time in quiet solitude within your own space. Cultivate your contemplative practice by setting aside specific periods of time for journaling and inner reflection. Spend some time alone, walking and thinking. Swimming in a pool or bathing in a tub immerses you in the feminine vibration of being.

Turtle Affirmation

I am determined and have the strength to follow through with the next best thing. I am strong, healthy, and unwavering in my body, mind, and spirit. I am comfortable and feel at home in my skin. My connection with the cycles of the moon and planets is strong. I enjoy a regular meditation practice.

Message from Prasiolite

You may be feeling weakened in body, mind, or spirit. If you are depleted and need a bit of determination and strength, spend time in meditation to help recapture your ability to endure the demands of daily life and energize your mental strength for life on all levels. Take time to find and eat the right foods to provide your body with the core nutrients it is craving.

Additional Vibrational Matching Gemstones for Turtle

Bloodstone, girasol quartz, howlite, labradorite, moonstone, optical calcite, prehnite, selenite, and unakite.

82. VULTURE AND JET

Has the time come to clear away toxins or toxic behaviors? How well do you care for the environment? Do you reduce, reuse, and recycle? Are you grieving a loss?

Vulture totem is an ally for you when you need to clean up some aspect of your life so that the cycles of life can continue. The value of vultures in our environment should not be underestimated. Vultures are scavenger animals, feeding on carcasses and keeping our environment free of decay and bacteria. They serve the ecosystem by consuming rotted meat that could be toxic to other animals. Vultures live in flocks and feed together on the carcass of a dead animal. When engaging in this behavior, the flock is called a wake.

Call on the energy of Vulture when you want to be more community-minded and mindful of the environment. Let Vulture's scavenging actions be a model for community gatherings where all participants work together to care for the environment—clean up, recycle, and reduce waste.

Vulture may also signal a loss in life and the grieving process. When Vulture flies into your life, it signals that you may be in a period of mourning. The loss or removal of someone or something in your life is initially uncomfortable and sad. Let Vulture be your ally to help you release the vibration of sadness as you uncover the opening in your life that has come about as a result of the loss.

Vultures live up to 70 years and stay mated for life, which makes Vulture an ally that supports your experience or desire for a lifelong mate.

Vulture's Vibrational Matching Gemstone: Jet

Jet is a fossilized wood that has turned to coal. This stone is helpful for supporting the removal of toxins in the body, especially in the case of food poisoning, drug abuse, alcoholism, and smoking. Use this stone to aid you during your detoxification process. Jet supports and encourages the removal of waste or nonproductive matter through purification and clearing on an energetic level. On an emotional level, jet supports the process of letting go of negative emotions, knee-jerk reactions, and nagging thoughts replaying in your consciousness. Use jet when you are adjusting to the end of a relationship, regardless of the manner in which it ended.

Divine Influence

Call on Archangel Raphael to help you understand the evolutionary cycles of life and to bring in the transformative power of Divine healing.

Vulture's Location on the Wheel of Life

Vulture is located on the south path, where transformation and transmutation occur for the evolution and healing of relationships.

Contemplate This

Are you a conscious steward of the earth? Do you compost and recycle? Does part of your life need purification? Take responsibility for your footprint on this planet. Learn to reuse and repurpose items you no longer need. It may be time to let go of something that is no longer a vital, healthy part of your life. Let yourself release what is no longer useful, and clean it out to make way for the new.

Message from Vulture

Release belief systems that hold you back. Uncover negative beliefs you may have about being in a lifelong, loyal romantic partnership in order to attract that love into your life and enjoy a loving partnership for the rest of your life. Remember to value and spend time in groups in order to establish a supportive community around you. Find value in your ability to integrate and process matters of the past that once seemed like toxic influences but from which you can now garner wisdom.

Vulture Affirmation

I accept the impermanent nature of life. I am a stew-
ard of the earth. It is easy for me to "think green."
I reduce the amount of waste produced in my house-
hold. I reuse and recycle everything I can. I leave our
planet a better place and in better condition than be-
fore I arrived. I am clear-headed and aligned with my
natural rhythms.

Message from Jet

You may be in the process of healing after the loss of a job, relationship, pet, or loved one. It is important to reestablish your equilibrium—physically, mentally, and emotion-ally—after periods of intensity. It's time to cultivate a deeper relationship with yourself. Uncover what you can do to increase your happiness. As you deepen self-love and self-ac-ceptance, love and relationships cycle back into your life.

Additional Vibrational Matching Gemstones for Vulture

Apache tears, brown agate, chlorite phantom quartz, green moss agate, Kambamba jasper, moss-included dogtooth calcite, rhodonite, rose quartz, tree agate, and ruby in zoisite.

83. Walrus and Howlite

Are you able to share parts of yourself with the world for the greatest good of all? Do you have prominent positive attributes to sustain you and raise you up? Have you incorporated a gratitude practice for the great magnitude of abundance in your life?

Walrus totem is an ally for you when you are ready to embrace your positive attributes and the ways in which they contribute to making the world a better place. Walrus encourages you to give freely of your talents, skills, and resources to encourage a constant flow of prosperity and abundance. Walrus has given its body to humankind over millennia to provide sustenance—art, bones, fat, food, skin, and material for boats and clothing. Use the plentiful vibration of Walrus when you consciously wish to attract extraordinary wealth.

Walrus uses its tusks to make holes in frozen surfaces and climb out of the water below. Symbolically, this represents your ability to pull yourself out of deep emotions using your determination and physical power. When Walrus bores a hole into your life, it signals a time for you to pull yourself up and out onto the next level. Water, as symbolized by Walrus, assists in regaining emotional balance. You have a lot of value and so much to share. Nurture and tend to the foundation of your being on all levels. You will always feel fulfilled when you believe in yourself and embrace your emotions.

Walrus forages on the sea floor, which moves nutrients into the water for the good of the community. By immersing yourself in water, you can feed your emotional body and bring balance into your life. Spend time at the water's edge in order to regain emotional balance. This will help clear away any negative energy you may have accumulated from unsettling conversations or negative internal dialogue.

Walrus's Vibrational Matching Gemstone: Howlite

Howlite reminds you to include prayer and gratitude practices in your daily routine and to respect your elders and the environment. Howlite is helpful for cooling heated emotions and regaining emotional balance. The calming, white energy of this stone relieves intense pressure during potentially explosive situations. This stone also has a cleansing vibration. It provides you with a higher understanding of the source of emotional stress, giving you a new, lighter perspective. Use howlite when you need to detoxify and release noxious thoughts and emotions.

Divine Influence

Call on the Angel of Abundance to help you attract abundance on all levels and the Angel of Gratitude to help you notice the magnitude of blessings in your life.

Walrus's Location on the Wheel of Life

Walrus is located on the northwest quadrant, where the depth of emotions is understood and gratitude for life's bounty is expressed.

Contemplate This

Do you rely on your deeper nature to sustain yourself, physically and emotionally? Feed your soul, and share the overflowing blessings pouring through you. Share yourself and any excess material objects with someone who needs a little help in their life. When you are willing to share the gift of who you are, you become a blessing for this world. Let go, and give. Recognize that you always have all you need, and more. Knowing this, you can relax.

Message from Walrus

Become aware of your emotions. Define them. Learn to observe them and detach from them. Notice the overflowing abundance and good fortune that exists in your life. Determine how you can gift items or parts of yourself to others for the highest good of the community. Be happy for other people's good fortune and blessings. With an open heart, reflect on how blessed you are!

Walrus Affirmation

I enjoy financial abundance. Everything I need to know is stored within me. Blessings flow through me like a healing river. I am fluid. I am pure and clear. I take the time I need to relax in a pool, bath, or body of water. I drink the right amount of water to maintain a fluid, healthy body.

Message from Howlite

Make sure that you are drinking enough water. Take time to immerse yourself in healing waters, such as a bath or a refreshing pool. Water purifies your body and mind. Hydrate yourself inside and out in order to maintain fluidity at all levels of consciousness. Allow the natural flow to detoxify your body, mind, and emotions. Bring the nurturing power of healing to the forefront in order to regenerate and rejuvenate your body, mind, and spirit as well as your financial security. Learn the lessons of mindfulness and respect for all life in alignment with God, Goddess, and Creator.

Additional Vibrational Matching Gemstones for Walrus

Aquamarine, blue goldstone, citrine, emerald, epidote, green tourmaline, green goldstone, larimar, peridot, pyrite, and yellow chrysoprase.

84. WEASEL AND MUSCOVITE

Do you surround yourself with people of integrity? Have you noticed that someone in your midst appears to be kind and innocent but is proving to be deceitful? Do you have an acute sense of smell?

Weasel totem is an ally that helps you discover someone's true nature. Weasel looks sweet and cuddly, but it can be quite vicious, reminding you that appearances aren't always indicative of a person's personality. Weasels are predators that need to eat half their body weight every day and kill small animals such as chickens and rabbits, so they've developed a reputation for being treacherous vermin.

When Weasel weasels its way into your life, take note if there are manipulative people around you. Weasels employ devious techniques for survival. A charismatic colleague might conspire to have you do something that doesn't feel right, or chaotic shenanigans might be used as a ploy to distract you from the truth or underhanded intentions. On the other hand, check in with yourself to be sure that you aren't being charmingly deceitful in order to get your own way.

Weasel is associated with a superior sense of smell, including clairolfaction (the ability to intuitively pick up a smell that doesn't physically exist and which provides some sort of guidance or clue into a situation at hand). If something doesn't smell right to you, pay attention and sniff out the facts. Make it your intention to understand the underlying cause of a challenging situation so that you are better able to move through it with ease and grace.

Weasel's Vibrational Matching Gemstone: Muscovite

Muscovite's shimmering protective energy reminds you that where there is love, there can only be goodness and well-being. Its silver energy helps you connect with your innate receptive and intuitive nature. With muscovite and Weasel as allies, trust your intuition and ferret out the facts for self-preservation. Use muscovite as an instrument for self-observation and self-reflection so that you can uncover parts of your personality and underlying intentions, leading to personal growth and development. Muscovite can be used to help you honor your feelings and sort out your thoughts and emotions when chaos is afoot, enabling you to know and express the truth. It also helps you open your ears and other senses, right down to your physical nerve endings, to be able to hear and grasp what others are communicating.

Divine Influence

Call on Archangel Haniel to help you connect with the truth and Archangel Sabrael to help reveal situations that involve jealousy, negativity, or underhanded maneuvers.

Weasel's Location on the Wheel of Life

Weasel is located on the western portion of northwest quadrant, where the path of truth and authenticity is revealed.

Contemplate This

Do you act with integrity and authenticity? Are your thoughts, words, and actions aligned with your morals and values? Come from a place within yourself that is filled with honesty and ethical behavior. Hold the intention that you attract and are surrounded by people of integrity in all aspects of your life. Determine if the truth about a certain matter needs to be spoken. Have the courage to speak up with grace and set boundaries to improve your life circumstances.

Message from Weasel

Do the research to uncover what you need to know about a person, place, or situation for your safety and well-being. Avoid taking things at face value, and step away from any confusion that may have been consciously created by a supposed friend or colleague. Focus on your goals and intentions with clarity regarding your underlying and overlying intentions. Reflect on your honor. By so doing, you will broadcast a vibration that will attract trustworthy people and colleagues into your life.

Weasel Affirmation

I honor my emotions. I stand up for myself. I say what I need to say. I surround myself with people who willingly speak their truth. It is easy for me to reflect on both the blessings and challenges in my life as an objective observer. My observations strengthen my spiritual nature and improve my inner foundations for knowledge and wisdom.

Message from Muscovite

Take time for inner reflection and self-observation to expand your spiritual foundation. Look deep within your soul at your personal motivations. Uncover parts of your consciousness that might be drawing in jealousy from or for others, self-sabotage, and impatience. Stay focused on the goodness in your life. Instead of focusing on other people's good fortune, focus on the blessings in your own life. Step away from anyone who is resentful of your purpose and destiny.

Additional Vibrational Matching Gemstones for Weasel

Amazonite, angelite, aquamarine, aragonite, blue topaz, celestite, clear quartz, gold tiger's eye, hematite, labradorite, and peridot.

85. WHALE AND HEMIMORPHITE

How loud are your thoughts? Do you realize that you are emitting a frequency that is being picked up by those around you as well as people who are far away? Are you ready to sing to yourself for happiness and love?

Whale totem is an ally that assists you in becoming more conscious of the effects of the thoughts, emotions, and words you think, feel, and say. Everything is energy, and all energy has a vibration. The vibrations of your thoughts and emotions are as significant as the words you say aloud. Just as whales broadcast low-frequency messages across long distances, you, too, are broadcasting your thoughts, feelings, and emotions far and wide. As an ally, Whale reminds you to be mindful of your thoughts and what you are emitting. Call on Whale to help you understand that the energy of your thoughts returns to you—it is a creation of your reality and affects everything.

When Whale swims into your life, begin observing the beliefs and thoughts you have been broadcasting into the universe throughout your life. Contemplate if you are contributing to world peace with your thoughts or if you are creating more angst in the world with worrisome thoughts. Shift your awareness. Make a conscious note of the thoughts you carry around with you, and recognize that your thoughts are affecting more than just your reality. Your thoughts and feelings are contributing to your community and the whole world.

Whales communicate through reverberations that sound like songs. Like most songs, Whale's song has definite patterns and repetitive melodies. You also have repetitive thoughts and patterns of thinking. Whale's song teaches you to listen to the repetitive nature of your thoughts. Through awareness and observation, you can "change your tune" and broadcast what is for your highest good as well as for the highest good of all.

Whale's Vibrational Matching Gemstone: Hemimorphite

The ocean-blue variety of hemimorphite helps realign and balance your emotions and communications. Take time to nurture yourself and know that you are loved by the Divine. Open your heart chakra by showing yourself and others more compassion. Hemimorphite reminds you that it is always time to restore your well-being. A joyful outlook on life can be yours. Focus on how you want your reality to manifest. With Whale and hemimorphite as allies, you are able to remember that your thoughts and beliefs create reality. So change your thoughts, stop worrying, and manifest the life you truly want for yourself, thereby affecting everyone else's life too. Have courage and faith as you navigate your way through life. Telepathically send out the message of all you wish to be and create, and believe in your ability to attract those things into your life.

Divine Influence

Call on Archangel Muriel to help you establish emotional balance and connection with the creatures of the sea.

Whale's Location on the Wheel of Life

Whale is located on the eastern portion of the northeast quadrant, where the knowledge and wisdom of ancestors are restored.

Contemplate This

Are you sensitive to sound? Do you realize that your thoughts, emotions, and words are broadcast and create your reality? Be mindful of what you are thinking. Use the power of your intention to maintain focus on creating your world. Find your "inner song" within the depths of your being, and sing your reality into existence. Take the necessary steps to shift your focus from that which troubles you to that which brings you joy. Recognize that life flows in circles and all cycles shift and change.

Message from Whale

You may be wondering, "Why is this happening to me?" Recognize that you are the creator of your life. Clear your consciousness of negative energy from conversations, experiences, and your own internal dialogue. Release emotionally charged thoughts. Water assists in regaining emotional balance. Engage in nurturing and nourishing practices, such as taking a long bath and drinking water frequently. Sing a song to yourself and find inner peace and love within.

Whale Affirmation

It is easy for me to hear subtle sounds that help me create my reality. I receive messages and guidance through intuitive hearing or sound, even those that are not physical sound waves. I traverse the inner depths of my consciousness in order to remember my truth and align my soul. My emotional body is awash with positive cleansing energy. I enjoy a wonderful sense of emotional balance.

Message from Hemimorphite

Your emotions may be in turmoil, or you might simply be feeling uneasy. Think about the last time you went to the seaside or another large body of water. Spend time at the water's edge to regain emotional balance. This will help clear away any negative energy you may have accumulated from unsettling conversations or negative internal dialogue.

Additional Vibrational Matching Gemstones for Whale

Amazonite, angelite, aquamarine, aragonite, blue topaz, celestite, chrysocolla, chrysoprase, elestial, larimar, tabular quartz, turquoise, and unakite.

86. Wolf and Elestial Quartz Crystal

Do you enjoy being part of a community? Are you sociable? Do you consider yourself a leader or a follower? Are you flexible?

Wolf totem is an ally for times when you need to be a leader or follow a leader. It represents the viability of a strong community. Wolf medicine encourages you to be sociable and active in your community. Wolves are social, intelligent, and affectionate. They enjoy being part of the pack. They have a variety of personalities and are flexible regarding their hierarchy or status among the members of their pack. While there are occasions for the "lone wolf," most wolves are part of a community. In the wild, lone wolves are often older females who have been rejected by the pack or young wolves looking for new territory.

When Wolf walks into your life, take time to reflect on your circle of friends, family, and colleagues. Wolf brings the energy of a solid family connection as well as support for each individual. If you are seeking assistance with building a strong family foundation, Wolf as your ally helps you find a way to create that reality.

Notice the pecking order within your social groups, including your workplace, and realize that there will be times when it is appropriate for roles to change or shift depending on the situation. Tap into your intelligence and your memory and recall how past circumstances were resolved so that you can apply that experience to a current situation with confidence. Wolf helps you to be flexible enough to be the leader or the follower with ease and grace. If you need to be a follower, be a supportive member of the pack.

Wolf's Vibrational Matching Gemstone: Elestial Quartz Crystal

Elestial quartz crystals are the teachers of the crystal and gemstone kingdom. Their energy provides support to groups through alignment with legions of angels. Whether your group is your family unit, your work unit, or your community unit, use the vibe of this crystal to maintain a sense of balance and emotional calm. Elestial quartz helps you understand that angels work together for the good of all humankind and throughout the cosmos. This quartz crystal helps you think and act with Wolf's pack mentality for a positive outcome. Elestial quartz also helps you be a good role model and trailblazer.

Divine Influence

Call on Archangel Sandalphon to help support the energy of groups and communities for healing and personal alignment.

Wolf's Location on the Wheel of Life

Wolf is located on the northeast quadrant, where social understanding and integration of the connection with all life is realized.

Contemplate This

Are you in a position of leadership, such as a teacher or owner of a company? Are you a sociable member of your community? Tap into the part of you that is outgoing as well as the part that is a storyteller. Tell your stories to others, and listen to the stories others tell. Be a positive role model for others? People do notice you and observe your manner of interaction, your achievements, and your participation. Allow for emotional connection with others, and find fulfillment in that connection.

Message from Wolf

Enjoy the company of your community, and spend quality time with family and friends. The gift of your time cultivates the various relationships in your life. Honor and respect each person in your life for who they are, as well as for their contributions to the whole. Recognize individual talents, and encourage each person to be all they can be. Understand that there will be disagreements on occasion; assertiveness is healthy, but try to avoid overly aggressive behavior. Shine your light brightly, and make a wonderful contribution to all that is good in your community.

Wolf Affirmation

I find comfort in the harmony of my community. I am a respected member of society, and I honor others for who they are and what they can do. I have a peaceful relationship with my family. It's easy for me to share and teach through storytelling. I am extremely intuitive and heed the messages of higher wisdom and knowledge.

Message from Elestial Quartz Crystal

Cultivate healthy, harmonious relationships. Leave a healthy amount of space between you and your relationships with colleagues, friends, and family. Respect the members of your community, and honor their talents and magnificence as they presently exist. Cultivate and nurture the loving relationships in your life. To attract new love or renew existing love, alter your mindset to think in terms of "we" rather than "me."

Additional Vibrational Matching Gemstones for Wolf

Amber, clear quartz cluster, dumortierite, golden sheen obsidian, golden topaz, pink calcite, relationship quartz crystal, and purple-dyed agate

87. WOODPECKER AND PETRIFIED WOOD

Do you want to unearth the belief systems hidden in your subconscious in order to understand what might be holding you back? When was the last time you participated in a ceremonial drumming circle? Are you seeking to strengthen your spiritual connection and faith?

Woodpecker totem is an ally that assists when you need to chisel something out of whatever is blocking it. This typically relates to truth or hidden agendas. Woodpecker energy also helps when you need to get down to the deeper levels of your mind and emotions.

Woodpecker's beak serves as a chisel and a crowbar. This bird takes percussive action against the wood to get at what's underneath when it requires nourishment. When Woodpecker knocks on your symbolic tree, it is inviting you to delve into yourself to find spiritual sustenance. One of the ways to accomplish this is to participate in a ceremonial-type drumming circle focused on drumming out the old energies, and then, in a separate round of drumming, inviting in the reality you want to experience.

As you drum, the energy of the percussion—the sound and the force—empowers you to feel your feelings and bang "it" out on an energetic level to help you when you have to face a situation or person on a physical level. You don't need to drum as fast as a woodpecker pecks wood! Some woodpeckers can peck up to 20 times per second! The transformational potential and release through drumming is cathartic, and a safe and effective way to face emotional debris that is buried deep within you.

Woodpecker's Vibrational Matching Gemstone: Petrified Wood

Petrified wood teaches you that much of what you need to realize, understand, remember, or know is buried deep within your body, mind, and soul. On a spiritual level, uncovering the layers of years of processing can be achieved through spiritual healing practices like drumming, yoga, tai chi, rebirthing (conscious connected breathwork), past-life regression therapy, meditation, and shamanic journeywork. Petrified wood reminds you that all the knowledge and wisdom you need is available within the recesses of your mind. These fossilized remains assist you in the process of clearing out the clutter that no longer serves you. Both Woodpecker and the good energy of petrified wood support you as you remove the extraneous from your life and uncover the hidden information you need.

Divine Influence

Call on Archangel Auriel to help you conjure the courage to face your buried fears and emotions and Archangel Seraphiel to help you replace those fears with peace and blessings.

Woodpecker's Location on the Wheel of Life

Woodpecker is located on the southeast quadrant, where the light can shine into places previously hidden so that they can be healed and transformed.

Contemplate This

What's buried deep within your consciousness? Do you have something so stagnant within your belief system you can't break out of the mold? Are you petrified of something? Step outside yourself, and observe the generational patterns in your ancestral history. Sometimes, it's hard to recognize that a belief is holding you back. It takes courage, persistence, and spiritual fortitude to discover it. Weed out what no longer serves you, and embrace what does.

Message from Woodpecker

You can create a happy and healthy life by clearing out negative thoughts and replacing them with positive thoughts and belief systems. Enter the deeper layers of your mind and emotions. Implement spiritual discipline. Be consistent. Ground yourself in a daily spiritual practice, creating the stability needed to maintain mindfulness and single-pointed focus. Let go of procrastination, and add energy and enthusiasm to your spiritual practice.

Woodpecker Affirmation

I am focused and grounded. I stay with the task at hand until it is complete. Everything I need to know is stored within me. I easily tap into my inner wisdom and knowledge. I have the courage and self-confidence to create my world. I am motivated. I take action. I am passionately persistent.

Message from Petrified Wood

Prepare yourself to be nourished by prosperity. Use the knowledge you've gained from the work you've been doing over the past as the foundation of your success. Be aware that work you've done in past lives is part of your knowledge base. It is time to bring to the surface embedded feelings in your subconscious so that you can remove unnecessary limits on your potential. Let go of these unhealthy emotions.

Additional Vibrational Matching Gemstones for Woodpecker

Amber, ametrine, azurite-malachite, chrysocolla, elestial quartz crystal, green moss agate, smoky quartz, red tiger's eye, and tree agate.

88. Zebra and Zebra Jasper

Are things either black or white to you? Do you realize how unique you are? Are you surrounded by supportive friends and family?

Zebra totem is an ally that helps you embrace your distinctive characteristics, especially if you feel that your differences make you stand out too much. Zebra's striped pattern symbolizes how unique and irreplaceable you are. When Zebra canters into your life, it is reminding you to embrace your particular personality and unique vibrations. Embrace the masculine (white) and feminine (black) energy within yourself to better understand the duality of life. On Planet Earth, there is both darkness and light. Zebra teaches you to stay focused on the light while embracing the darkness. The division into two mutually exclusive, opposed, or contradictory groups—light and dark—is a point of contemplation. Uncover what that means and how to find the fine balance between these opposing forces.

Zebras use their stripes and their family group as a form of protection from predators. When they stand together, their stripes create an illusion so that predators are unable to discern the number of zebras in the herd. Zebra offers you the vibration of camouflage when you need to deflect the negativity of people, places, or situations that are a threat to you on a mental, emotional, spiritual, or physical level. As an ally, Zebra helps you remember to stand together with your community, family, or group of friends to support and protect each other.

Zebra's Vibrational Matching Gemstone: Zebra Jasper

Zebra jasper carries the energy of mental clarity, giving you the ability sort through all of the details of a project. When things aren't black and white, this stone helps you sort through all the shades of gray. Zebra jasper enhances your physical endurance when you need to stay focused on what needs to get done while maintaining the motivation to do it. It is a good stone to have on hand if you get easily distracted. It helps you concentrate on what you need to do in the moment rather than every other thing you need to get done later. In this way, zebra jasper is beneficial for a writer who is avoiding "putting pen to paper."

Divine Influence

Call on Archangel Ariel to help you realign with your feminine energy and release subconscious fears and Archangel Camael to help balance feelings of anger, aggression, and fear.

Zebra's Location on the Wheel of Life

Zebra is located on the east path, where perspective and clarity are gained.

Contemplate This

Can you see the writing on the wall, or are you caught up in illusion? Spend time thinking about how many perspectives there are in the world and that things aren't always what they seem to be at first glance. Open new pathways of spiritual thought and connection. Remember, there is always darkness within light. Embrace the darkness to enhance the clarity in your life.

Message from Zebra

Embrace the polarities of life. Contrast offers more clarity over time. Maintain a focus on doing one thing at a time, and finish what you start. Find comfort and security within your family and group of friends. Darkness accentuates brightness so that we can clearly see situations, people, and circumstances for what they are.

Zebra Affirmation

I'm a self-motivated person. I get things done. I am very perceptive and discerning in all areas of my life. I see things from varying perspectives. I recognize the choices of paths available to me. I have mental clarity. I courageously see through the darkness of adversity in order to make positive changes. I feel safe and secure. I see myself, situations, and others clearly.

Message from Zebra Jasper

You may be used to seeing things as either black or white. Consider the possibility that some things can also be a combination of these two shades. It is important to clearly define some things in your life while remaining open to the various shades of gray—in other words, look for the common ground and that unique "in-between" point of view. Use black-and-white energy to clarify which spiritual path to focus on during rites of passage.

Additional Vibrational Matching Gemstones for Zebra

Azurite-malachite, cobaltoan calcite, Dalmatian jasper, girasol quartz, moonstone, orthoceras, ruby, shell fossil, and snowflake obsidian.

Appendices

Easy Reference Guides

APPENDIX A
GEMSTONE LISTING FOR ANIMAL TOTEM

Ant.   Azurite-malachite, blue lace agate, blue calcite, clear quartz singing crystal, celestite, Picasso stone, red calcite

Antelope.   Fluorite, Mookaite jasper, red calcite, red jasper, red tiger's eye, sapphire, sunstone, tiger iron, golden topaz, ruby vanadinite

Armadillo.   Ametrine, black tourmaline, charoite, desert rose, golden calcite, danburite, hematite, orange calcite, pyrite, yellow jasper

Badger.   Amazonite, ametrine, black obsidian arrowhead, charoite, chrysocolla, dogtooth calcite, emerald, rhodochrosite, selenite rose

Bat.   Azurite-malachite, blue lace agate, blue calcite, clear quartz singing crystal, celestite, galena, Picasso stone

Bear.   Azurite, brown agate geode, brown jasper, honey calcite, lodestone, magnetite octahedron, moonstone, muscovite, golden sheen obsidian, rainbow obsidian, sodalite

Beaver.   Agate, amber, carnelian, epidote, fluorite, honey calcite, petrified wood, orange calcite, pyrite, rose quartz, pyrite, sardonyx

Bee.   Amethyst, blue calcite, citrine, golden calcite, golden topaz, honey calcite, magenta-dyed agate, malachite, red calcite

Beetle.   Amber, amethyst, black onyx, black tourmaline, charoite, girasol quartz, galena, hematite, magenta-dyed agate, red tiger's eye

Bluebird.   Apophyllite, clear quartz, citrine, gold tiger's eye, golden calcite, kyanite, peacock copper, peridot, rhodonite, rose quartz, selenite

Blue jay.   Amazonite, angelite, aquamarine, blue calcite, blue lace agate, celestite, citrine, indicolite, lapis lazuli, sodalite

Buffalo.   Amethyst druzy, angelite, celestite, copper, jade, howlite, rose quartz, ruby in zoisite, sardonyx, seraphinite, serpentine

Butterfly.   Amethyst, ametrine, charoite, green aventurine, green calcite, orange calcite, pietersite, phantom quartz, pink calcite, purple-dyed agate, tiger's eye

Camel.   Azurite-malachite, emerald, green aventurine, green tourmaline, Isis clear quartz point, jade, leopardskin jasper, Mookaite jasper, tree agate, pyrite, rutilated quartz, tourmalinated quartz, azurite-malachite

Cardinal.   Andulasite, blue calcite, clear quartz, fluorite, garnet, green tourmaline, lapis lazuli, red jasper, Mookaite jasper, pyrite, red goldstone, ruby, tabular quartz, vanadinite

Cat.   Amethyst druzy, azurite-malachite, hiddenite, labradorite, leopardskin jasper, lapis lazuli, lepidolite, moonstone, selenite, trilobite, unakite

Clam.   Amber, ammonite, clear quartz, elestial quartz crystal, magnesite, orthoceras fossil, petrified wood, smoky quartz, turquoise, yellow jasper

Coyote.   Amazonite, ammonite, angelite, blue lace agate, chevron amethyst, malachite, Picasso stone, tabular quartz, turquoise, vanadinite

Crab.   Aragonite, black tourmaline, Botswana agate, elestial quartz crystals, jasper, howlite, orange calcite, smoky quartz, trilobite, unakite

Crocodile.   Blue calcite, blue lace agate, Botswana agate, optical calcite, orange calcite, peridot, turquoise orange calcite

Crow.   Black obsidian, black tourmaline blue lace agate, celestite, cathedral quartz, fluorite, lodestone magnetite octahedron, moldavite, scolecite, selenite

Deer.   Amber, amethyst, ametrine, blue calcite, citrine, golden calcite, golden topaz, orange calcite, red goldstone, rhodochrosite sunstone

Dog.   Citrine, Dalmatian jasper, green aventurine, green tourmaline, emerald, iolite, jade, lapis lazuli, pink calcite, rose quartz, sapphire, sardonyx

Dolphin.   Amazonite, angelite, apophyllite, blue lace agate, blue calcite, brucite, celestite, indicolite, kyanite, larimar

Dove.   Amazonite, amethyst, blue calcite, celestite, clear quartz, danburite, Herkimer diamond, kunzite, optical calcite, rose quartz, scolecite, selenite

Dragonfly.   Amethyst cathedral ,chevron amethyst, dioptase, Herkimer diamond, labradorite, opal, opalite, peacock copper, pietersite, rainbow moonstone, window clear quartz

Duck.   Chrysoprase, magenta-dyed agate, pink calcite pink tourmaline, relationship quartz crystal, rhodochrosite, rhodonite, rose quartz, ruby, tabular quartz, unakite, watermelon tourmaline

Eagle.   Amethyst, apophyllite, citrine, danburite, gold tiger's eye, Herkimer diamond, golden calcite, indochinite tektite, kyanite, moldavite, sapphire, selenite rose, window quartz

Earthworm.
Amber, aragonite, channeling quartz, chrysanthemum stone, green moss agate, Laser wand, orthoceras, record keeper quartz crystal, selenite, stromatolite, tree agate

Elephant.   Angelite, amazonite, bloodstone, clear quartz crystal, girasol quartz, jade, laser wands, moonstone, opal, pink calcite, rhodochrosite, selenite, tabular quartz, turquoise, variscite

Elk.   Brecciated jasper, carnelian, citrine, clear quartz cluster, garnet, golden topaz, red jasper, ruby, ruby in fuchsite, ruby in zoisite, sunstone

Finch.   Amazonite, angelite, blue calcite, blue lace agate, blue topaz, celestite, citrine, green aventurine, jade, kunzite, rose quartz, turquoise

Firefly.   Apophyllite, citrine, clear quartz, golden calcite, golden topaz, labradorite, sunstone, tiger's eye, yellow jasper, selenite

Flamingo.   Danburite, emerald, garnet, green tourmaline, Herkimer diamond, kunzite, Mookaite jasper, pink opal, pink calcite, rhodochrosite, rose quartz, ruby, ruby in fuchsite, ruby in zoisite, watermelon tourmaline

Fox.   Aragonite, citrine, fluorite, green calcite, labradorite, lapis lazuli, moldavite, rhodochrosite, sapphire, septarian, shell fossil

Frog.   Aquamarine, charoite, green aventurine, green-dyed agate, green tourmaline, emerald, enhydro-quartz crystals, elestial quartz crystals, larimar, seraphinite

Giraffe.   Azurite-malachite, apophyllite, blue tiger's eye, Botswana agate, dioptase, dolomite, gold tiger's eye, labradorite, lapis lazuli, leopardskin jasper, red tiger's eye, smoky quartz point

Goat.   Ametrine, amethyst, aquamarine, blue chalcedony, chalcopyrite, covellite, golden sheen obsidian, fluorite, phantom quartz, pyrite, red tiger's eye

Goldfish.   Citrine, golden calcite, fire agate, gold beryl, golden topaz, green aventurine, green goldstone, labradorite, red goldstone, jade, sunstone

Gorilla.   Amethyst, black onyx, blue calcite, chrysoprase, green moss agate, hematite, kyanite, red jasper, red tiger's eye, ruby

Grasshopper.
          Amethyst, chalcopyrite, charoite, copper, Herkimer diamond, lapis lazuli, phantom quartz, pyrite, rutilated quartz, singing laser quartz wands, vanadinite

Hawk.   Apophyllite, aragonite cluster, azurite-malachite, chevron amethyst, clear quartz, gold tiger's eye, hawk's eye aka blue tiger's eye, kunzite, labradorite, lapis lazuli, optical calcite, rose quartz

Horse.   Carnelian, garnet, green moss agate, moss-included dogtooth calcite, pyrite, red goldstone, red jasper, ruby, sunstone, tree agate

Hummingbird.
          Apophyllite, chevron amethyst, dumortierite, green aventurine, infinite, jade, labradorite, lepidolite, moonstone, peacock copper

Jaguar.   Axinite, cathedral quartz, cobaltoan calcite, fluorite, golden calcite, golden topaz, Herkimer diamond, hematite, leopardskin jasper, magenta-dyed agate, sapphire, tiger's eye, tiger iron

Ladybug.   Black tourmaline, golden sheen obsidian, green aventurine, green moss agate, heliodor, jade, magenta-dyed agate, red jasper, ruby, smoky quartz, tree agate

Leopard.   Bismuth, black obsidian, fluorite, golden sheen obsidian, iolite, leopardskin jasper, phantom quartz, pyrite, snowflake obsidian, rutilated quartz, tourmalinated quartz, leopardskin jasper

Lizard.   Amethyst, black obsidian, dioptase, Herkimer diamond, howlite, iolite, labradorite, lapis lazuli, moonstone, peridot, pietersite, window quartz crystal

Lion.   Ametrine, citrine, gold tiger's eye, golden sheen obsidian, golden topaz, rutilated quartz, sunstone

Mockingbird.
            Amazonite, angelite, apatite, aquamarine, blue calcite, brucite, celestite, dioptase, iolite, larimar, sapphire, turquoise, vanadinite

Monkey.   Black tourmaline, brown agate, blue goldstone, carnelian, clear quartz cluster, golden sheen obsidian, green goldstone, red goldstone, orange calcite, rhodonite, selenite, turquoise

Moose.   Apophyllite, bismuth, blue lace agate, blue tiger's eye, cathedral quartz, charoite, chrysanthemum stone, garnet, magenta-dyed agate, morganite, prasiolite, selenite, sugilite

Moth.   Blue tiger's eye, honey calcite, hiddenite, girasol quartz, howlite, labradorite, magnesite, moonstone, phantom quartz, snowflake obsidian

Mouse.   Amethyst, bismuth, blue chalcedony, celestite, Dalmatian jasper, Herkimer diamond, fluorite, larimar, scolecite, selenite, yellow jasper

Ostrich.   Amethyst, apatite, black tourmaline, citrine, citron chrysoprase, chrysocolla, golden calcite, green calcite, peridot, prehnite, red jasper, ruby, turquoise

Otter.   Aragonite, aquamarine, citrine, chalcedony, cobaltoan calcite, gold tiger's eye, golden calcite, golden topaz, larimar, magenta-dyed agate, moonstone, pink tourmaline, silver topaz unakite

Owl.   Cathedral quartz, channeling quartz, clear quartz, golden sheen obsidian, indicolite aka blue tourmaline, kyanite, lapis lazuli, moonstone, record keeper quartz, sapphire, selenite, sodalite

Panther.   Ammonite, black obsidian, blue topaz, cathedral quartz, jet, kyanite, malachite, lapis lazuli, rutilated quartz, silver topaz, time link quartz

Parrot.   Angelite, bi-color tourmaline, blue lace agate, chalcopyrite, green moss agate, green tourmaline, larimar, peacock copper, peridot, turquoise, watermelon tourmaline

Peacock.   Angelite, blue-dyed agate, celestite, citrine, clear quartz, copper, howlite, iolite, kyanite, lapis lazuli, sodalite, peacock copper, sapphire, rhodochrosite, selenite rose

Penguin.   Aquamarine, bloodstone, green calcite, green tourmaline, kunzite, larimar, magenta-dyed agate, pink calcite, pink tourmaline, relationship quartz crystal, rhodochrosite, rose quartz, ruby in zoisite, unakite

Pig.   Amethyst, carnelian, fluorite, golden topaz, hiddenite, indochinite tektite, labradorite, moldavite, red calcite, red jasper, selenite, sugilite

Porcupine.   Amethyst, black kyanite, black obsidian arrowheads, black tourmaline, golden sheen obsidian, hematite, jet, lapis lazuli, purple-dyed agate, shungite, tourmalinated quartz

Praying Mantis.
        Blue calcite, green calcite, indochinite tektite, Isis quartz crystal, Mookaite jasper phantom quartz crystal, optical calcite, orange calcite, pink calcite, red calcite

Rabbit.   Botswana agate, cobaltoan calcite, carnelian, girasol quartz, moonstone, petrified wood, opal, pink calcite, rhodochrosite, selenite

Raccoon.   Amazonite, amethyst druzy, angelite, apophyllite, black tourmaline, fluorite, hiddenite, labradorite, lapis lazuli, petrified wood, selenite, trilobites

Ram (Big Horned Sheep).
        Ammonite, carnelian, carborundum, emerald, garnet, orbicular jasper, red calcite, red jasper, pyrite, ruby

Raven.   Axinite, bismuth, celestite, channeling quartz crystal, elestial quartz crystal, hematite, iolite, Isis quartz crystal, lapis lazuli, moqui marbles, morganite, pietersite, phantom quartz

Rhinoceros.
        Axinite, brown agate, cathedral quartz point citrine, golden calcite, golden topaz, green moss agate, rutilated quartz, septarian, tree agate, yellow jasper

Sandpiper.   Andalusite, aquamarine, aragonite, chlorite phantom quartz, elestial quartz crystals, green moss agate, larimar, orange calcite, peridot, smoky quartz, unakite

Seagull.   Amazonite, ametrine, aquamarine, blue lace agate, celestite, epidote, larimar, moldavite, peridot, rhodochrosite, unakite

Sea Lion.   Azurite-malachite, carnelian, celestite, chrysoprase, chrysocolla, garnet, golden calcite, golden topaz, lapis lazuli, ruby

Skunk.   Amethyst, azurite, blue-dyed agate, chlorite phantom quartz, green most agate, kyanite, labradorite, moonstone, optical calcite, pietersite, selenite, tree agate

Snake.   Amethyst, apophyllite, black obsidian arrowhead, golden sheen obsidian, jet, selenite, snowflake obsidian, unakite

Spider.   Aquamarine, Botswana agate, bloodstone, carnelian, covellite, girasol quartz, golden topaz, heliodor, labradorite, Picasso stone, rainbow moonstone, red goldstone, yellow jasper

Squirrel. Clear quartz, elestial quartz crystals, chlorite phantom quartz, green moss agate, moss-included dogtooth calcite, moldavite, indochinite tektite, peacock copper, selenite, tree agate

Starfish. Aquamarine, blue topaz, brucite, chrysanthemum stone, elestial quartz crystals, howlite, larimar, moonstone, smoky quartz, unakite

Swan.   Amethyst, danburite, girasol quartz, green kyanite, howlite, kunzite, magenta-dyed agate, moonstone, morganite, pink calcite, pink tourmaline, rose quartz, scolecite, selenite

Tiger.   Blue lace agate, celestite, citrine, gold tiger's eye, golden topaz, iolite, lapis lazuli, moldavite, pyrite, sapphire, selenite rose

Turkey.   Apatite, golden calcite, dioptase, green aventurine, green calcite, green chrysoprase, grossular green garnet, jade, peridot, petalite, rutilated quartz, serpentine

Turtle.   Bloodstone, girasol quartz, howlite, labradorite, moonstone, optical calcite, prasiolite, prehnite, selenite, unakite

Vulture. Apache tears, brown agate, chlorite phantom quartz, green moss agate, jet, Kambamba jasper, moss-included dogtooth calcite, rhodonite, rose quartz, tree agate, ruby in zoisite

Walrus.   Aquamarine, blue goldstone, citrine, emerald, epidote, green tourmaline, green goldstone, howlite, larimar, peridot, pyrite, yellow chrysoprase

Weasel.   Amazonite, angelite, aquamarine, aragonite, blue topaz, celestite, clear quartz, gold tiger's eye, hematite, labradorite, muscovite, peridot

Whale.   Amazonite, angelite, aquamarine, aragonite, blue topaz, celestite, chrysocolla, chrysoprase, elestial, hemimorphite, larimar, tabular quartz, turquoise, unakite

Wolf.   Amber, clear quartz cluster, dumortierite, elestial quartz crystal, golden sheen obsidian, golden topaz, pink calcite, relationship quartz crystal, purple-dyed agate

Woodpecker.
          Amber, ametrine, azurite-malachite, chrysocolla, elestial quartz crystal,
          green moss agate, petrified wood, smoky quartz, red tiger's eye, tree agate
Zebra.   Azurite-malachite, cobaltoan calcite, Dalmatian jasper, girasol quartz,
          moonstone, orthoceras, ruby, shell fossil, snowflake obsidian, zebra jasper

Appendix B
Animal Listing
for Gemstones

Agate.   Beaver

Amazonite.   Badger, Blue Jay, Coyote, Dolphin, Dove, Elephant, Finch,
                          Mockingbird, Raccoon, Sea Gull, Weasel, Whale

Amber.   Beaver, Beetle, Clam, Deer, Earthworm, Wolf, Woodpecker

Amethyst.   Bee, Beetle, Buffalo, Butterfly, Cat, Coyote, Deer, Dove,
                          Dragonfly, Eagle, Goat, Gorilla, Grasshopper, Hawk,
                          Hummingbird, Lizard, Mouse, Ostrich, Pig, Porcupine,
                          Raccoon, Skunk, Snake, Swan

Amethyst Cathedral.   Dragonfly

Amethyst Druzy.   Raccoon, Buffalo, Cat

Ametrine.   Armadillo, Badger, Butterfly, Deer, Goat, Lion, Sea Gull,
                          Woodpecker

Ammonite.   Clam, Coyote, Panther, Ram

Andulasite.   Cardinal

Angelite.   Blue Jay, Buffalo, Coyote, Dolphin, Elephant, Finch,
                          Mockingbird, Parrot, Peacock, Raccoon, Weasel, Whale

Apache Tears.   Vulture

Apophyllite.   Bluebird, Dolphin, Eagle, Firefly, Giraffe, Hawk,
                          Hummingbird, Moose, Raccoon, Snake

Aquamarine.   Blue Jay, Frog, Goat, Mockingbird, Otter, Penguin, Sandpiper,
                          Sea Gull, Spider, Starfish, Walrus, Weasel, Whale

Aragonite.   Crab, Earthworm, Fox, Hawk, Otter, Sandpiper, Weasel, Whale

Axinite.   Jaguar, Raven, Rhinoceros

Azurite.   Bear, Skunk

Azurite–Malachite.   Ant, Bat, Camel, Cardinal, Cat, Giraffe, Hawk, Sea Lion,
                          Woodpecker, Zebra

Bi-Color Tourmaline.   Parrot

Bismuth.   Leopard, Moose, Mouse, Raven

Black Kyanite.   Porcupine

Black Obsidian.   Crow, Leopard, Lizard, Panther, Porcupine, Snake

Black Obsidian   Arrowhead. Badger

Black Onyx.   Beetle, Gorilla

Black Tourmaline.   Armadillo, Beetle, Crab, Crow, Ladybug, Monkey, Ostrich, Porcupine, Raccoon

Bloodstone.   Elephant, Penguin, Spider, Turtle

Blue Calcite.   Ant, Praying Mantis

Blue Chalcedony.   Goat, Mouse, Otter

Blue Lace Agate.   Ant, Bat, Blue Jay, Coyote, Crocodile, Crow, Dolphin, Finch, Moose, Parrot, Sea Gull, Tiger

Blue Topaz.   Finch, Panther, Starfish, Weasel, Whale

Botswana Agate.   Crab, Crocodile, Giraffe, Rabbit, Spider

Brecciated Jasper.   Elk

Brown Agate Geode.   Bear, Monkey, Rhinoceros, Vulture

Brown Jasper.   Bear

Brucite.   Dolphin, Mockingbird, Starfish

Carborundum.   Ram

Carnelian.   Beaver, Elk, Horse, Monkey, Pig, Rabbit, Ram, Sea Lion, Spider

Cathedral Quartz.   Crow, Jaguar, Moose, Owl, Panther, Rhinoceros

Celestite.   Ant, Bat, Blue Jay, Buffalo, Crow, Dolphin, Dove, Finch, Mockingbird, Mouse, Peacock, Raven, Sea Gull, Sea Lion, Tiger, Weasel, Whale

Chalcopyrite.   Parrot, Goat, Grasshopper

Channeling Quartz.   Earthworm, Owl, Raven

Charoite.   Armadillo, Badger, Beetle, Butterfly, Frog, Grasshopper, Moose

Chevron Amethyst.   Coyote, Dragonfly, Hawk, Hummingbird

Chlorite Phantom
    Quartz.   Sandpiper, Skunk, Squirrel, Vulture

Chrysanthemum Stone.   Earthworm, Moose, Starfish

Chrysocolla.   Badger, Ostrich, Sea Lion, Whale, Woodpecker

Chrysoprase.   Duck, Gorilla, Ostrich, Sea Lion, Turkey, Walrus, Whale

Citrine.   Bee, Bluebird, Blue Jay, Deer, Dog, Eagle, Elk, Finch, Firefly, Fox, Goldfish, Lion, Ostrich, Otter, Peacock, Rhinoceros, Tiger, Walrus

Clear Quartz.   Bluebird, Cardinal, Clam, Dove, Dragonfly, Firefly, Hawk, Owl, Peacock, Squirrel, Weasel

Clear Quartz Cluster.   Elephant, Elk, Monkey, Wolf

Clear Quartz Singing
    Crystal.   Ant, Bat

Cobaltoan Calcite.	Jaguar, Otter, Rabbit, Zebra
Copper.	Buffalo, Grasshopper, Peacock
Covellite.	Goat, Spider
Dalmatian Jasper.	Dog, Mouse, Zebra
Danburite.	Armadillo, Dove, Eagle, Flamingo, Swan
Desert Rose.	Armadillo
Dioptase.	Dragonfly, Giraffe, Lizard, Mockingbird, Turkey
Dogtooth Calcite.	Badger
Dumortierite.	Hummingbird, Wolf
Elestial Quartz Crystal.	
	Clam, Crab, Frog, Raven, Sandpiper, Squirrel, Starfish, Whale, Wolf, Woodpecker
Emerald.	Badger, Camel, Dog, Flamingo, Frog, Ram, Walrus
Enhydro-Quartz Crystals.	
	Frog
Epidote.	Beaver, Sea Gull, Walrus
Fire Agate.	Goldfish
Fluorite.	Antelope, Beaver, Cardinal, Crow, Fox, Goat, Jaguar, Leopard, Mouse, Pig, Raccoon
Galena.	Bat, Beetle
Garnet.	Cardinal, Elk, Flamingo, Horse, Moose, Ram, Sea Lion
Girasol Quartz.	Beetle, Elephant, Moth, Rabbit, Spider, Swan, Turtle, Zebra
Gold Beryl.	Goldfish
Gold Tiger's Eye.	Bluebird, Eagle, Giraffe, Hawk, Lion, Otter, Tiger, Weasel
Golden Calcite.	Armadillo, Bee, Bluebird, Deer, Eagle, Firefly, Goldfish, Jaguar, Ostrich, Otter, Rhinoceros, Sea Lion, Turkey
Golden Sheen Obsidian.	
	Bear, Ladybug, Leopard, Lion, Monkey, Owl, Porcupine, Snake, Wolf
Golden Topaz.	Bee, Deer, Elk, Firefly, Goldfish, Jaguar, Lion, Otter, Pig, Rhinoceros, Sea Lion, Spider, Tiger, Wolf
Green Aventurine.	Butterfly, Camel, Dog, Finch, Frog, Goldfish, Hummingbird, Ladybug, Turkey
Green Calcite.	Butterfly, Fox, Ostrich, Penguin, Praying Mantis, Turkey
Green Kyanite.	Swan
Green Moss Agate.	Earthworm, Gorilla, Horse, Ladybug, Parrot, Rhinoceros, Sandpiper, Squirrel, Vulture, Woodpecker

Green Tourmaline.   Camel, Cardinal, Dog, Flamingo, Frog, Parrot, Penguin,
                       Walrus,
Grossular Green Garnet.
                       Turkey
Heliodor.   Ladybug, Spider
Hematite.   Armadillo, Beetle, Gorilla, Jaguar, Porcupine, Raven, Weasel
Herkimer Diamond.   Dove, Dragonfly, Eagle, Flamingo, Grasshopper, Jaguar, Lizard,
                       Mouse
Hiddenite.   Cat, Moth, Pig, Raccoon
Honey Calcite.   Bear, Beaver, Bee, Moth
Howlite.   Buffalo, Crab, Lizard, Moth, Peacock, Starfish, Swan, Turtle,
                       Walrus
Indicolite.   Blue Jay, Dolphin, Owl
Indochinite Tektite.   Eagle, Pig, Praying Mantis, Squirrel
Infinite.   Hummingbird
Iolite.   Dog, Leopard, Lizard, Mockingbird, Peacock, Raven, Tiger
Isis Clear Quartz Point.
                       Camel, Praying Mantis, Raven
Jade.   Buffalo, Camel, Dog, Elephant, Finch, Goldfish,
                       Hummingbird, Ladybug, Turkey
Jasper.   Crab
Kunzite.   Dove, Finch, Flamingo, Hawk, Penguin, Swan
Kyanite.   Bluebird, Dolphin, Eagle, Gorilla, Owl, Panther, Peacock,
                       Skunk
Labradorite.   Cat, Dragonfly, Firefly, Fox, Giraffe, Goldfish, Hawk,
                       Hummingbird, Lizard, Moth, Pig, Raccoon, Skunk, Spider,
                       Turtle, Weasel
Lapis Lazuli.   Blue Jay, Cardinal, Cat, Dog, Fox, Giraffe, Grasshopper, Hawk,
                       Lizard, Owl, Panther, Peacock, Porcupine, Raccoon, Raven, Sea
                       Lion, Tiger
Larimar.   Dolphin, Frog, Mockingbird, Mouse, Otter, Parrot, Penguin,
                       Sandpiper, Sea Gull, Starfish, Walrus, Whale
Laser Wand.   Earthworm, Elephant, Grasshopper
Leopardskin Jasper.   Camel, Cat, Giraffe, Jaguar, Leopard
Lepidolite.   Cat, Hummingbird
Lodestone.   Bear, Crow
Magenta-Dyed Agate.   Bee, Beetle, Duck, Jaguar, Ladybug, Moose, Otter, Penguin,
                       Swan

Magnesite.	Clam, Moth
Magnetite Octahedron.	Bear, Crow
Malachite.	Bee, Coyote, Panther
Moldavite.	Crow, Eagle, Fox, Pig, Sea Gull, Squirrel, Tiger
Mookaite Jasper.	Antelope, Camel, Cardinal, Flamingo, Praying Mantis
Moonstone.	Bear, Cat, Elephant, Hummingbird, Lizard, Moth, Otter, Owl, Rabbit, Skunk, Spider, Starfish, Swan, Turtle, Zebra
Moqui Marbles.	Raven
Morganite.	Moose, Raven, Swan
Moss-Included Dogtooth Calcite.	
	Horse, Squirrel, Vulture
Muscovite.	Bear, Weasel
Opal.	Dragonfly, Elephant, Rabbit
Opalite.	Dragonfly
Optical Calcite.	Crocodile, Dove, Hawk, Praying Mantis, Skunk, Turtle
Orange Calcite.	Armadillo, Beaver, Butterfly, Crab, Crocodile, Deer, Monkey, Praying Mantis, Sandpiper
Orthoceras.	Clam, Earthworm, Zebra
Peacock Copper.	Bluebird, Dragonfly, Hummingbird, Parrot, Peacock, Squirrel
Peridot.	Bluebird, Crocodile, Lizard, Ostrich, Parrot, Sandpiper, Sea Gull, Turkey, Walrus, Weasel
Petalite.	Turkey
Petrified Wood.	Beaver, Clam, Rabbit, Raccoon, Woodpecker
Phantom Quartz.	Butterfly, Goat, Grasshopper, Leopard, Moth, Praying Mantis, Raven, Sandpiper, Skunk, Squirrel, Vulture
Picasso Stone.	Ant, Bat, Coyote, Spider
Pietersite.	Butterfly, Dragonfly, Lizard, Raven, Skunk
Pink Calcite.	Butterfly, Dog, Duck, Elephant, Flamingo, Penguin, Praying Mantis, Rabbit, Swan, Wolf
Pink Opal.	Flamingo
Pink Tourmaline.	Duck, Otter, Penguin, Swan
Prasiolite.	Moose, Turtle
Prehnite.	Ostrich, Turtle
Purple-Dyed Agate.	Butterfly, Porcupine, Wolf
Pyrite.	Armadillo, Beaver, Camel, Cardinal, Goat, Grasshopper, Horse, Leopard, Ram, Tiger, Walrus
Rainbow Moonstone.	Dragonfly, Spider

Rainbow Obsidian.   Bear
Record Keeper Quartz Crystal.
                          Earthworm, Owl
Red Calcite.   Ant, Antelope, Bee, Pig, Praying Mantis, Ram
Red Goldstone.   Cardinal, Deer, Goldfish, Horse, Monkey, Spider
Red Jasper.   Antelope, Cardinal, Elk, Gorilla, Horse, Ladybug, Ostrich, Pig,
                          Ram
Red Tiger's Eye.   Antelope, Beetle, Giraffe, Goat, Gorilla, Woodpecker
Relationship Quartz Crystal.
                          Duck, Penguin, Wolf
Rhodochrosite.   Badger, Deer, Duck, Elephant, Flamingo, Fox, Peacock,
                          Penguin, Rabbit, Sea Gull
Rhodonite.   Bluebird, Duck, Monkey, Vulture
Rose Quartz.   Beaver, Bluebird, Buffalo, Dog, Dove, Duck, Finch, Flamingo,
                          Hawk, Penguin, Swan, Vulture
Ruby.   Antelope, Cardinal, Duck, Elk, Flamingo, Gorilla, Horse,
                          Ladybug, Ostrich, Ram, Sea Lion, Zebra
Ruby in Fuchsite   Elk, Flamingo,
Ruby in Zoisite.   Buffalo, Elk, Flamingo, Penguin, Vulture
Rutilated Quartz.   Camel, Grasshopper, Leopard, Lion, Panther, Rhinoceros,
                          Turkey
Sapphire.   Antelope, Dog, Eagle, Fox, Jaguar, Mockingbird, Owl, Peacock,
                          Tiger
Sardonyx.   Beaver, Buffalo, Dog
Scolecite.   Crow, Dove, Mouse, Swan
Selenite.   Bluebird, Cat, Crow, Dove, Earthworm, Elephant, Firefly,
                          Monkey, Moose, Mouse, Owl, Pig, Rabbit, Raccoon, Skunk,
                          Snake, Squirrel, Swan, Turtle
Selenite Rose.   Badger, Eagle, Peacock, Tiger
Septarian.   Fox, Rhinoceros
Seraphinite.   Buffalo, Frog
Serpentine.   Buffalo, Turkey
Shell Fossil.   Fox, Zebra
Shungite.   Porcupine
Silver Topaz.   Owl, Panther
Smoky Quartz.   Clam, Crab, Giraffe, Ladybug, Sandpiper, Starfish, Woodpecker
Sodalite.   Bear, Blue Jay, Owl, Peacock

Stromatolite.	Earthworm
Sugilite.	Moose, Pig
Sunstone.	Antelope, Deer, Elk, Firefly, Goldfish, Horse, Lion
Tabular Quartz.	Cardinal, Coyote, Duck, Elephant, Whale
Tiger Iron.	Antelope, Herkimer Diamond
Time Link Quartz.	Panther
Tourmalinated Quartz.	Camel, Leopard, Porcupine
Tree Agate.	Camel, Earthworm, Horse, Ladybug, Rhinoceros, Skunk, Squirrel, Vulture, Woodpecker
Trilobite.	Cat, Crab, Raccoon
Turquoise.	Clam, Coyote, Crocodile, Elephant, Finch, Mockingbird, Monkey, Ostrich, Parrot, Whale
Unakite.	Cat, Crab, Duck, Otter, Penguin, Sandpiper, Sea Gull, Snake, Starfish, Turtle
Vanadinite.	Antelope, Cardinal, Coyote, Grasshopper, Mockingbird
Variscite.	Elephant
Watermelon Tourmaline.	
	Duck, Flamingo, Parrot
Window Clear Quartz.	Dragonfly
Yellow Chrysoprase.	Walrus
Yellow Jasper.	Armadillo, Clam, Firefly, Mouse, Rhinoceros, Spider
Zebra.	Zebra Jasper

Appendix C
Wheel of Life Location for Animal Totems

This appendix gives you an easy way to look up where animals are located on the wheel of life.

East Path: Bluebird, Deer, Giraffe, Hummingbird, Mockingbird, Ostrich,
                      Parrot, Peacock, Pig, Seagull, Zebra

Eastern Quadrant: Eagle, Hawk, Owl

Eastern Portion of the Southeast Quadrant:
                      Crab, Frog

Eastern portion of the Northeast Quadrant:
                      Ant, Elephant, Finch, Firefly, Grasshopper, Ram, Sandpiper,
                      Tiger, Whale

South Path: Beetle, Coyote, Dog, Dove, Duck, Flamingo, Goldfish, Otter,
                      Porcupine, Praying Mantis, Snake, Vulture

Southern Quadrant: Blue Jay

Southern Portion of the Southwest Quadrant:
                      Badger, Beaver

Southeast Quadrant: Crow

Southwest Quadrant: Camel, Cat, Crocodile, Dragonfly, Ladybug, Monkey, Penguin,
                      Swan

West Path: Bat, Gorilla, Horse, Mouse, Rabbit, Spider

Western Portion of the Southwest Quadrant:
                      Armadillo

Western Portion of the Northwest Quadrant:
                      Fox, Skunk, Squirrel, Turkey, Turtle, Weasel

Western Portion of the Northern Quadrant:
                      Bee

North Path: Butterfly, Jaguar, Raven

Northwest Quadrant: Bear, Cardinal, Earthworm, Goat, Lizard, Rhinoceros, Walrus

Northern Portion of the Northwest Quadrant:
                      Antelope, Elk, Sea Lion

Northeast Quadrant: Buffalo, Clam, Dolphin, Leopard, Lion, Moose, Moth, Panther,
                      Starfish, Swan

APPENDIX D
ARCHANGELS AND ANGELS
FOR ANIMAL TOTEMS

Angels are messenger of love and light. They are God's messengers and guardians that watch over us. Archangels answer prayers. There are legions of angels for each and every one of us for various purposes, many of which exist on the higher realms, higher up in the kingdom, closer to the Supreme Being. As humans, our connection with these celestial ones is with the lowest two tiers of the heavenly organization chart. The lowermost levels are the archangels followed by the angels. This section provides you with an overview of the archangels, a few masters mentioned in this book, and the legions of angels. This is followed by the matching animal vibrations.

Archangels and Masters

Archangel Ariel:	Ant, Antelope, Duck, Elk, Goat, Gorilla, Ram, Zebra
Archangel Auriel:	Deer, Dragonfly, Elephant, Rabbit, Woodpecker
Archangel Camael:	Antelope, Cat, Sea Lion, Zebra
Archangel Chamuel:	Cardinal, Duck, Flamingo, Penguin
Archangel Gabriel:	Bat, Crocodile, Crow, Dove, Dragonfly, Lizard, Moth, Parrot, Spider, Swan
Archangel Haniel:	Badger, Clam, Crow, Dove, Eagle, Finch, Mockingbird, Sea Lion, Weasel
Archangel Jophiel:	Armadillo, Hummingbird, Moose
Archangel Michael:	Eagle, Hawk, Lion, Owl, Panther, Peacock, Porcupine, Rhinoceros, Tiger
Archangel Muriel:	Duck, Monkey, Otter, Sandpiper, Seagull, Whale
Archangel Raphael:	Beaver, Coyote, Frog, Horse, Praying Mantis, Vulture
Archangel Raziel:	Lizard, Pig, Raven
Archangel Sabrael:	Bluebird, Weasel
Archangel Sandalphon:	Earthworm, Squirrel, Wolf
Archangel Seraphiel:	Armadillo, Swan, Woodpecker
Archangel Thuriel:	Dolphin, Sandpiper
Archangel Uriel:	Antelope, Bee, Firefly, Grasshopper, Jaguar, Moose, Sandpiper, Squirrel, Turkey
Archangel Zaphkiel:	Monkey, Raccoon, Skunk
Blessed Mother Mary:	Ladybug
Divine Mother:	Jaguar
Metatron:	Jaguar, Moose

Angels

Angel of Abundance: Camel, Walrus

Angel of Adaptability: Camel

Angel of Awakening: Snake

Angel of Balanced Emotions: Crab, Otter

Angel of Blessings: Goldfish

Angel of Communication: Blue Jay, Parrot

Angel of Creative Intelligence: Fox

Angel of Divine Remembrance: Ant

Angel of Emotional Balance: Starfish

Angel of Flexibility: Cat

Angel of Fun and Play: Otter

Angel of Good Fortune: Goldfish, Ladybug

Angel of Gratitude: Buffalo, Walrus

Angel of a Happy Home: Cardinal

Angel of Health, Wealth, and Happiness: Goldfish, Grasshopper, Ladybug

Angel of Inner Knowing: Giraffe

Angel of Inner Strength: Leopard, Rhinoceros

Angel of Intelligence: Pig, Raccoon

Angel of Intuition: Moth

Angels of Loving Relationships: Flamingo

Angel of Loyalty: Dog

Angel of Meditation and Contemplation: Skunk, Turtle

Angel of Nature: Horse

Angel of Opportunity: Leopard

Angel of Perspective: Giraffe

Angel of Physical Strength: Leopard

Angel of Prosperity: Walrus

Angel of Protection: Porcupine

Angel of Relationships: Cardinal

Angel of Romance: Flamingo

Angel of Romantic Partnership: Hawk

Angel of Setting Boundaries: Rhinoceros

Angel of Sound Sleep: Gorilla

Angel of the Dreamtime: Moth

Angel of Transformation: Snake

Angel of Unconditional Love: Dog

Guardian Angel: Blue Jay, Gorilla, Seagull

GLOSSARY

Angels. Luminous beings—neither masculine nor feminine—that act as Divine messengers. There are many types of angels, including Archangels, guardian angels, seraphim, and cherubim. They act and react based on thought forms (mental energy) and their charges' specific requests. Because humans have free will, angels need to be asked to assist us or intervene on our behalf.

Animal Medicine. The healing aspects that a particular animal provides in order to bring something to your awareness. By understanding the messages and mannerisms of various animals whose energy enters your life, either physically or mentally, you can make necessary adjustments in how you perceive yourself and reality. This concept is associated with Native American spirituality and the spirituality of many indigenous tribes around the world.

Animal Totems (Power Animals). The essence of animal energy that aids you in your everyday life. Similar to spirit guides, animal totems energetically travel with you to enhance your efforts in your spiritual pursuits and practices such as shamanic journeywork to find answers for self-improvement. This concept is associated with Native American spirituality and the spirituality of many indigenous tribes around the world.

Anthropomorphic. Personification. Depicts the forces of nature, along with animals and plants, in storytelling as a literary device. It is traditionally used in fables and has ancient roots in literature.

Chakra. A Sanskrit word for "wheel" or "vortex." The seven main chakras, or energy centers, that make up your body begin at the base of the spine with the root chakra and end at the head with the crown chakra, and all of them are energetically connected. When one or more of your chakras becomes blocked or out of alignment, it affects your mental state or your emotional balance. It can also affect you spiritually. Eventually, the blockage presents itself on the physical level with imbalance or some health condition that seems to show up out of nowhere. Read my book Chakra Awakening, for a deep understanding of the chakras.

Clairaudience. The ability to receive messages or guidance through intuitive hearing or sound that has not been produced by physical sound waves. The voice within is the connection to the higher self and to one's guides and angels.

Claircognizance. The ability to know something intuitively.

Clairgustation. The intuitive ability to recognize a taste in the mouth that provides insight into a matter at hand. Medical intuitives often use this sensory gift to identify their clients' physical challenges.

Clairolfaction. The ability to intuitively pick up a smell that doesn't physically exist as scent particle, which provides some sort of guidance or clue into a situation at hand.

Clairsentience. The ability to clearly sense, or feel, and therefore know.

Clairvoyance. The ability to receive intuitive messages through visions in the mind's eye, including dreams and daydreams, through the vibration or energy of spiritual sight. This vibration resides primarily at the third eye.

Consciousness. Awareness in relationship to oneself and the surrounding world and inside world. It is a compilation of one's belief systems and thoughts that are part of the natural thinking process. The foundations of consciousness are established early in life, yet can be realigned and changed with intent. Other terms associated with consciousness are mindfulness, wakefulness, sense of self, perceptions of reality, and philosophical outlook.

Crystal Alignment. The use of crystals placed on and around the body to clear, balance, and align the chakras. It usually includes a guided-imagery meditation, in which the participant is instructed to envision the results they are seeking.

Crystals. Minerals with smooth sides, points, and edges.

Devic Forces. See Elemental Spirits.

Divine Feminine. The universal mother, or Great Mother, represented by any and all of the following: the Goddess, Gaia, Isis, Mary Magdalene, Mother Mary, Lady Nada, Kuan Yin, the Asteroid Goddesses as they are represented from an astrological viewpoint (Pallas Athena, Juno, Vesta, and Ceres), and many others. The Divine Feminine represents the state of receptivity and being-ness.

Elemental Spirits. A force in nature or energy, with or without intelligence, related to the four elements—earth, air, fire, and water. Names given to these forces include gnomes and dwarves to represent earth; sylphs to represent air; salamanders to represent fire; and undines, nymphs, and mercreatures to represent water.

Essential Oils. The oils and other constituents of distilled organic compounds, such as plant hormones, vitamins, and phytochemicals, which can be used in a carrier oil and applied to the skin for rebalancing the physical, mental, and emotional bodies.

Feng Shui. The ancient Chinese art of placement used in designing buildings and arrangement of furniture and objects within living quarters. A bagua is a map of the space being energetically arranged.

Fossil. The preserved remains, partial or whole, of a once-living organism.

Gemstone. A broad term that includes both organic materials and man-made inorganic gemlike materials.

Labyrinth. A maze with a single path to the center and back. This type of maze symbolizes our ability to learn things about ourselves that bring us within and then back out again with answers and a new personal truth. Walking a labyrinth can be a spiritual, meditative, and contemplative process.

Medicine Wheel. A teaching tool in the shape of a wheel that contains 36 positions, each one providing a story and connection with the many cycles of life that we spiral through daily, monthly, yearly, and throughout a lifetime. The teachings of the medicine wheel provide a map to understanding all life.

Meditation. A practice of quieting the mind. It's called a practice because it takes practice with every moment of the experience to stay focused on nothing. There are various forms of meditation using guided imagery to enable the practitioner to focus on calming thoughts to attain higher states of awareness. A goal of meditation is often geared toward attaining compassion and understanding.

Metaphysical. Beyond the physical. This concept encompasses what the physical and scientific world cannot define yet clearly exists. Many of the principles and discussions within this book are metaphysical.

Monkey Mind. A Buddhist term and animal metaphor used to express that the mind is restless, chattering, unsettled, confused, and difficult to control.

No Mind. The complete absence of thought.

Obsidian. Natural glass formed during the cooling of volcanic lava.

Oracle. A person, place, or thing through which advice or prophecy is given.

Quartz. Silicon dioxide that crystallizes and is also found in masses; found in many forms and color—examples include amethyst, citrine, smoky quartz, rose quartz, and rock crystal quartz.

Rock. A mineral aggregate.

Self-actualization. The realization of one's ultimate true potential. Maslow's hierarchy of needs theory brought this concept to full prominence.

Self-awareness. The knowledge of your intentions, feelings, and desires.

Self-knowledge. The understanding of yourself and your underlying motives and intentions.

Self-observation. A tool to awaken your conscious awareness, which when activated, can help you more effectively use the power of your thoughts to create reality. Self-observation is the intentional act of observing your behaviors, reactions, and actions as an interested, objective observer—that is, without judgment.

Self-realization. A fulfillment of life's purpose and your highest potential.

Shamanic Journeywork. A journey to the center of one's self, which may be achieved in various ways. Many shamanic journey practitioners use drumming, at the rate of the heartbeat, to induce a trancelike state. In this state, the practitioner usually connects with either the subconscious (the lower word) or the super-conscious (the upper world) to find answers, understand, and healing.

Spirit Guides. Disincarnate beings that exist in another dimensional reality. These guides become allies when we consciously choose to invite them into our spiritual circle of consciousness. It is important to choose your spirit guides wisely, just as you choose your friends wisely.

Tabular. A crystal that forms in the shape of a tablet. In quartz crystals, two of the six sides are much wider than the other four.

Telepathy. Communication without the use of the spoken word; a form of mental energy used for mind-to-mind and heart-to-heart communication.

Thought forms. Mental energy.

Wheel of Life. The experience of life through the seasons of the year and the experience of death and rebirth to continue to experience the evolution of the soul.

Word Patrol. The practice of employing awareness when speaking or thinking so that your words and thoughts create a desired reality rather than an unwanted situation. For example, when employing word patrol, you would say, "I'm hungry," rather than saying, "I'm starving" to avoid creating a reality in which the body goes into starvation mode and begins to store fat.

BIBLIOGRAPHY & REFERENCES

Books

Andrews, Ted. Animal-Speak: *The Spiritual & Magical Powers of Creatures Great & Small.* St. Paul, Minnesota: Llewellyn Publications, 1993.

___. *Animal-Wise: The Spirit Language and Signs of Nature.* Jackson, Tennessee: Dragonhawk Publishing, 1999.

Ash, Steven and Renate Ash. Sacred Drumming. New York, New York: Sterling Publishing Company, Inc., 2001.

Coomaraswamy, Ananda K. and The Sister Nivedita. *Myths of the Hindus & Buddhists.* New York, New York: Dover Publications, Inc., 1967.

Nequatewa, Edmund. *Truth of a Hopi: Stories Relating to the Origins, Myths and Clan Histories of the Hopi.* London, England: Forgotten Books, 2008.

Sams, Jamie. *The 13 Original Clan Mothers: Your Sacred Path to Discovering the Gifts, Talents, & Abilities of the Feminine through the Ancient Teachings of the Sisterhood.* New York, New York: Harper San Francisco, 1993.

Waters, Frank. *Book of the Hopi.* New York, New York: Penguin, 1977.

Articles

Animals of the Inuit. https://sites.google.com/site/inuitforkids. Accessed October 13, 2017. https://sites.google.com/site/inuitforkids/home/animals-of-the-inuit

Basic Facts About Elephants. http://www.defenders.org. Accessed August 29, 2017. http://www.defenders.org/elephant/basic-facts

Basic Facts About Gorillas. http://www.defenders.org. Accessed August 25, 2017. http://www.defenders.org/gorilla/basic-facts

BioExpedition. Ladybug. http://www.bioexpedition.com/ April 13, 2012. Accessed August 16, 2017. http://www.bioexpedition.com/lady-bug/

Bradford, Alina. "Zebra Facts." https://www.livescience.com/. October 17, 2014. Accessed August 15, 2017. https://www.livescience.com/27443-zebras.html

___. "Facts About Rhinos." March 23, 2016. https://www.livescience.com. Accessed September 13, 2017. https://www.livescience.com/27439-rhinos.html

___. "Rams: Facts About Male Bighorn Sheep." July 31, 2014. https://www.livescience.com. Accessed September 12, 2017. https://www.livescience.com/27724-rams.html

Brown, Sarah F. Pig "Characteristics and Traits - Understanding Their Behavior Will Help You To Take Care of Pigs." http://ezinearticles.com/ August, 31, 2010/. Accessed August 5, 2017. http://ezinearticles.com/?Pig-Characteristics-and-Traits—-Understanding-Their-Behavior-Will-Help-You-To-Take-Care-of-Pigs&id=4956451

California Sea Lion. https://seaworld.org. Accessed September 14, 2017. https://seaworld.org/en/animal-info/animal-infobooks/california-sea-lion/.

Common Sandpiper. http://www.nationalgeographic.com/ Accessed September 14, 2017. http://www.nationalgeographic.com/animals/birds/c/common-sandpiper/

Coyote. http://www.nhptv.org/natureworks. Accessed August 9, 2017. http://www.nhptv.org/natureworks/coyote.htm

Crocodile. https://animalcorner.co.uk. Accessed October 11, 2017. https://animalcorner.co.uk/animals/crocodile/

Description of Vultures. http://animals.mom.me. Accessed October 13, 2107. http://animals.mom.me/description-vultures-5097.html

Facts about Otters. www.otter-world.com/. Accessed August 5, 2017. www.otter-world.com/ag/characteristics/

Fossey, Dian. "Making Friends With Mountain Gorillas." January 1970 issue of National Geographic Magazine. Accessed August 28, 2017. http://www.nationalgeographic.com/magazine/1970/01/mountain-gorillas-study-dian-fossey-virunga/

Fox Family Life and Fox Lifecycle. http://www.newforestexplorersguide.co.uk. Accessed August 11, 2017. http://www.newforestexplorersguide.co.uk/wildlife/mammals/foxes/family-life.html

Gorillas. http://www.berggorilla.org. Accessed October 11, 2017. http://www.berggorilla.org/en/gorillas/

Hadley, Debbie. "10 Fascinating Facts About Ants." https://www.thoughtco.com/. April 24, 2017. https://www.thoughtco.com/fascinating-facts-about-ants-1968070

Hess, Dr. Laurie DVM, DABV. "Want a Backyard Goat? 10 Things to Consider." http://www.vetstreet.com/. June 23, 2016. Accessed August 19, 2017. http://www.vetstreet.com/our-pet-experts/want-a-backyard-goat-10-things-to-consider

Hiskey, Daven. "Ostriches Don't Hide Their Heads in the Sand." http://www.todayifoundout.com. August 12, 2010. Accessed August 15, 2017. http://www.todayifoundout.com/index.php/2010/08/ostriches-dont-hide-their-heads-in-the-sand/

Horowitz, Kate. "7 Fierce Facts About Weasels." http://mentalfloss.com. May 20, 2015. Accessed August 29, 2017. http://mentalfloss.com/article/64193/7-fierce-facts-about-weasels

"How Elephants Communicate." https://www.elephantvoices.org. Accessed August 30, 2017. https://www.elephantvoices.org/elephant-communication/why-how-and-what-elephants-communicate.html

Kelly. "Year of the Monkey — Fortune, Career, Health, and Love Prospects in 2017." https://www.chinahighlights.com. Accessed August 20, 2017. https://www.chinahighlights.com/travelguide/chinese-zodiac/monkey.htm

Konkel, Lindsey. "7 Things You Don't Know About Moths, But Should."
https://www.livescience.com. July 27, 2012. Accessed August 29, 2017.
https://www.livescience.com/21933-moth-week-facts.html

Laboratory of Behavioral Ecology and Evolution at Seoul National University. "Camouflage of moths: Moths actively seek out best hiding places." July 31, 2012.
https://www.sciencedaily.com/. Accessed October 15, 2017.
https://www.sciencedaily.com/releases/2012/07/120731123521.htm

Lawton, Dan. "Physical Characteristics of Woodpeckers."
https://www.backyardchirper.com. Accessed July 29, 2017. https://www.backyard-chirper.com/bird-info-148.html

Livescience. "Mussels and Clams Can Clean Up Polluted Water." August 21, 2014.
https://www.seeker.com/. Accessed July 29, 2017. https://www.seeker.com/mussels-and-clams-can-clean-up-polluted-water-1768972732.html

Matriarchy. http://www.newworldencyclopedia.org/. Accessed August 30, 2017.
http://www.newworldencyclopedia.org/entry/Matriarchy

Mayntz. Melissa. "20 Fun Facts about Flamingos: Trivia About Flamingos."
https://www.thespruce.com. Updated April 28, 2017. Accessed August 16, 2017.
https://www.thespruce.com/fun-facts-about-flamingos-385519

___. "25 Fun Facts About Hummingbirds: Do You Know Your Hummer Trivia?"
https://www.thespruce.com. Updated 7/22/17. Accessed August 17, 2017.
https://www.thespruce.com/fun-facts-about-hummingbirds-387106

___. "How Hummingbirds Fly: What Makes Hummingbird Flight Unique?"
https://www.thespruce.com. Updated 4/4/17. Accessed August 17, 2017.
https://www.thespruce.com/how-hummingbirds-fly-386446

Monkey Worlds. Accessed August 24, 2017. http://www.monkeyworlds.com/

Mooseworld Staff. "Moose as Metaphor." http://www.mooseworld.com/ Accessed October 15, 2017. http://www.mooseworld.com/

Northern Cardinal - Cardinalis cardinalis. http://www.nhptv.org. Accessed September 5, 2017. http://www.nhptv.org/natureworks/cardinal.htm

O'Connell, Rebecca. "Gigantic Facts About Moose." October 20, 2014. http://mentalfloss.com/ Accessed October 15, 2017. http://mentalfloss.com/article/59461/10-gigantic-facts-about-moose

Oliver, Gary, Ph.D. "7 Keys to Building Strong Families." http://www.imom.com/ Accessed August 15, 2017. http://www.imom.com/7-keys-to-building-strong-families/#.WZMMClWGOUk

Otter. https/seaworld.org. Accessed August 5, 2017. https/seaworld.org/en/animal-info/anima-infobooks/otters/behavior

Our Lady's Bug. http://catholicism.org. October 20, 2004. Accessed August 16, 2017.
http://catholicism.org/our-ladys-bug.html

Owl. www.pure-spirit.com. Accessed August 5, 2017. www.pure-spirit.com/more-animal-symbolism/400-owl

Penguin. Physical Characteristics. www.seaworld.org. Accessed August 9, 2017. www.seaworld.org/en/animal-info/animal-infobooks/penguin/physical-characteristics

Pigs Can't Look Up Into the Sky. www.didyouknow.it/.Accessed August 5, 2017. www.didyouknow.it/animals/pigs-cant-look-up/

Praying Mantis. www.keepinginsect.com. Accessed August 9, 2017. www.keepinginsect.com/praying-mantis/breeding/ and www.keepinginsect.com/praying-mantis/general/ and www.keepinginsect.com/praying-mantis/6-astonishing-mantis-facts/

Raccoon. http://www.nhptv.org./ Accessed August 9, 2017. http://www.nhptv.org/natureworks/raccoon.htm

Saleem, Maria. "Hawks Bird Facts, Hawks Pictures." http://www.liveanimalslist.com February 14, 2014. Accessed October 13, 2107. http://www.liveanimalslist.com/birds/hawks.php

Steen, David. "Seagulls in the Ecosystem." Guest Post. June 19, 2013. http://www.livingalongsidewildlife.com. Accessed September 14, 2017. http://www.livingalongsidewildlife.com/2013/06/seagulls-in-ecosystem-guest-post.html

Stephens, Christina. "Information About the Mockingbird." http://animals.mom.me. Accessed August 20, 2017. http://animals.mom.me/information-mockingbird-3913.html

"The 7 Characteristics Of An Eagle And Why They Are Lessons For Good Leadership Politics." Nairaland. http://www.nairaland.com. Accessed August 14, 2017. http://www.nairaland.com/1145749/7-characteristics-eagle-why-lessons

"The Intriguing Mysteries of Nazca Lines in Peru." http://www.ancientsummit.com. Accessed August 24, 2017. http://www.ancientsummit.com/the-intriguing-mysteries-of-nazca-lines-in-peru/

"The Weasel Personality." http://animalinyou.com. Accessed August 29, 2017. http://animalinyou.com/animals/weasel

Whale Communication. http://www.whale-world.com/ Accessed August 15, 2017. http://www.whale-world.com/whale-communication/

Whale Facts and information http://www.whale-world.com/ Accessed August 15, 2017. http://www.whale-world.com/

"What does peacock feather symbolize?" www.chinabuddhismencyclopedia.com/.Accessed August 8, 2017. www.chinabuddhismencyclopedia.com/en/index.phop/What_Does_Peacock_Feather_Symbolize

FINDHORN PRESS

Life-Changing Books

Consult our catalogue online
(with secure order facility) on
www.findhornpress.com

For information on the Findhorn Foundation:
www.findhorn.org